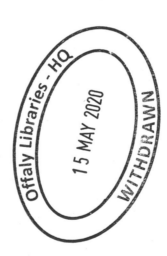
Irish Film 100 Years

The dramatic seaweed gathering scene from *Man of Aran*

4

Dedicated to
Noel and Andrea, two regular film buffs

We thank the following for supplying photographs and other material

Samson Films

Clarence Pictures

Little Bird

Warner Bros.

Rank Organisation

Castlerock International

Pembridge Productions

Mercurian Productions

Ferndale Films

Paramount Pictures

Palace Pictures

RTE

British Film Institute

Ardmore Studios

ProMedia

Hell's Kitchen

O'Sullivan Productions

Treasure Films

Temple Films

The Irish Film Board

United Artists

20th Century Fox

Spelling Films

Universal Pictures

Trilogy Entertainment Group

MGM/UA Studios

Contents

Acknowledgements

I would like to acknowledge the help of a large number of people and organisations without which this book would not have been written. I would like to begin with the people who gave me interviews about their experiences of film-making in Ireland, including Patrick Carey, Neil Jordan, Tomas MacAnna, Justin Collins, Martin Ritt, John Ford, John Huston, Louis Marcus, Harry Alan Towers, Colm O'Laoghaire, Annie O'Sullivan, George Morrison, Fred O'Donovan, Roger Corman, Cyril Cusack, Joseph Strick, Hilton Edwards, Kieran Hickey, Seamus de Burca, Liam O'Leary, Noel Purcell, Dermot Breen, Dan O'Herlihy, Patrick Dawson, Michael O'Herlihy, O.Z. Whitehead, John Boorman, Kevin Barker, Commandant Peter Young, Army Archives, John Lynch, Tony Barry and Paddy Breathnach.

I owe a debt of thanks to Fr. J.A. Gaughan, Morgan O'Sullivan, Dermot Doolin, Bob Quinn, Vincent Corcoran and Sheamus Smith for reading and commenting on the initial text; Kevin Moriarty Ardmore Studios, Wicklow Film Commission, the staff of the National Film Institute, the National Library, Gael Linn, Bord Scannan na hEireann, The Arts Council, Radio Telefís Éireann, Strongbow, Ferndale Films, Michael Kelleher and Eileen Murray (Bray Library), John Keenan, Pat Johnson (Civic Museum), Garrett Flynn, Blaise Treacy, Ed Guiney, Brendan O'Connor, Arthur Lappin, Geraldine Flynn, Gladys Sheehan, Michael Judge, Barry Flynn, Brian White, Michael O'Hógain, Noel Rowsome, Susan Harnett, Mary Crotty, Irish Film Centre and Henry Cairns (Town Hall Bookshop); to Eamonn O'Higgins and Gerald Connolly for proof-reading and especially to Patricia O'Reilly for her help and guidance: to the Irish Times, Sunday Tribune, The Bray People, Irish Independent, Irish Press, Film Ireland and Film West.

11

Preface

My love for cinema began as a child in Bray, County Wicklow. I was a regular matinee goer to the Royal and Roxy, and savoured the adventures of Roy Rogers, the Marx Brothers and Humphrey Bogart chasing the Maltese Falcon. Some years later, with the opening of Ardmore Studios on my doorstep, I could actually see films in production. I remember the awe of watching Robert Mitchum and a youthful Richard Harris being directed in a scene in a ditch on the banks of the Dargle; of seeing James Cagney barking orders on a hilltop in Gleencree; of witnessing spectacular dog-fights over Calary Bog, and of observing Laurence Harvey in a makeshift graveyard beside the gasometer. I saw how a scene was created from words on a script, how sets were erected, and how the tricks of the trade, like back-projection and painted backdrops, deceived me and most cinema-goers.

Later, I conducted interviews with stars and directors for a series of newspapers and magazine articles. I also wrote a book on Irish Films for Folens's Irish Environmental Library Series. This gave me a deeper insight into the motivations and philosophies of film-makers. A number of people spoke to me of the need for a history of film-making in Ireland and suggested I should write it. This book is the result of a five-year labour of love. In it, I have outlined the development of film-making in Ireland from the first screening at the Star of Erin Music Hall in Dame Street on 20 April 1896, through the jerky one-reeler at the turn of the century to the multi-million dollar productions of today. I have also detailed the efforts of an emerging band of contemporary vibrant young Irish film-makers.

My task was to write a history of film-making in Ireland, which is mainly the story of the making of feature films by foreign directors. Up to the late 1970s the Irish contribution was confined almost entirely to shorts and documentaries. Native feature film-making only began on an acceptable level after the foundation of the Irish Film Board. At various stages throughout the years, important one-off works did emerge from Irish directors. One of the earliest examples was *The Dawn* in 1936, acted by amateurs in Killarney and directed by Tom Cooper. Unfortunately there was no follow-up.

Arthur Flynn - Author

The notable point about the pre-Ardmore days was that the majority of films shot on location had an Irish setting, e.g. *Odd Man Out, The Quiet Man* and *Captain Boycott* . There were a few exceptions such as Huston's *Moby Dick* and Olivier's *Henry V.* When Ardmore opened, the balance swung in the opposite direction with settings as varied as Germany, France, China and America. During the seventies, Dublin was the location for a series of quickie Italian and German films. I outline the turbulent thirty-eight year history of Ardmore Studios in which it changed ownership several times with a number of receivers to its present capacity bookings. I describe the films produced there by leading directors ranging from Carol Reed, Martin Ritt, Henry Hathaway to John Huston, John Boorman and Stanley Kubrick. A little known fact is that a neat thriller entitled *Dementia,* made at the studio in 1963, was directed by Francis Ford Coppola - ten years before he directed *The Godfather.* Ardmore brought in the big names Cagney, Mitchum, Burton, Hepburn, Harvey, O'Toole and Connery. But it was only a service industry which supplied facilities for visiting production companies; it did nothing to foster an indigenous Irish film industry.

The early 1990s saw the first indications of an unprecedented upturn in the fortunes of film-making in Ireland by both indigenous directors and foreign companies availing of the tax breaks of Section 35 of the Finance Act and locations in the country. A number of facts contributed to this welcome development, beginning with the two Oscars for *My Left Foot,* the nomination of Richard Harris for *The Field* and Neil Jordan's Oscar for the screenplay of *The Crying Game.* Coinciding with these achievements, Michael D. Higgins, on his appointment as Minister for Arts, Culture and the Gaeltacht, took a keen interest in the film industry. He immediately re-established the Film Board and set various training programmes in motion, dealing with all aspects of film. This resulted in a number of important films being produced in Ireland from Mel Gibson's *Braveheart* to Gerry Stembridge's *Guiltrip* and Neil Jordan's *Michael Collins.*

The book includes a filmography of all feature films, made partly or entirely in Ireland, complete with date, director and stars.

Chapter 1

Birth of the Cinema

No one man invented the 'motion picture'. It was the product of scientists, artists and businessmen working independently in many parts of the world.

The magic lantern, which appeared in the sixteenth century, was the precursor of the film. It consists of a series of drawings which, when spun and viewed through slits, gave the illusion of motion. A form of this technique - little figures on the corners of copy-book pages - have amused children for generations.

The next development was the replacement of the drawings with photographs. This process, called chronophotography, was developed by a number of scientists towards the end of the nineteenth century. Continuous research and advancing technology led the American, George Eastman, to perfect a system of printing images onto a continuous roll of celluloid film. Numerous variations on this format were made, including Thomas Edison's Kinetoscope, a type of peep-show through which moving pictures could be viewed.

It seemed a natural progression to project the moving images onto a screen large enough for an audience to view. The efforts to do so turned into a world-wide race with many countries intent on being the first onto the field. The blueprints and experiments of the competitors were closely guarded secrets.

Finally, on 20th February 1896, at the Grand Cafe, Boulevard des Capucines in Paris, Louis and Auguste Lumière showed the first moving pictures to a paying public. This new form of entertainment was an instant success with the audience clamouring for more. Depicted in those first films were action sequences of people and transport and newsreel footage of processions and meetings.

The success of the Paris cinema led to the opening of many more around the world. Outside the major cities, films were screened wherever a showing could be arranged - in parish halls, fairgrounds, music halls, markets and anywhere people were liable to gather. Films were sometimes included in music-hall bills. In the initial years cinema passed into the hands of the travelling fairground showmen who transformed their puppet shows and lit-up theatres. This was

Louis and Auguste Lumière

particularly the case in Ireland. By 1908, permanent cinemas were being built on a wide scale.

In May 1897, the gradually developing cinema in France suffered a severe blow when a projectionist's carelessness resulted in a fire which claimed one hundred and forty lives. Following this, the authorities imposed more stringent controls on public performances. France was also to the forefront in producing the first dramatic film, *The Story of a Crime*, in 1901; America followed two years later with Edwin Porter's *The Great Train Robbery*.

James Joyce followed the progress of this new industry with interest. His sister, Eva, was a regular cinema-goer. When she pointed out that it was unusual to find a city the size of Dublin without a cinema, he saw this as both a challenge and an opportunity. Any mention of Dublin normally fired his imagination. He immediately set about planning a cinema for his native city. However, his intention was to make money rather than to bring a novel artistic experience to Dubliners.

Joyce was living in Trieste at the time and he persuaded a group of local businessmen to finance the venture. He found no difficulty in

acquiring a suitable premises, the necessary licences, the staff and the films. The cinema, which he named the Volta, was situated in Mary Street. It opened on 20th December 1909. Most of the films shown were continental with Italian titles. The opening programme consisted of a number of one-reelers, *The First Paris Orphanage, La Pouponniere, Devilled Crab, The Bewitched Castle* and *Beatrice Cenci*.

The venture proved successful and people flocked to see each new film. Joyce enjoyed his role as a prosperous businessman and even planned to expand and open cinemas in Cork and Belfast. However, on his return to Trieste the business declined through mismanagement and had to be sold.

The earliest producers in England had been in the main either enthusiastic photographers or inventors who created short films at very little cost and were astonished at the profits they could make on a success. Cecil Hepworth, one of the most prominent film pioneers in England, was responsible for many of the first shorts filmed in Ireland. In 1905 he was to make England's first dramatic film, *Rescued by Rover*.

In Ireland, films began to be made from the end of the nineteenth century. They were in the main current affairs shorts that dealt with meetings, exhibitions, races and visits of prominent people. There was even a brief record of the Dublin Horse Show. Most of these films were combined to form an evening's entertainment. Dan Lowry exhibited them at the Star of Erin Music Hall in Dame Street on 20th April 1896, when it was temporarily converted into a cinema. The following year the tinted films of Professor Joly of Paris were shown. Later that year, films were also shown at the Rotunda and Gaiety.

What must be the earliest Irish newsreel of any length was a documentary on the state visit of Queen Victoria to Dublin in 1900, starting with her arrival at Kingstown (now Dún Laoghaire) and following her progress through streets lined with flag-waving crowds. Incidental films of Irish scenery and topicalities, such as the *Fire Brigade Going Out on a Call, A View from the Train on the*

Blackrock Line, Demolition of a Building and *The Gordon Bennett Motor Race in Kildare,* were also shot around the turn of the century.

On 2nd January 1905, a pictorial record of the major events of that year was shown in the Town Hall in Rathmines by the Irish Animated Photo Company. The programme featured the ceremonies of the Consecration of Saint Patrick's Cathedral, Armagh, with close-ups of the prelates assisting at the event, and His Eminence, Cardinal Vanutell giving the Papal Blessing to the multitude. Local shots included congregations leaving churches in Rathgar and Rathmines in which individuals were clearly recognisable. The motion in them was jerky, the people goose-stepping much as they were to do in the later Mack Sennett comedies.

In America, production companies mushroomed and there was a vigorous battle to gain control of the booming film business. By 1909 there were at least nine separate companies. D.W. Griffith emerged as the architect of that country's supremacy in the cinema. His pioneering forms and techniques were to remain largely unchanged for the next half century. Initially, film production was based in New York, mainly because

D.W. Griffith

the leading actors worked on Broadway, but a number of factors, including better weather conditions and lower costs, soon drew the film-makers to Hollywood.

Nineteen hundred and ten is another important date in the history of the cinema, as it was the first occasion when an American film company travelled outside the States to film on location. The company was Kalem, founded in 1907 by Frank Marion, Samuel Long and George Klein. In the spring of 1910 Marion called Sidney

Sidney Olcott

Olcott, their top director, to his office. Opening a large map of the world in front of him, he asked Olcott to choose whichever country he would like to visit with a full film-making unit. Olcott promptly pointed to the small island, where his mother was born, on the west coast of Europe - Ireland. (She was born in Dublin.)

Olcott, who ranked second only to Griffith, was one of the most creative directors in America.

He had begun his career as an actor and had directed the first screen version of *Ben Hur* in 1907. His brief was to look for new material and subsequently to produce films with suitable themes.

Kalem's *Robert Emmet, Ireland's Martyr*

In August 1910, Olcott landed at Queenstown (now Cobh) and remained for a short while at the Victoria Hotel in Cork. Having toured Ireland, Olcott went to Killarney, where he stayed at the Glebe Hotel. He brought with him Gene Gauntier, his leading lady, Robert Vignola, and George Hollister, his cameraman. Miss Gauntier later wrote *Blazing Trail*, describing her work with Olcott. The manuscript is on display in the Museum of Modern Art Film Library in New York. She and Olcott also collaborated on film ideas and scenarios, and they were two of the first people in the world to write specifically for the cinema.

Olcott's first film in Ireland was *The Lad from Old Ireland*, described as 'Kalem's Great Trans-Atlantic Drama'. A number of shorts on Irish beauty spots such as Blarney Castle, Glengarriff and the Lakes of Killarney followed. Leaving Ireland the company moved to England, where they filmed *The Irish Honeymoon* and to Germany to make *The Little Spreewald Mädchen*.

The Lad from Old Ireland was such a huge success with Irish immigrants in America that Kalem decided to send a larger company the following year. In addition to Gauntier, Vignola and Hollister, Olcott brought Jack P. McGowan from Australia, Alice Hollister (the cinema's first Vamp), Alice Maples, Jack Clarke, Pat O'Malley, Allan Farnham, Arthur Donaldson and Helen Lindroth.

They returned in June 1911, staying in Killarney for a few days, but Olcott felt that a country setting would better suit his purpose. One day, while touring in a jaunting car, he discovered the village of Beaufort, about eight miles from Killarney and decided it was an ideal location. His efforts to explain his intentions caused much amusement among the locals as they knew nothing about motion pictures. Olcott enquired if they had ever seen a magic lantern show. Yes, they knew about lantern entertainments. 'Well', said Olcott, 'films are like magic lantern slides, but they move'. They were still just as bewildered but were willing to help Olcott and learn about this amazing new invention

In Beaufort the company stayed at the hotel of Patrick O'Sullivan and his daughter, Annie. Olcott and his crew worked all through the summer of 1911. They took the interiors on a platform they had built behind the O'Sullivan house and travelled throughout the country for exteriors.

In his superbly documented book, *The Rise of the American Film,* Lewis Jacobs describes the work of Olcott. His first production in 1911 centred on the adventures and trials of the rebels of 1798 and principally those of Rory O'Moore, the romantic Emmet-like figure. The film made for boisterous, fast-moving entertainment. A copy of it is in the British Film Institute Distribution Library. It is worth noting that this copy does not include the closing scene in which Rory departs by sailing-boat for America. This sequence was filmed at Queenstown. At the time, Olcott was unaware of the explosive content of the material. The controversy that followed its release greatly annoyed the British Home Office.

The film also displeased the local clergy. The

Sunday after the film was completed, the O'Sullivans with Sidney Olcott and some of his crew attended Mass in the local Catholic Church. The Parish Priest of Tuogh, Fr. Daly, in his sermon spoke of the evil element in the village represented by the Kalem Company, whose players dressed as priests and nuns. The village was shocked and a group of local men threatened to 'beat up' the sinners from America. Filming could not continue until Olcott and the American Consul in Queenstown had been to see the local bishop and the latter instructed the parish priest to apologise for his remarks. Kalem became apprehensive and wanted to recall Olcott, but Olcott admitted his gaffe and promised to stay clear of such delicate subject matter in future. He was allowed to remain in Ireland.

From then on, the O'Kalems (as they jokingly called themselves) and the villagers became firm friends. There was no shortage of villagers willing to play small parts in the films at five shillings per day. Some even played quite

Sidney Olcott's *The Kerry Dancer*

important roles: Annie O'Sullivan was one of the female leads in *The Gypsies of Old Ireland*. Most of the films were made in Beaufort, Dunloe and Killarney while much of the travelling was done on sidecars. On one occasion they travelled fifty miles to Dingle only to discover on arrival they had forgotten the camera.

Olcott then turned his attention to Dion Boucicault's melodramas and filmed *The Colleen Bawn* starring Brian MacGowan. Olcott himself played the part of Danny Mahon. Then followed *Arrah-na-Pogue* with music specially composed by Walter Cleveland Simon. Other films included: *Robert Emmet, Ireland's Martyr,* starring Jack Melville and Pat O'Malley, *You'll Remember Ellen* (from Thomas Moore's poem), *The O'Neill* (from *Erin's Land*), *The Kerry Gow, A Girl of Glenbeigh, The Fishermaid of Ballydavid, Shaun the Post, The Kerry Dancer, The Shaughraun, Conway* and *Ireland the Oppressed.*

Sidney Olcott and Gene Gauntier left Kalem in 1912 and formed the Gene Gauntier Feature Players. They returned to Beaufort in 1913, together with Jack J. Clarke, whom Miss Gauntier had married during the making of *From Manger to Cross* the previous year. The people of Beaufort believed Olcott was deeply in love with Miss Gauntier, and that he would have married her but for the fact that he was a devout Catholic and she had been divorced.

In August 1914, hundreds of Volunteers from all over Kerry and many other parts of the province of Munster marched through the streets of Killarney, which were lined with cheering people. The local Killarney company stole most of the show on the day because it was the only fully-armed group in the whole parade. Because of the difficulty in obtaining arms the Volunteers had been using dummy rifles for training but the Killarney company was now equipped with rifles and bayonets. Members of the Royal Irish Constabulary were as baffled as the other on-lookers as to where the arms came from. The explanation was simple. The rifles and bayonets were props of the Kalem Company. This was Olcott's discreet revenge for the earlier interference by the British authorities. The competitions in signalling and drilling were filmed by Kalem.

That same year Olcott formed Sid Films, and returned yet again to Beaufort to make a series of films starring Valentine Grant, who later became his wife. Olcott at this time talked of building a permanent film studio there to enable him to film all year round. He consistently claimed that he found it easy to direct the Irish people as they were natural actors and actresses. Unfortunately, the outbreak of World War I put an end to his plans. In his eighteen weeks' stay in Beaufort, he made almost one film per week, each about three reels long and running approximately three quarters of an hour. Lewis Jacobs maintains that these films succeeded in killing off the idea of the stage Irishman because they showed people in a realistic way.

Annie O'Sullivan later spoke of how much the Kalem Company loved Beaufort and how they would pretend that their birthdays fell during their visit as an excuse to celebrate. Both Robert Vignola and Olcott kept up a correspondence with Miss O'Sullivan until their deaths. Alice Hollister recalled how she and Pat O'Malley had got together shortly before the latter's death in 1966, and talked about Beaufort all night. None of the O'Kalems are alive today. Valentine Grant died in 1949; Jack P. McGowan died in 1952; Robert Vignola passed away in 1962 and Gene Gauntier in 1967. After her death, Olcott went to live with Vignola. A few weeks before Christmas of that year, Olcott wrote out his Christmas cards and parcelled up his wife's jewellery to be sent to individuals he felt Valentine would want to give them to.

A few days before Christmas, Annie O'Sullivan found two letters for her in the post. One was from Vignola telling her of Olcott's death. The second was from Olcott and enclosed was a gold bracelet belonging to his wife. He had never forgotten Beaufort.

Miss Gene Gauntier and Jack Clarke in *You'll Remember Ellen*

Chapter 2

The Irish Pioneers

The outbreak of World War I was to remove European competition and establish America's dominance of world cinema. An American producer, Walter MacNamara, of MacNamara Feature Film Company, had come to Dublin in 1913, with the idea of making a film about Robert Emmet. He was introduced to P.J. Bourke, an actor/manager who lived in Dominick Street, and who not only provided him with a shooting script but also made the costumes for the production. Bourke was paid £3 per day for his efforts. The film *Ireland a Nation* which featured Barry O'Brien concentrated on the life and times of Emmet and also depicted more modern attempts to win Home Rule. It was shot in the vicinity of Baltinglass and Glendalough in County Wicklow and ran to five reels.

The film had only one public showing in Dublin in January 1917 at the Rotunda, because the British authorities quickly banned it. They felt it raised contentious issues and interfered with recruitment to the army. The critics were generous in their reviews. They found that the editing and cutting gave an exciting pace to the film and that only in the courtroom scene were the audience aware of a static camera. Techniques rare for the period were the close ups and the panning shots. However, the film did contain some anachronisms, e.g. the message containing the news of the Act of Union in 1801 was despatched to Father Murphy two years after his death; and some inaccuracies, such as Michael Dwyer marrying Anne Devlin and emigrating to Australia. In 1920 the Gaelic Film Company added scenes from contemporary Ireland to bring it up to date. These showed the

General Post Office, Dublin, 1916

Auxiliaries, the Black and Tans, and the death of the Lord Mayor of Cork, Terence MacSwiney.

From 1913 onwards, most of the major events and leading figures in the national struggle were filmed. Unfortunately quite a considerable amount of film was either lost or destroyed. Part of what was preserved was used in George Morrison's two outstanding films, *Mise Eire* (1959) and *Saoirse?* (1961).

Around this time native film-makers, fascinated by this new medium, began to emerge. Some had theatrical backgrounds and some even combined the roles of actor and director. Of course there were also those who saw the possibilities strictly in commercial terms. It was not difficult to set up a production company. The initial outlay was on the camera, film, processing facilities and also, possibly, costumes. Actors were readily available, particularly from the Abbey Theatre. Many actors received no payment and others only requested a small remuneration. For many, the

Poster for *In the Days of St. Patrick*

In the Days of St. Patrick - The Chariot Race (Courtesy George Morrison)

excitement of being in a film and seeing themselves on the screen was reward enough.

Producers believed they had a ready market for their films in America, Italy, England, Australia and France, and more companies kept emerging. Just before the Easter Rising in March 1916, the Film Company of Ireland was established by James Mark Sullivan, an American diplomat and lawyer. Consisting mainly of actors from the Abbey Theatre, this company produced such films as *O'Neill of the Glen* and *The Miser's Gift*, both directed by, and starring, J.M. Kerrigan. Other titles from this company included *Woman's Wit, Food of Love, Widow Malone* and *The Eleventh Hour*. In all they made nine films. Like Olcott, they intended to show to the world that there was more to Ireland than the stereotype of the 'pigs in the parlour'. They also planned to build a large studio that winter and to install the best equipment available. This plan did not materialise but they continued in production . On 26th October 1916, the Dame Street Picture House showed *The Miser's Gift*, describing it as the first comedy production by the Film Company of Ireland. The same cinema, in the following month, showed another of their productions, *An Unfair Love Affair*, directed by J.M. Kerrigan and starring Nora Clancy and Fred O'Donovan. The versatile Kerrigan also directed and starred in *Puck Fair Romance*, co-starring Kathleen Murphy. Another important production in 1916 was *Molly Bawn*, directed by Cecil B. Hepworth and starring Alma Taylor and Stewart Lowe.

The General Film Company of Ireland headed by Norman Whitton, with J.W. Mackey from Galway in charge of production and J. Gordon Lewis as cameraman, made an important film in 1917. It was *In the Days of St. Patrick*, directed by Whitton and starring a well-known Queen's Theatre actor, Ira Allan, in the title role. Alice Cardinall played his mother, George Griffin was King Laoghaire, Maud Hume the Queen, and T. O'Carroll Reynolds played Niall of the Nine Hostages. One of the slaves was a black boxer named Cyclone Billy Warren, a notable character around Dublin for a long time. The main location was in Rush, County Dublin and the ambitious production featured pirate galleys and chariots. It took a year of patiently watching the weather and seasons to get the proper conditions for filming. An interesting epilogue to the film showed some of the memorials to the saint: his grave at Downpatrick, his bell, pilgrims climbing and praying on Croagh Patrick, the Cathedral of Saint Patrick at Armagh and His Eminence Cardinal Logue blessing the children of Patrick's 'Children of Erin' in all lands and on all seas. The results more than justified the difficult conditions and the critics gave it good reviews. It was well received throughout Ireland and England by trade and public alike.

Whitton also ran a newsreel called *Irish Events* for which he had his own laboratory in Pearse Street. At that time there were two other laboratories in Dublin: The Irish Animated Picture Company, also in Pearse Street, and the Gaumont Company in Lord Edward Street. They had newsreel film on Countess Markievicz and other prisoners and also of the surviving leaders of the Rebellion when they left prison in 1917. Other newsreel footage included the Conference of Ireland (excluding Sinn Féin members), which was convened by Lloyd George in Trinity College, and the funeral of Thomas Ashe. These latter films were preserved in the National Library.

Nineteen seventeen proved to be an extremely busy year with the following films in circulation: *The Upstart, Blarney, The Byeways of Fate* and *The Irish Girl*, all directed by J.M. Kerrigan, and *The First Irish National Pilgrimage to Lourdes*. The Film Company of Ireland announced their forthcoming films, *Rafferty's Rise*, directed by Kerrigan and a three-act comedy by Nicholas Hayes about a police man, *When Love Came to Gavin Burke*, directed by Fred O'Donovan and starring Brian Moore and Kathleen Murphy. Later that year O'Donovan directed a screen version of Charles Kickham's novel *Knocknagow* in which Cyril Cusack made a fleeting appearance as a five-year-old child evicted on to the roadside. William Moser was cameraman. Prominent members of the cast included Brian McGowan, J. McCarre and Alice Keating. It was filmed around Clonmel where it had its first showing. Other films were a comedy, *A Passing Shower*, and two dramas, *A Man's Redemption* and *Cleansing Fires*.

Quite a number of the same names continually appear in the credits of productions around this period because something of a repertory group of actors and directors had been assembled. They worked well together and moved from film to film. In 1917 the Irish Film Company announced they had built up a library of 10,000 feet of Irish scenery and had compiled *A Serial of Twenty Irish Scenics*. Whitton's company produced other films of local interest, such as a visit to Patterson's match factory entitled *Matchmaking in Ireland*. He was approached by the Court Laundry to make a film of their operation and Dubliners saw for the first time how their clothes were cleaned. Ireland's first cartoon film, 450 feet in length, entitled *Ten Days Leave*, was also produced that year. It received its first public showing in the Bohemian Cinema, Phibsboro. Frank Leah was the animator and Jack Warren the director. Warren, an Englishman, was editor of an Irish magazine, *The Irish Limelight*, and Leah was one of its regular contributors.

In 1915, some thirty years before *Hungry Hill* and *Odd Man Out,* the famed Abbey actor F.J. McCormick directed and acted in a film called *Fun at Finglas Fair*, concerning the antics of two escaped convicts. It was written by Cathal MacGairbhigh and starred the Columbian Players. The film was

Billy Power's Shop

shown to the manager of the Masterpiece Cinema in Talbot Street, but was never screened publicly as British soldiers broke into the cinema during the 1916 Rising and accidentally destroyed the prints. McCormick appeared in some later films of the Irish Film Company including *Irish Destiny* and *The Life of Michael Dwyer*. These films were shot mainly around Dublin and although there were not many cars in use at the time an occasional one appeared by accident in a film which had a period setting.

Over forty years before the opening of Ardmore Studio, Bray played a significant part in early film production. William Power, who returned from Manchester with the intention of making films to meet the demand for Irish pictures, was the leading figure in this respect. He ran a barber's shop on Novara Road, which was as much a film studio and laboratory as it was a hairdresser's. He set up a Dramatic Society in 1917 so as to have a recruiting ground for his films. One year later he wrote, produced and directed a short comedy with the intriguing title *Willie Scouts while Jesse Pouts.* He was pleased with the results and received such support locally that he founded the Celtic Film Company. His second project was a more ambitious two hour film, *Rosaleen Dhu*. This was the tale of a Fenian exiled from Ireland who joins the Foreign Legion. He meets and marries an Algerian girl who turns out to be an heiress to a vast Irish estate.

The film was shot mainly in the Bray area although they did go as far as Arklow for the desert scenes and to Kilmacanogue for a crossroads dancing sequence. Long before Huston, Kubrick and Boorman, Power had realised the potential of the Wicklow landscape.

These early films were shot mainly by a camera in a fixed position but Power, with great foresight, invested in a camera capable of panning (for the princely sum of £88). But if no expense was spared on the camera and film, the props and cast cost nothing. Extras were selected from amongst the eager onlookers. Sometimes the company would neglect to ask permission to use private property. For example, a thatched cottage on Bray Head was used for an eviction scene unknown to the owner, a farmer who was milking his cows in an adjoining field. The hero's farewell took place on a coalboat which had been anchored in Bray Harbour for over a week. Power left a man half shaved in the barber's chair when he got word that the boat was about to sail. He gathered his crew, rushed to the harbour and shot the scene.

The film was processed in wooden barrels in a small yard at the rear of the barber's shop and later sub-titled in the tiny lab. *Rosaleen Dhu* was premiered in Mac's, a cinema housed in the old Turkish Baths in Bray. A warm reception from the local audience led to its screening nationwide. An even greater boost came from the offer of £2,000 for it from an American company.

All those connected with the Celtic Film Company were greatly encouraged by this success—and planned their second feature, *An Irish Vendetta*, with William Power himself in the leading role. He decided that those taking part in this production would receive shares and thus be fairly rewarded for their work. They were filming the story's climax on Leopardstown race course when tragedy struck. Power's horse bolted, throwing him onto the railings. He died two days

Jimmy O'Dea, Nan Fitzgerald and Fred Jeffs in
The O'Casey Millions

later, on 6th June 1920, in the Mater Hospital. Films and material connected with the Celtic Film Company fared no better than those of other groups in Irish film history. One copy of *Rosaleen*

Dhu was said to have been destroyed by the floods in Little Bray in 1935. Sadly, not a single still or frame of any of William Power's work has survived.

In 1922 Charles McConnell became chairman of another Irish film company, Irish Photoplays Ltd (capital £10,000). Other founders of this company were Fred Jeffs (real name Arthur O'Connor), Senator George Nesbitt, and Kenneth Hartley, a Londoner. They financed the making of three films: *The O'Casey Millions, Wicklow Gold* and *Cruiskeen Lawn*. The latter concerned horse-racing and was directed by Norman Whitton. Incidentally, Harry O'Donovan was property master for the company.

McConnell recalled those days:

We didn't make money from them, but we did cover ourselves. The stars of the films, as we liked to call them, were paid peanuts compared with even small time players of today. The 'extras' were often delighted to work just for the thrill of being in a film.

I remember Jimmy O'Dea quite well. He was very young and shy and mostly played straight parts, like in The Casey Millions when he was the romantic lead. He revealed great talent even at that early stage and I knew he would have a big future in films. I didn't see him then the great comedian he was later

Charles McConnell

to become, but he had a lively and lovable sense of humour.

We looked upon the film-making as an adventure and great fun. It was grand working with such dedicated people as Jimmy, Thomas Moran, Fay Sergeant, Chris Silvester, Nan Fitzgerald, Fred Jeffs, Kathleen Drago and Barrett McDonnell.

McConnell was proud of the fact that all those early films were scripted, photographed, produced and directed by an Irish film team:

I realised at the time that this small country could not compete with the film-makers of Britain

Frances Alexander in
Willy Reilly and his Colleen Bawn

and America with all their millions. But our little films - they ran for about an hour - were a success on the cinema circuit in Ireland and were actually shown in America. I must mention John McDonagh, who scripted and produced The Casey Millions. He was very gifted.

McDonagh, a well-known contributor to Radio Éireann, wrote the script for all three films. He later made *Paying the Rent* and *Willie Reilly and the Colleen Bawn* and was connected with many other films as writer, director, producer and actor. This latter film was one of the most popular and successful of the Film Company of Ireland's productions. Based on the 1855 novel by William Carleton, the film was shot at the height of the War of Independence. The story of a dispossessed Irish gentleman and his love for the Colleen Bawn, it makes a plea for better understanding between

Catholics and Protestants. The cast was headed by Brian McGowan and Frances Alexander.

From 1922, film-making in Ireland became a regular business as more ambitious projects went into production. John Hurley directed Mícheál MacLiammóir in *Land of Her Fathers* in 1924, with Phyllis Wakely, Frank Hugh O'Donnell and members of the Abbey Company. It was made by the Hepworth Company in Enniskerry and Killarney. The last print of this film was stolen in New York and has never since turned up. It was shot by one of D.W. Griffith's cameramen. The next year the Jessie Lasky Company filmed exteriors for *Irish Luck* in Killarney. This company, which included Cecil B. de Mille and Samuel Goldwyn amongst its directors, was one of the top film companies in the world. The same year I.G. Eppel made *Irish Destiny*, a love story set against the back ground of 'The Troubles' and featuring the burning of the Custom House. Exteriors were shot in Glendalough and Greystones and interiors in Shepherd's Bush Film Studio. The stars were

Mícheál MacLiammóir in a scene from film
Land of Her Fathers

Denis O'Dea, Una Shiels, Paddy Dunne Cullinan, Daisy Campbell and Maureen Delaney. The professionals were paid £6 per day and the amateurs in the cast received half that amount. In 1929, Lt. Colonel Victor Haddick from Limerick made another film about Saint Patrick. It was *Ireland - Rough-Hewn Destiny* with Gearoid O'Lochlinn, an Irish-speaking actor, playing the saint. Later that same year the Muintir Vitagraph Company made *Bunny Blarneyed*, the story of a girl's suitor who forces her father's consent by hanging him over the Blarney Stone. It starred John Bunny and was directed by Larry Trimble.

Some years after Frank O'Connor's first book of short stories was published in 1931, the

Barry Fitzgerald and Maureen Delaney in a scene from *Land of Her Fathers*

playwright, Denis Johnston, made the title story, 'Guests of the Nation', into a silent film, using actors mainly associated with the Gate Theatre, including Barry Fitzgerald, Shelagh Richards and Esther Cunningham. Set in 1921, the film depicts the relationship between two captured British soldiers and their IRA captors. When the British authorities refuse to trade prisoners, the IRA men reluctantly execute the two soldiers. This was Denis Johnston's first venture into film-making and thereafter he was to concentrate mainly on playwrighting.

Scene from *Guests of the Nation* directed by Denis Johnston

Chapter 3

The Talkies

Some sound films were made from the mid twenties but the quality of sound was so poor that they were never released. On 6 October 1927 Warner Brothers screened *The Jazz Singer*, starring Al Jolson which changed the history of films.

By 1929 the attendance at picture showings had increased enormously in the USA owing to the popularity of 'the talkies'. In the transition years it seemed as if every second film was a musical with the advertising reading: ALL TALKING. . . ALL SINGING. . . ALL DANCING. . ALL COLOUR. Film producers saw the potential of Broadway stars and brought them to Hollywood for screen musicals. Not only were individual performers engaged but entire stage productions. However, many singers were apprehensive of the new genre and were reluctant to leave the stage.

One of the first to be enticed by the attractive salaries was Ireland's John McCormack, then ranked as one of the world's leading tenors. He received $50,000 a week for his ten weeks' work on his sound début in the Fox musical *Song of my Heart* (for which locations were filmed near Bray). The film, directed by Frank Borzage, also featured the young Irish actress Maureen O'Sullivan, who was beginning to make an impression in Hollywood. She played the daughter of a family threatened with ruin whose fortunes are restored by a John McCormack fund-raising recital. She was later to gain world-wide fame as Jane in the *Tarzan* films. Although *Song of my Heart* received good reviews from the critics, the public were not too enthusiastic: they enjoyed McCormack on records and in concert, but were not so keen on him as a stocky leading man.

Some years later McCormack co-starred with Henry Fonda and Annabella in *Wings of the Morning* which was filmed partly in Killarney. Directed by Harold Schuster, it was a melodrama, with a mixture of gypsies, romance, songs and horsemanship. It had the distinction of being the first technicolour film made in the British Isles. Other notable films produced during 1936 included Brian Desmond Hurst's *Irish Hearts* based on Dr Abrahamson's novel, *Night Nurse*. The cast included Nancy Byrne, Lester Matthews, Sara Allgood and Arthur Sinclair. Hurst followed this with a film version of John Millington Synge's classic, *Riders to The Sea*, starring Sara Allgood, Kevin Guthrie, Ria Mooney and Shelagh Richards.

Scene from *Man of Aran*

It was filmed in Renvyle, County Galway. Sponsored by singer Gracie Fields, this was one of a number of films in which companies and individuals invested in return for a percentage of the profits.

On a boat trip from America to Europe, the renowned documentary film-maker, Robert Flaherty, heard a young Irishman describe the Aran Islands off the west coast of Ireland, where life was so primitive that the islanders had to make soil by hauling seaweed up the cliffs and mixing it with sand to form a top-soil in which to grow their potatoes. This impressed Flaherty who saw the

Tiger King in *Man of Aran*

region as the location for man's struggle against the elements and he began to research the subject. Michael Balcon, production-chief of Gaumont-British, became interested in the project and allotted £10,000 for *Man of Aran,* as a sound film, which was less than the cost of Flaherty's silent picture *Nanook of the North*, ten years before. Flaherty cast islanders in all the roles. He spotted Mikaleen Dillane, a young boy he wanted for one of the main characters. His parents were reluctant to allow the boy to appear and Flaherty had to resort to dubious methods to get their consent. Maggie Dirrane was cast as the mother and the most difficult character to cast, the father, was finally found in the person of Tiger King. Flaherty

Maggie Dirrane in *Man of Aran*

was an intolerable man to work for. In the course of filming, John Taylor, his assistant, was fired twice and quit once but never stopped working. The islanders, for people who astonishingly could not swim, performed the most amazing feats of bravery, encouraged by Flaherty's unflagging enthusiasm. In the film, Flaherty gambled with the lives of people living at starvation level and was in constant fear that tragedy would strike. He spent eighteen months filming on Inishmore and shot over 200,000 feet of film which was processed on the island in a small studio he had built. The film ran over budget and Gaumont-British felt that Flaherty was shooting the same material over and over again and suggested that Balcon should stop production.

Flaherty did not object as he was glad to be relieved of the compulsion to continue. The film won the Grand Prix Award at the 1934 Venice Film Festival—and a secure place in the history of cinema as one of the greatest documentaries of all time.

Almost thirty years after Olcott's pioneering venture, filming was resumed in Killarney by a local garage proprietor, Tom Cooper, who produced and directed with the co-operation of two hundred and fifty eager amateurs from the surrounding districts, a somewhat remarkable picture called *The Dawn*. Cooper himself headed the excellent cast which also included Eileen Davis, Brian O'Sullivan, Donal O'Cahill and Jerry O'Mahoney. Cooper had no formal training or experience in the technique of film other than being a keen film-goer who appreciated the work of D.W. Griffith and Eisenstein. Originally titled *I am Tainted*, the film took from 1933 to 1936 to shoot as filming was limited to Sunday afternoons and off-peak hours. The consumption of electricity for the indoor scenes equalled the output for the entire Killarney area. There was no basic script and scenes and dialogue were planned only days in advance in local pubs.

As it was made on a modest budget, very few members of the company received a wage, but some of 'the stars' received payment in kind for their service. The completed film was cut, edited, printed and developed in an old shed behind the cinema. The only editing implement was a scissors and the one lensed camera did all the shots—close up and long range. It was a dramatic sound film, based on IRA activity in the Kerry area during the Black and Tan War. There was an extra degree of realism in the fact that it was actually made by people who took part in that campaign. One critic summed it up as 'too bad to be true and too good to miss'.

In an ambush sequence, an IRA unit opens fire on a Crossley tender carrying Black and Tans. It was intended that six of the Tans were to be killed in the exchange and the remainder were to run for cover. For the first take none of the Tans 'died'. Cooper instructed that six were to die in the next take but this time all twelve were dramatically killed. While Cooper in desperation was choosing the six to be killed the next time a gun was accidentally discharged (the signal to open fire) and the third ambush was enacted without being filmed. There was no ammunition left and filming had to be abandoned. One particularly memorable scene involved the striking use of a silhouette representing the rebels marching to battle on a hilltop.

The following is the correspondence between Tom Cooper and Frank Aiken, Minister for Defence, concerning props for *The Dawn*.

Hibernia Film Studios, Killarney

To Frank Aiken Esq.
Minister of Defence
Leinster House
Dublin
5th January 1935

A Chara,

Further to my interview with you at Leinster House some time ago regarding getting from your Department the use of military equipment for the purpose of the production of a film of the Black and Tan days in Ireland, I would be very much obliged if you would kindly arrange to put at our disposal the following:

A quantity of service rifles (war time pattern). A quantity of revolvers, a hotchkiss gun and some machine guns. Also a small quantity of short, service rifles similar to R.I.C. Carbines, as well as a number of old pattern rifle similar to those issued to the Irish Volunteers in the early days of the Movement. A supply of blank ammunition for the above will also be necessary. I would be obliged also if you could arrange to let us have a number of ammunition belts similar to those used by British Tommies, and two officers uniforms complete with belts similar to British officers dress.

I would also be obliged if you would be good enough to arrange to loan us for a short time two Crossley Tenders and one Armoured Car.

The advice of your Department will also be very much appreciated with regard to the correctness of all the equipment and dress outlined above.

I regret having to give you so much trouble but I am sure you will understand that we have no other means of procuring this equipment except through your Department.

For your information I would add that our film will be dated between the years 1918 and '21. A very small portion of the entire film will be dated 1866, and I would be very much obliged for the advice of your Department as to what arms the R.I.C. would carry at about that period.

I am taking up the matter of a permit for the use of the equipment with the Superintendent, Garda Siochana, Killarney, and I would suggest that all arms and ammunition, etc. while here should be under the control of the garda authorities.

I would much appreciate your early attention to this matter as we are now ready to commence filming the production in question.

Thanking you.

Mise le meas,

T. Cooper

DEPARTMENT OF DEFENCE
Dublin

23rd January 1935

A Chara,

I am desired by Mr. Aiken to refer to your letter of the 5th instant requesting the loan of certain military equipment and in reply to say that the Department invariably requests payment in advance for services of this nature. The cost involved in this instance will be a charge at the rate of 1 shilling per mile per vehicle used in the transport of the equipment loaned. Any ammunition used must also be paid for and any loss of or damage to equipment arising out of the loan will require to be made good.

With regard to your request for one Armoured Car I am to inform you that it is the custom always to send two of these cars on a journey and these together

with other vehicles, guns and ammunition which may be loaned to you will require to be returned to military custody at Ballymullen Barracks Tralee each night during the period for which they are loaned.

As all the equipment you require may not be in stores the Minister considers it advisable for you to go into this aspect of the matter in detail with the Quartermaster General's staff here and if you will communicate the day and hour which would be convenient for you an interview will accordingly be arranged.

Mise, le meas,

J.J.J.
Secretary to the Minister

Norris Davidson wrote about The Dawn in World Film News in 1939:

By now the story of its production is fairly well known; short lengths of film developed in a chemist's shop, experiments with more or less home-made sound equipment. The tiny studio is lit by converted trawler lights, the home-made microphone boom squeaked when moved so speakers could not be followed about the studio, the tripod of the Studio Debrie was made in the director's garage, there is not one professional actor in the whole bunch - and with that The Dawn began. It began with either blind arrogance or in the courageous spirit of Flaherty returning to the Far North to re-make Nanook after the destruction of the first negative. This film is Ireland and the incredible

Scene from *The Dawn*

thing is that men who had actually lived a part of the story should not have been too close to it to distinguish between what was important to them and what is important to an audience. The film is not propagandistic, it has no star to create, often its apparent understatement reveals something with dazzling simplicity.

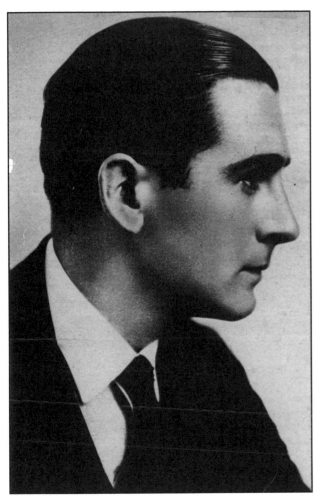

Director Rex Ingram

It was only in the late 1970s that Tom Cooper received a medal from Ardmore Studios in recognition of his contribution to Irish film.

Nineteen thirty-six saw the shooting of *The Early Bird* under the direction of Donovan Pedelty and starring Richard Hayward, Jimmy McGeehan and Charlotte Teddie. It was the first film made by Norris Davidson, who had assisted Flaherty on *Man of Aran*. Davidson collaborated with Lennox Robinson on a screenplay for *General John Regan*, based on a novel by George A. Birmingham, directed by and starring Henry Edwards. Co-stars were Chrissie White and W.G. Fay.

While Cooper was pioneering in Killarney, another Irishman, Rex Ingram, was gaining a reputation in Hollywood. Ingram, the son of a Church of Ireland minister, was born Reginald Ingram Hitchcock in Dublin on 18th January 1893. From an early age he showed an artistic flair and sold many of his drawings. Following the death of his mother he left for America in 1911. A chance meeting with the son of Thomas Edison, a pioneer of American film, gave him an insight into this new industry. He began as an actor but later wrote stories and screenplays and it was not long before he had a comprehensive knowledge of the skills of film-making.

In 1916 Ingram directed his first film, *The Great Problem*, from his own script. Then followed a series of distinguished titles including *Chalice of Sorrows*, *Black Orchids* and *Reward of the Faithless*. It was not until 1920, when he joined the Metro Company and directed *The Four Horsemen of the Apocalypse*, that he became one of the most highly rated and respected directors in Hollywood. This film was responsible for launching Rudolph Valentino as a world star and also Alice Terry, who married Ingram. Many more fine films followed— *The Conquering Power*, *The Prisoner of Zenda* and *Scaramouche*—but in 1924 Ingram grew disillusioned with Hollywood and left to open his own studio in Nice. It was here that he directed *Mare Nostrum* which he regarded as his best film. After making one sound film, *Baroud*, in which he played the leading part he retired from films and devoted his time to sculpting and writing. He died in July 1950. It is sad that such a talented film-maker never directed a film in his native country.

Two films, following in the wake of *The Dawn*, proved a disappointment to those hoping for a successful beginning to an Irish film industry. *Uncle Nick* directed by Tom Cooper was a stagey attempt which had all the crudities of his first film but none of its better qualities. It starred Val Vousden as Uncle Nick. The second film was *The Islandsman* directed by Patrick Heale from a scenario by Donal O'Cahill, who had broken with Cooper. It was badly devised and poorly acted by a cast which included Brian O'Sullivan and Gabriel

Fallon. It also featured Delia Murphy in a singing role.

Various other schemes were announced from time to time for Irish film productions of this period but as budget costs rose they became fewer. One which did get off the ground was *The Voice of Ireland,* directed by Colonel Victor Haddick, a writer, poet and soldier. It was a rather scrappy musical featuring Richard Hayward, Victor Haddick and Barney O'Hara. Then came *Sweet Inniscarra,* directed by Emmet Moore, an Irish-American who had made shorts here previously. The cast included Sean Rogers and Mae Ryan. Later titles included *The Luck of the Irish,* starring Hayward, Kay Walsh and Niall McGinnis, and *Irish and Proud of It,* produced in 1936 by Haddick, Hayward and Donovan Pedelty and starring Dinah Sheridan and Liam Gaffney.

In 1938 Jimmy O'Dea, Myretta Morven and Ronald Malcolmson starred in *Blarney,* directed by Harry O'Donovan. It concerned a salesman who mistakenly took a bag containing stolen gems. Four years previously, Jimmy had appeared in *Jimmy Boy* made by an English company, directed by John Baxter and co-starring Guy Middleton and Vera Sherburne. Jimmy played an Irish bootboy who unmasked a foreign film-star as a spy. *Irish for Luck* (1936), directed by Arthur Woods and starring Athene Seyler and Margaret Lockwood, had all the ingredients of films in vogue at the time: a poor Duchess, an orphan niece and a busker who wins fame on the BBC. *West of Kerry* (1938), directed by Dick Bird and starring Eileen Curran and Cecil Forde, concerns a girl from the Blasket Islands who falls in love with a visiting medical student.

The only person from this era to continue with production was Richard Hayward, who made *Devil's Rock,* starring himself, Geraldine Mitchell and Gloria Granger. It was directed by Germaine Burger. Hayward, better known as a writer than a film-maker also produced shorts on aspects of Irish life.

At the outbreak of the war, the Irish Army co-operated with newsreel camera man, Gordon Lewis, to make *Ireland's Call to Arms* in 1939 and

Step Together by Joe Evans. Other productions of this period included *Kilmainham Jail,* directed by Clifford Marston, a story of the Irish Bastille and *The Life of Michael Flaherty,* directed by John Eldright.

Following the successful screening of several of George Bernard Shaw's plays, the playwright's associate Gabriel Pascal, came to Dublin to set up a company in Ireland to film *Saint Joan* and a number of Shaw's other plays. Several Dublin business men, including Joseph McGrath of the Irish Hospitals' Sweepstake and Arthur Cox, an influential solicitor, were attracted by the enterprise. Shaw favoured the project and aroused the interest of de Valera's government in the possibility of an Irish film industry. De Valera instructed Dan Breen to travel to see Shaw at Ayot St. Laurence and a friendship developed between the two, but the scheme for the filming of Shaw's plays here was not put into effect. The reason was twofold. Firstly, sufficient capital was not forthcoming and secondly, the interest of the businessmen waned when it became evident that the church authorities of Pope Pius XII were reluctant to support the enterprise of a lapsed Protestant.

A letter from Shaw to Dan Breen gives an outline of their plans. It was addressed to 'Dan Breen, Esq. M.P. Dáil Eireann Leinster House, Dublin, Eire':

Dear Dan,

Get all this sentimental rubbish out of your blessed old noodle, I have no feeling in business. You can't humbug me; and it grieves me that you have humbugged yourself to the tune of £10,000.

I have given you time to do your damnedest to raise Irish capital. The result is £40,000. For film purposes it might as well be forty brass farthings; a million and a half is the least we should start with, and it would barely see us through two big feature films.

Shaw said that the only honourable thing for the company to do would be 'to wind up and pocket its losses'. On that he added:

But after the company has been advertised - as it has been - its failure would be a failure for Ireland. What is the available alternative?

First, to get rid of me and Pascal. The Protestant capitalists will not back me because I am on talking terms with you and do not believe that you will go to hell when you die.

The clergy, now that they know that I will not write up the saints for them, will not back up a notorious free thinker. The Catholic laity will not back up a bloody Protestant.

The capitalists, who have no religion and no politics except money making rule me out as a high brow in whom there is no money.

All of them object to Pascal because he is a foreigner who throws away millions as if they were threepenny bits. So out we go with our contracts torn up.

Shaw went on to declare that the company must cut out film production from its programme and become a studio-building company, raising capital wherever it can be got, 'from Rank, from Korda, Hollywood, Belfast, Ballsbridge, Paddy

Sara Allgood

Murphy, John Bull and Solomon Isaacs.

The studio, he said, would cost two million in two years but:

When they are ready the company will be an Irish landlord gathering rent from all the producing companies on earth.

I see no alternative to a winding up order except this. I have written it all to Dev; so don't try to gammon him about it; but believe me and face it . .

You all thought I was your ace of trumps; I know that I might be a drawback but I thought I might as well have a try. It has been a failure. I apologise and withdraw.

Still, ever the best of friends,

G. Bernard Shaw

Shaw's wishful thinking was confined to verbal exchanges and letter writing but apparently nothing more concrete emerged and their plans faded.

During the thirties, the Abbey Company made several tours of the United States and film producers began to take notice. When they toured America with Sean O'Casey's *The Plough and the Stars,* John Ford offered many of the cast roles in his film version of the play. Amongst those who accepted roles were Denis O'Dea, Barry Fitzgerald, F.J. McCormick and Sara Allgood. Initially they were only to appear in one film but some found life so comfortable and the offers so lucrative that they did not return to Ireland. Barry Fitzgerald is the best example of one who stayed and cornered the market in certain character parts, culminating in *Going My Way* for which he won a supporting actor Oscar. F.J. McCormick refused a five-year Hollywood contract and returned to the Abbey. Denis O'Dea appeared in some American films but would not make long-term commitments. In later years Irish actors and actresses including Mícheal MacLiammóir and Siobhan McKenna made one-off films but refused to be bound by restricting, though tempting, contracts.

In 1935 Ford directed the film of Liam O'Flaherty's novel *The Informer*, his next attempt to bring the best of Ireland's literature and theatrical tradition to the screen. It remains an all-time classic, best capturing the sense of place and period of 'The Troubles'. There was disappointment that this film, featuring Victor McLaglen's powerful performance as the mighty Gypo Nolan, was shot, not in Ireland, but on a Hollywood lot in an artificial mist. Still memorable are the wake scene, the court-martial with Gypo exposed as the informer and the finale where he staggers up the church aisle seeking forgiveness. It built and maintained a critical and popular reputation and went on to win four Academy Awards - Ford for direction, Dudley Nicholls for his adaptation, Victor McLaglen for Best Actor and Max Steiner for his musical score. Starring with McLaglen were Preston Foster and Heather Angel. In his critique in *The Spectator* Graham Greene wrote: *'Black and Tan patrols through the Liffey fogs, the watching secretive figures outside the saloons as the drunken informer drifts deeper and deeper with his cronies into the seedy night life of Dublin . . . a memorable picture of a pitiless war waged without honour on either side in doorways and cellars and gin shops.'*

The following year Ford again collaborated with screenwriter Dudley Nicholls to transform Sean O'Casey's ironic tragedy *The Plough and the Stars* into a romantic and sentimental celebration of the struggle for Irish independence. There was an excessive number of scenes with Barbara Stanwyck - RKO's price for allowing Ford to 'import the Abbey players intact' - as Nora Clitheroe and Preston Foster as her husband, Jack. The overall result was a stagey and exaggerated production.

Another renowned director to tackle an Irish classic was Alfred Hitchcock who directed O'Casey's *Juno and the Paycock* entirely in the studio in 1930. His stars were Sara Allgood, Edward Chapman, Sidney Morgan and Maire O'Neill. Hitchcock's film was a literal transcription of the Dublin slum play, which the director admitted he could find no way of narrating in cinematic form. The film was lavishly praised by the critics.

Victor McLaglen in a scene from *The Informer*

Chapter 4

Olivier in Ireland

Film producers were never keen to tackle Shakespeare's plays. Laurence Olivier, however, believed these classics had good potential at the box-office. His first venture was *Henry V*, a film which might never have been made had it not been for an Italian lawyer, Filippo del Giudice, who had persuaded Noel Coward to make *In Which We Serve* and was now looking for another patriotic vehicle to coincide with the D-Day landings in Normandy.

Olivier planned to cast Vivien Leigh as Princess Katherine but she was under contract to David O. Selznick who refused to allow her to appear in 'insignificant roles'. When he was unable to obtain the services of William Wyler as director, Olivier was forced to take on the functions of director, associate producer and leading actor himself. He cut the less heroic parts from the Bard's text, and added a spectacular Agincourt battle sequence and the death of Falstaff.

Film production in Europe at the time was greatly hampered by the war, but neutral Ireland offered facilities not readily available elsewhere. Extensive exterior filming was virtually impossible in Britain and France. In Ireland it presented no problem. Moreover, the absence of black-out restrictions here made it possible to shoot outdoor night scenes. Extras, labourers and horses could also be procured more easily in Ireland than in England.

Olivier explained his reason for choosing Ireland:

The greatest problem of all was finding a spot in England to film the battle. After all, this was the spring and early summer of 1943 and it was impossible to find anywhere that wasn't buzzing with aeroplanes or covered with modern military defences that would have looked odd in 15th century France. Where could we find a really poetic countryside?

The ideal location was Lord Powerscourt's estate, twelve miles south of Dublin, which was made available to the film unit. Olivier was enthusiastic about his find: *'A dream lay-out, exactly the place I had visualised to suit the fantasy of Shakespeare - the little hills, adjacent woods, positions for the French and English camps and a half mile run for the camera track. Finding it was an absolute fluke.'*

Laurence Olivier in *Henry V*

Every movement in the battle scene was planned. Olivier and a small team—associate producer Dallas Bower, art director Paul Sherriff and assistant Carmen Dillon, costume designer Roger Furse, musical director William Watson and film editor Reggie Beck—worked closely together. On the walls of Olivier's office were tiny reproductions on 33mm film of meticulous drawings of every shot in the action sequence. Included were scenes of the French knights floundering in a marsh, English archers and foot soldiers behind stakes, long shots of the French charge and a close-up of a cow's head.

The extras were an unkempt and motley crew as they were not allowed to shave or have a haircut for the duration of their contracts. Consequently, out of costume and dressed in civvies they looked like riff-raff. There were 510 footmen and 164 Defence Force (LDF) from nearby counties. The horsemen were recruited from the twenty-six counties and were paid £1 a day, double that of the others. Horsemen and

footmen slept and ate in separate tents but shared the same food and comforts. The general atmosphere was happy and relaxed. Horace B. Hammond, a Dublin archery expert, instructed the hundreds of mechanics, grocers, clerks, labourers and students in the art of the long bow for the dramatic sequence where the French army face the hail of English arrows. Horses were removed from under ploughs and milk carts. Even racing stables accommodated the film-maker. This new source of revenue, to the unemployed in particular, was most welcome. Chainmail was knitted in wool by girls from the Institute for the Blind and sprayed with aluminium paint.

In Ireland food supplies were plentiful and the weekly consumption was 20,000 eggs, 500 gallons of milk, 75 gallons of cream, 5,400 lbs of meat and 3,500 cabbages. The camp bar opened three nights a week, but those who had leave passes (issued on alternate nights to footmen, nightly to horsemen) patronised the three pubs in Enniskerry, or took the bus to Bray. Both towns profited from this influx of bearded men, whose total weekly salary cheque amounted to over £2,000. Enniskerry, with a population of 370, became a boom town and was unable to cope with the demand for supplies. The village's single taxi, owned by Joseph Troy, drove visitors several times a day to the location. Fifteen thousand people applied to see the filming but permits were granted sparingly. Security was tight on the gates and all permits were checked.

The weather was unsettled, brilliant blue skies being followed by banked clouds and squalls of wind and rain. Thus Olivier, after patiently rehearsing hundreds of horsemen and extras, had often to postpone shooting. He said dejectedly: *'The trouble is that the horses are inclined to get tired and the horsemen to forget.'* Hatless, dressed usually in a leather lumber jacket, riding breeches and golf stockings, and carrying a megaphone, Olivier appeared to be everywhere at once, instructing, coaxing, demonstrating how he wanted a scene enacted. In spite of the frustrating weather and the onerous responsibility of his first directing job, Olivier maintained an even temper. When rehearsing extended formations of horsemen his voice flowed from a dais in tones of politeness: *'Everybody please halt except Section 8 - I'd like you to try it at a steady trot this time, please.'* After each day's shooting he ordered a glass of Guinness for every extra. For this and other reasons he was popular with the men

While he was filming in Ireland, Olivier was unaware that money to keep the film going was in

E.J. McCormick and James Mason in *Odd Man Out*

danger of running out. The production company, Two Cities, had to approach the Rank Organisation for extra funds. Rank financed them to the tune of £300,000, but emphasised that there would no further payments. The final budget was £475 ,000. The actual battle cost £80,000 to film and represented fifteen minutes of screen time in a film lasting two and a half hours. The acting from the entire cast, including Robert Newton, Leslie Banks and Rene Asherton, was superb, with Olivier himself winning an Oscar. Along with Olivier, the credit went to director of photography, Robert Krasker and the mood-catching score of William Walton. The actual Battle of Agincourt segment deservedly belongs with the great moments in cinema history. The critical success of *Henry V* encouraged Olivier to make *Hamlet* and later *Richard III* and *Othello* .

Another significant new talent to emerge in the British film industry during the war years was Carol Reed. In 1946 he chose Belfast as the location for *Odd Man Out*, a Rank Organisation film with interiors shot in Britain. It depicts the last hours of a seriously injured IRA chief wounded in a payroll raid on a mill and the ensuing drama played out against the backcloth of the night-time city. Once again Robert Krasker was director of photography and his versatility is strikingly displayed in the contrast between *Odd Man Out* and *Henry V.*

Reed and Krasker captured magnificently the bleak yet multitudinous city where the wounded man, Johnny McQueen, seeks refuge in his slow journey towards death. *Odd Man Out,* based on the novel by F.L. Green, established Reed as one of Britain's top directors and will be long remembered for the marvellous portrayal of the dying rebel by James Mason and for the last great screen performance of the Abbey Theatre's F.J. McCormick. Irish actor Dan O'Herlihy played his first screen role in this film and was soon after to receive an Academy Award nomination for his role as Robinson Crusoe in the Bunuel film (a role originally intended for Orson Welles). Other important parts were played by Robert Newton, Kathleen Ryan, Noel Purcell, Albert Sharpe and Eddie Byrne. Almost painful in its suspense and tragedy, *Odd Man Out* is a drama not easily forgotten. Reed won his first British Academy

F.J. McCormick in *Odd Man Out*

Michael Scott and Deborah Kerr in *I See a Dark Stranger*

Award for Best Picture with it. Incidentally, his next two films, *The Fallen Idol* and *The Third Man*, also won that award.

During the forties several other less impressive films, many with Irish subject matter, were made here. Frank Launder and Sidney Gilliat Productions produced two films in the mid-forties. Their productions frequently suffered from over scripting so that the dialogue tended to kill the pace as was the case with their first Irish film, *I See A Dark Stranger,* in 1946. Siobhan McKenna was originally offered the starring role, but turned it down when she was advised by F.J. McCormick to remain at the Abbey for three years and become a real actress. She was replaced by Deborah Kerr, starring as a young Irish girl with red hair, a brogue and a temper who is motivated by her patriotism to spy for Germany. Her co-star was Trevor Howard. It also featured Liam O'Gorman, Liam Redmond, Breffni O'Rourke, Cecil Forde and Eithne Dunne. Shot in County Wicklow and set during the Emergency, it depicts the romance between Bridie Quill (Kerr) who is a spy for Germany and Bayne (Howard), a British officer on leave. The film proved more popular in America than Britain.

Launder and Gilliat's next venture *Captain Boycott*, directed and co-written by Launder and Wolfgang Wilhem, was based on the novel by Philip Rooney and filmed in Counties Wicklow, Westmeath and Mayo. It is the story of a struggle against tyranny in 1880 when a wealthy landowner in Ireland threatened to evict his tenants and the farmers in the district stand up to him - they 'boycott' him. It was a compact historical drama in which the principals turned in good performances. It starred Stewart Granger as the Irish hero, Cecil Parker as Captain Boycott and Kathleen Ryan as a farmer's daughter installed in one of Boycott's vacated farms. Other leading roles were taken by Alistair Sims as the parish priest, Noel Purcell as the local teacher and Mervyn Johns as the bailiff. Cameo roles were played by Robert Donat as Parnell and Joe Linnane as an auctioneer.

A unit of the Irish Army was employed for some sequences for which they went under canvas in the mountains. It rained almost continuously and their theme song was 'When it rains, it rains pennies from Denham' (the name of the production company). When the unit moved to Mullingar to film a race meeting, the producers invited local participation. The entire town closed down and turned out in force to be 'in the pictures'. Those in costume were paid twice the fee of those in civvies. The parish priest had to plead with the producers to release the grave diggers to dig a grave.

Brian Desmond Hurst, born in Cork in 1900, began his film-making career in Hollywood in 1925 when he became assistant director to John Ford. He returned to County Kerry to do a stint of location work in 1945 on *Hungry Hill* which was based on the novel by Daphne du Maurier. It starred Margaret Lockwood, Dennis Price and Cecil Parker again. The Irish members of the cast included Eileen Crowe and Arthur Sinclair. Siobhan McKenna, on holidays from the Abbey, made her screen début in a small part. F.J. McCormick also featured. Because *Odd Man Out* and *Hungry Hill* were being filmed at the same time, McCormick moved from one to the other. He was not able for the strain and died less than a year later at the age of fifty-five. Shot partly in Glengarriff, County Cork, *Hungry Hill* was a rambling Victorian melodrama which chronicled two Irish families, the Brodericks and Donovans, over three generations of feuding and bitterness.

In 1948, British director Charles Crichton chose Dublin and Greystones for location work on a mediocre film called *Another Shore*, starring Robert Beatty, Moira Lister and Stanley Holloway. Based on a novel by Kenneth Reddin, it was the tale of a Dublin man's dream to get away to the South Seas. The following year another British company arrived to make *Saints and Sinners*, starring Cork-born Kieron Moore and Christine Norden, with Noel Purcell and Eddie Byrne in support. Other character roles were filled by members of the Abbey company. This was a comedy drama concerning a successful businessman who returns to his native Irish village to find that things have changed. Direction was by Leslie Arliss from a screenplay by Paul Vincent Carroll.

Other feature films made in Ireland during the forties include *Crime on the Irish Border* (or *The Voice Within*), a tale of smuggling on the border (1946), directed by Maurice J. Wilson and starring Kieron Moore, Barbara White, Shaun Noble and Breffni O'Rourke. In 1947 Desmond Leslie directed *Stranger at My Door*, also called *The Iron Staircase*. Four years later, Leslie returned to Dublin to direct a thriller, *At A Dublin Inn*, the story of an ex-convict who becomes a burglar to help a blackmailed girl, featuring Joseph O'Connor, Valentine Dyall and Agnes Barnhill. In 1948, Patrick McCrossan directed two films. The first, *My Hands Are Clay*, with a weak plot and not very imaginative direction, starred Shelagh Richards, Bernadette Leahy and Cecil Brook, and was partly filmed in Dublin and Enniskerry. The second, *Dublin's Fair City*, was never completed.

The highly respected team of Michael Powell and Emeric Pressburger shot sequences for *Black Narcissus* in Killarney and Tipperary in 1946. The film, starring Deborah Kerr, Sabu and David Farrar, was a sentimental melodrama about a group of nuns who open a school and hospital in a hill village in India. Only one or two minutes of the original print survive. The same year also saw the arrival of another leading British director, Herbert Wilcox, to film a segment for one of his highly successful films of the period, *The Courtneys of Curzon Street*. It starred his wife, Anna Neagle, as an Irish maid, with co-star Michael Wilding and Gladys John. It was a musical spanning the years 1899-1945 which followed the saga of the family of a nobleman. It became the top money making film of that year in the British Isles. Richard Massingham directed a children's story entitled *The Greedy Boy* in Wexford in 1947, starring Sile Nic a Bhaird, Joyce Sullivan and Terry Wilson, which won an award at the Venice Film Festival. That same year, American stars Gene Kelly and Betsy Blair came to Shannon Airport to film scenes for *Transatlantic Flight* under the direction of Joseph Ryle.

The fifties began with a number of less significant films. Nineteen fifty saw a drama, *The Strangers Came*, directed by Alfred Travers, with a cast headed by Seamus Mac Locha and Gabriel Fallon. The following year *The Promise of Barty O'Brien*, directed by George Freedland, described how Marshall Aid was put to use in Ireland. Frank O'Connor was responsible for the script which featured such veteran players as Eric Doyle, Harry Brogan, Eileen Crowe, Doirin Ní Mhaidin and Philip O'Flynn. Alfie Byrne, one of the most famous and popular Lord Mayors of Dublin, made a guest appearance. The plot concerns Barty O'Brien's determination to become an electrical engineer and his father's opposition to it. *La Jeune*

Brian O'Higgins, Jack McGowran, Noel Purcell and Michael Gough in *No Resting Place*

Folle was a French production set during 'The Troubles' and was partly filmed in Dublin in 1952 by director Ives Allegret. In 1953 Gerald Healy directed two films, *Cosc an Gadai* and *Turas Tearnaimh* featuring the Abbey players.

Paul Rotha, an authority on the cinema, having written many books on the subject, produced a sensitive film about Wicklow tinkers titled *No Resting Place* in 1950. It is the grim story of a group of itinerants, the Kyles, and particularly of one, Alec Kyle, who is forced to become a fugitive with his family when he accidentally kills a gamekeeper in retaliation for an attack on his young son. One Guard named Mannigan (Noel Purcell), becomes obsessed with tracking down Alec for murder. It also starred Eithne Dunne, Brian O'Higgins, and Jack McGowran. The film proved once again that an artistic film could be

produced on a modest budget. It was the first feature by Rotha and also the first British film made without the use of a studio.

Another small, yet distinguished, film which cannot be overlooked is *A Jack Of All Maids*, about a man who loved women, starring Jack McGowran. It was directed by Abbey Theatre director Tomas MacAnna in the cafe of the old Abbey Theatre in the summer holidays of 1951. MacAnna had previously directed two other films — a documentary called *Wicklow Gold* and an uncompleted documentary about Maynooth College. He then came to the juncture where he had to decide between the cinema and the theatre. Fortunately for the Abbey and its audiences, he opted for the latter.

The participation of the Irish defence forces in film-making began in 1943 with the LDF in *Henry V*, and continued successfully on a regular basis with Irish soldiers doubling as British, German and French troops in a number of major films. Whenever possible, depending on the availability of manpower, the Department of Defence has acceded to requests for the deployment of troops in films. It is Department policy to scrutinise scripts to ensure there is no propaganda or other element which would cause embarrassment before making a commitment. Generally payment is made directly to the Department of Defence by the film companies and they in turn decide the sum to be paid to the respective ranks.

Chapter 5

John Ford's Irishmen

One of the most successful films ever made in Ireland was produced in 1951 when John Ford moved into Counties Galway and Mayo to direct *The Quiet Man*. The eye-patched American director (real name John Feeney), the son of an Irish immigrant, wished to take a break from filming the westerns - *She Wore a Yellow Ribbon, Wagonmaster* and *Stagecoach* - which had established him as the supreme master of the genre. The story of *The Quiet Man*, which Ford termed 'a mature love story', may have attracted him because it concerned an Irish-American returning to the 'ould country'. Characters and acting combined to make *The Quiet Man* the most autobiographical film he ever made. Ford had regularly included a stage-Irish bit character in his films. Following *The Quiet Man* this element became more prominent.

Ford, whose family came from Spiddal, County Galway, had discussed the possibility of making the film with his friend, Lord Killanin, as far back as 1936. The war intervened and it was not until fifteen years later, when producer Herb Yates provided the finance, that filming began in Connemara in locations chosen by Killanin.

The Quiet Man was based on a short story by Maurice Walsh. Ford asked Welsh author Richard Llewellyn, who had written *How Green Was My Valley*, to expand it into a novel and set the story in 1922 at the time of 'The Troubles'. The original draft featured the Black and Tans, but Ford felt that the scenes of violence destroyed the mood and they were eliminated. Frank and John Nugent wrote the screenplay. The cast was led by John Wayne in what was for him an unusual role, Maureen O'Hara in character as a fiery redhead, Barry Fitzgerald outstanding as Michaeleen Og Flynn, a match-making jarvey, and Victor McLaglen giving a likeable performance as the burly villain of the piece.

Having cast the main roles, Ford auditioned actors from the Abbey Theatre to make the film as authentic as possible. In supporting roles were Ward Bond, Eileen Crowe, Mildred Natwick, Francis Ford, Jack McGowran, Arthur Shields, Charles Fitzsimons and May Craig, along with a host of Irish character actors. The nostalgic music was by Victor Young, who scored it with Irish folk songs including 'Galway Bay', 'The Wild Colonial Boy' and 'The Isle of Innisfree', which was written by Richard Farrelly, a Dublin garda.

It was to be the first Republic Picture made outside America and the most expensive film they had ever produced at $1,175,000. Wayne was paid $100,000 and waived his usual percentage. Shooting began in June 1951, in the village of Cong, County Mayo. In spite of careful preparations it was a difficult picture to make. The vagaries of the Irish weather during the six-week

Maureen O'Hara

Irish schedule made it difficult to match the lighting. Yates was determined that it should remain within budget and scrutinised the spending of every penny. While filming in Ireland Ford received his highest military honour, by being named an admiral. To celebrate the occasion John Wayne pushed Ford into Galway Bay.

Wayne played Sean Thornton, a successful boxer in America, who accidentally kills an opponent in the ring. To forget the tragedy he returns to settle in his native Innisfree. Soon he falls in love with a fiery girl, Mary Kate (O'Hara), but her brother, Red Will Danaher (McLaglen), the local squire, refuses to allow him to marry her.

All is settled happily in the end but not before Thornton, overcoming his fear of killing another man, challenges Danaher to a fight—which results in what must be the longest, toughest, most memorable screen fight of all time.

Yates told Ford that the film was not to run any longer than 120 minutes or he would cut it. Ford edited the film to 129 minutes but Yates insisted on 120 minutes. At the preview Ford cut the final nine minutes, the entire fight sequence. Yates relented and Ford got his way.

The Quiet Man was an instant box-office success. For Bord Fáilte (the Irish Tourist Board)

John Wayne in *The Quiet Man*

it proved one of the most valuable publicity films ever, as it brought throngs of foreign tourists, particularly Americans, to the bleak west coast to visit the tiny village of Cong (the focal point of the film), to see the breath-taking beauty of Lough Corrib and find the thatched cottage in the wilds of Connemara which was Wayne's house in the film.

While in Ireland the film raised many a belly-laugh, in America it raised the hackles of Irish people living there for its 'stage Irishness'. It won for Ford the Best Director's Academy Award and Winton C. Hock the Best Cinematography Award. Another positive side-effect of its success was that it made Republic Studios solvent following a bad period with *The Masked Marvel* and other cliff-hangers.

Later Ford, Lord Killanin and Brian Desmond Hurst were involved in setting up an

Irish film company, Four Provinces Productions. They intended to establish an Irish film industry to bring to the screen some of the classics of Irish literature, including works by James Joyce, Liam O'Flaherty and Sean O'Casey. The plan was to

Director John Ford

make their headquarters in a provincial town - preferably one like Galway, which had a variety of locations within easy reach. Unfortunately, owing to his commitments with the International Olympic Committee from 1952, Killanin had to curtail his involvement in film-making.

In 1952 *The Gentle Gunman* was shot on location in the Dublin Mountains and Wicklow area by the successful British team of director Basil Dearden and producer Michael Ralph who later went on to revolutionise the British cinema with such wide-ranging films as *Victim, Violent Playground* and *League of Gentlemen.* It starred John Mills and Dirk Bogarde, both then at the height of their popularity in Britain. In support were Robert Beatty, Gilbert Harding, Michael Golden, Joseph Tomeity, Elizabeth Sellars and Barbara Mullan. Set in 1941, it concerned a small group of IRA men engaged in planting bombs in London. It was, in essence, a plea to the Irish not to blow up London. Bogarde and Mills played Irish

brothers with the latter replacing the former as an activist when he deserts the IRA on realising the futility of violence. The original play by Roger MacDougall may have been a serious study of pacifism and the moral ironies of war but it lost much of that in its transformation to the screen.

In 1953 Hilton Edwards, who, with his partner Mícheál MacLiammóir, was a founding figure of the Gate Theatre in Dublin, directed a short film, *Return to Glenascaul*, which received widespread cinema release and was nominated for a Hollywood Academy Award. The script, written by Edwards and based on a well known Irish ghost story, told of strange happenings to a man one winter's night. At the time of making the film Edwards was in Rome making *Othello* with Orson Welles. He asked Welles, who had encouraged him to direct films, to play in the prologue and epilogue and he agreed. This section Edwards directed in the Scalera Studios before returning to Dublin with cameraman George Fleischmann to shoot the remainder of the film in the Phoenix Park and in an old house in Milltown. The only difficulty he encountered was in matching the car he used in Dublin with the one he had already used in Rome, but this was effectively done by the addition of a Mercedes radiator cap. Welles was in fact returning a favour: he had made his first major stage appearance at the Gate Theatre under Edwards' direction in 1931. Welles played a man who is told a ghostly personal adventure by a man to whom he gives a lift one night as he drives towards Dublin. It was a chilling ghost story, expertly produced. The film was financed by a local theatre owner, Louis Elliman, who was dabbling in film production.

Once again it proved that a wholly Irish made film could become a reality, given the right facilities and the necessary financing. While most European countries established viable film industries, an indigenous feature film still remained a once-in-a-decade undertaking in Ireland. Edwards was later to attempt a second film entitled *Stone in the Heather* (changed to *Cross my Heart*) using an early Irish myth as his theme. Louis Elliman was producer and Edwards wrote the script with the assistance of George Morrison and filmed it in the Dublin Mountains. Unfortunately it did not achieve the same results as his first venture. Although it did have some interesting moments, it did not satisfy Edwards in the cutting. In a frank interview he admitted he did not have enough money to finish it to his liking. Another short film he directed, also with George Fleischmann as camera man, was a record of the Gate Company preparing for their trip to Elsinore in Denmark where Mícheál MacLiammóir and company played *Hamlet* at the invitation of the Danish government. Edwards learned much from Orson Welles and whenever people mentioned that Welles was responsible for the direction of his films, he would express pleasure before modestly admitting they were all his own work.

Powerscourt demesne in County Wicklow in 1953 was again to hear the pounding of hooves and the clanging of steel when the crew of *The Knights of the Round Table* moved in. This was a straight version of the later Richard Harris musical *Camelot*, and the epic *Excalibur* (made in the same location), all based on the Arthurian legend. The film perceived the tale of Lancelot, Guinevere and King Arthur through the eyes of Hollywood. Starring Robert Taylor, Ava Gardner and Mel Ferrer, it was directed by Richard Thorpe. Local men again grew beards and repeated the film experience they had with Olivier. Out came the horses and anything else that could be hired to the film-makers. The locals once more enjoyed being 'in the films'.

The next film unit to visit Ireland came also for a period film. John Huston transformed Youghal, County Cork, into the waterfront of New Bedford, Massachusetts, in 1850, when it was the world's foremost whaling station, to bring Herman Melville's classic novel *Moby Dick* to the screen. Huston could not use the real New Bedford because it was modernised. Youghal was Sir Walter Raleigh's first landfall after his 1551 voyage of exploration to the Americas, when, in return, a grateful Queen Elizabeth gave him Youghal and land in County Cork amounting to 40,000 acres. Another problem the film-makers had was to find an authentic whaler of the period. This was solved by buying the 'Hispaniola' - the ship Walt Disney

On location in Youghal, County Cork with
Moby Dick

built specially for *Treasure Island*. They converted her into a three-masted schooner - the whaling ship 'Pequod'. The harbour at Youghal had to be dredged to take the ten-foot draught of the 'Pequod' and other craft. Though outwardly the ship appeared authentic to the last detail, internally it had make-up rooms, wardrobes, hairdressing rooms, and kitchens to feed the unit while on location. Ray Bradbury wrote the screenplay that centred on Captain Ahab's maniacal chase of the giant white whale that had mutilated him. To capture the conflict Huston used a muted technicolour process. What *The Quiet Man* did for Connemara three years previously, Huston's film was to do for this small, south coast fishing resort. Visitors flocked to see the company at work, view the buildings camouflaged with false fronts and catch a glimpse of the stars. It was a star-studded, all-male cast led by Gregory Peck as the sadistic, one-legged Captain Ahab and supported by Richard Basehart, Leo Genn, Noel Purcell and the well known Dublin journalist, Seamus Kelly. Orson Welles made a short but dramatic appearance as the hell-fire preaching Father

Maureen Potter and Jimmy O'Dea in *The Rising of the Moon*

Jack MacGowran, Fergus McQuade and Paul Farrell
in *Rising of the Moon*

Mapple. Many yarns are told about the production, particularly about boats picking their way among dummy whales.

Another costume drama, *Captain Lightfoot*, was shot in 1954 with locations in Counties Meath, Dublin, Wicklow and Louth. It featured the Four Courts, the beach at Clogherhead, a chase at Slane Castle, and inevitably Powerscourt. It was a swashbuckling story in the true Errol Flynn/ Douglas Fairbanks tradition about a legendary Irish highwayman during the redcoat era. The script took many liberties with Irish history. Handsome Hollywood star, Rock Hudson, played the title role with Barbara Rush as his leading lady. The supporting cast was headed by Jeff Morrow, Finlay Currie, Denis O'Dea and Kathleen Ryan. The film was directed by American Douglas Sirk, a greatly under estimated figure in English and American film literature. As he showed in this film, he was a master of creating and sustaining mood and in handling actors, exposing depths in their performances with a consistency that few other directors had been able to achieve.

Four years after *The Quiet Man*, John Ford returned to Ireland and the west coast to make *The Rising of the Moon*, also known as *Three Leaves of Shamrock*. The film was a trilogy based on works by Irish writers. The first episode, an adaptation of Frank O'Connor's story, *The Majesty of the Law*, was a comedy of pride which featured Noel Purcell as Old Dan, the last survivor of a noble family, now alone in his crumbling ancestral tower. He is arrested for assaulting a seller of bad poteen. The central episode was based on Michael McHugh's one-act play, *A Minute's Wait*, and the comedy derives from the manner in which the Dublin train's brief halt at a country station is extended into an hour of jollity and general chaos. Lady Gregory's one-act play provided the basis for the final episode from which the film took its title. Set during 'The Troubles' of 1921, it describes the rescue from jail of a condemned IRA man, played by Donal Donnelly. The three stories contrasted

immensely in content. In a departure from his normal practice, Ford used no big star names (except an introduction by Tyrone Power) and instead relied on established Irish actors to fill all the roles. The officers of Irish Actor's Equity must have been pleased as practically every actor, actress and extra on their books was employed. The list was impressive, containing names such as Noel Purcell, Donal Donnelly, Frank Lawton, Cyril Cusack, Denis O'Dea and Maureen Potter. The main locations were in Counties Galway and Clare. Unlike *The Quiet Man*, this was one of Ford's less successful films, but he did manage to recreate an authentic atmosphere of the period for the Black and Tan episode. One of the main criticisms was that he attempted to condense too much into too short a time.

Jacqueline, made in 1956 by Roy Baker, was based on a screenplay by Liam O'Flaherty and Patrick Kirwan with additional dialogue supplied by Patrick Campbell and Catherine Cookson. The plot concerns the McNeils, a Protestant family

John Wayne and Maureen O'Hara in *The Quiet Man*

living in Belfast, where Mike, the father, works in the shipyards. He becomes ill and begins to drink heavily. Fired from his job, with his wife despairing of his alcoholism, his situation seems hopeless. However, all is made right by his young daughter, Jacqueline, whose charms persuade the shipyard owner, Mr. Lord, to give Mike a better job, on a country farm far from the shipyards. British actor John Gregson played Mike McNeil. It was the screen début of young Dublin actress Jacqueline Ryan and her performance won much praise; however, her fame was short-lived and she faded after this single film. Among the cast list were Noel Purcell, Cyril Cusack, Liam Redmond, Máire Kean and Kathleen Ryan as Jacqueline's mother. It gave some dismaying insight into what the Rank Organisation thought life in Northern Ireland was like in the fifties.

In the same year *The March Hare*, directed by George More O'Farrell, came to Ireland for location work. It was a comedy about horse-racing, starring Terence Morgan, Peggy Cummins and Cyril Cusack, which did little more than give employment to bit-part players. In 1958 a second-feature thriller entitled *Dublin Nightmare* was filmed in the capital under the direction of John Pomeroy. It describes how a photographer, while visiting Ireland, is drawn into political conflict and violent struggle of which he has no real understanding. The stars were William Sylvester, Marla Landi and Richard Leech.

In the late fifties, producers turned to popular Abbey Theatre plays in the hope that they might be as successful on the big screen. Two such plays, filmed as low budget second-features, were George Sheils' *Professor Tim* and *Boyd's Shop*, both produced by Emmet Dalton and directed by Henry Cass. The principal scenes were filmed around the village of Enniskerry and the interiors were shot in England. *Professor Tim* starred Ray McAnally and Máire O'Donnell and *Boyd's Shop* starred Eileen Crowe, Geoffrey Golden and Aideen O'Kelly. The supporting cast in both films read like a Who's Who of the Abbey Theatre, with the company shaping up as quite a repertory group for visiting film companies. Hardly a film was produced in Ireland without the names of a handful of their players appearing in the credits. Neither of these films did anything either to enhance the reputation of the National Theatre or to encourage the foundation of an Irish film industry. They did succeed in pointing to need for the setting up of a film studio in Ireland. Why should films with an Irish setting, Irish actors and an Irish producer have to move to England for studio facilities?

The majority of films with Irish settings were criticised for dwelling too much on the proverbial 'stage Irishman' with his exaggerated gestures and expressions. A prime example of this paddywhackery was the Rank Organisation's *Rooney* (1957). This was the last film shot on location in Ireland before the opening of Ardmore Studio the following year. Interiors were filmed at Pinewood Studios and the Dublin locations included Rathmines, the quays and Mount Street, and scenes were filmed during an actual All-Ireland Hurling Final in Croke Park. This lightweight comedy was directed by George Pollock, best known as director of the *Miss Marple* series of the sixties. It centred on Rooney, a Dublin dustman, who, to avoid the attentions of his landlady, takes a room in the O'Flynn household. However, he is rejected when the family discovers the nature of his work and his only friends are the old grandfather and a young cousin, Máire. Later all the grandfather's money is inherited by Máire and Rooney proposes to her. He also fulfils his ambition to play in the All-Ireland Final. John Gregson, again cast as an Irishman, played the dustman and was ably abetted by Noel Purcell, Eddie Byrne, Jack McGowran, Philip O'Flynn and Liam Redmond. The women in his life included Muriel Pavlow, June Thorburn, Máire Kean and Pauline Delaney. As usual, Barry Fitzgerald stole the film as the lovable grandfather. Some critics argued that Dublin bin-collectors were depicted in the film as far too polite and mannerly, thus diminishing the reality of the plot.

John Wayne and Barry Fitzgerald in *The Quiet Man*

John Gregson, Eddie Byrne, Jack McGowran and Noel Purcell in *Rooney*

Chapter 6

Ardmore Studios

In 1958 Ireland got its own film studio -Ardmore Studios in Bray, County Wicklow - which was officially opened in May that year by Séan Lemass, then Minister for Industry and Commerce. Up to that time film-making in Ireland was confined to location shooting which, while expensive to the producers and lucrative to the local communities, represented only a small proportion of the completed films. The heavy cameras, the massive arc lamps, the cumbersome sound booms, all required that interiors should be shot in studio. With the opening of Ardmore, producers could come to Ireland and carry out the full process of film production. Since 1914, when Sidney Olcott dreamt of having his own studio, numerous attempts had been made to build one but had all fallen through. Most collapsed through lack of financial backing. Now that obstacle had been surmounted. The Industrial Credit Company (now defunct) advanced £217,750 by way of a debenture loan, with an additional grant of £45,000 from the Industrial Development Authority - a total investment of £262,750.

Many factors contributed to the establishment of Ardmore Studio. In 1954 an

Sean Lemass, the then Minister for Industry and Commerce who officially opened Ardmore Studios in 1958

enquiry was set up by the government to examine film-making. Lord Killanin and film director, Brian Desmond Hurst headed it. While little was achieved by this group, a move by Fred O'Donovan was indirectly responsible for the setting up of the studios. He made a deal with an American film company to produce thirteen films in Ireland based on Irish classics and to use in the main Abbey actors. O'Donovan went as far as to sign up the entire Abbey Company for the project, but the plan collapsed through destructive criticism, indifference and lack of interest in Ireland. However, the idea was not entirely lost as Major-

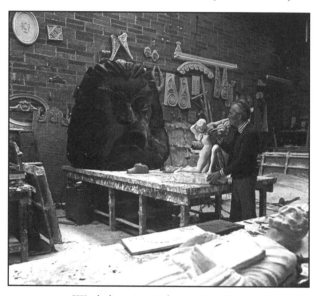

Workshop in Ardmore Studios

General Emmet Dalton, an important figure in the foundation of the state and now a film producer, saw the scope for such an undertaking and pursued it on a smaller scale. His productions of *Professor Tim* and *Boyd's Shop* served as trial runs for shooting a film entirely in Ireland. To date Ireland had been used as a location for visiting film-makers who returned to England or America for studio facilities. The only exceptions had been *The Dawn* and some of the early films, notably those of Olcott.

The enterprise which led to the setting up of Ireland's first feature studio was one of the proposed industry's greatest events. The joint managing directors were Emmet Dalton and impresario Louis Elliman. The other two directors were A.B. Elliman and C.P. McGrath. The studio

manager was Captain Justin Collins, a son-in-law of Dalton. It was a completely self-contained film centre, located one mile outside Bray town at the top of Ardmore Valley. It stood on a site of approximately ten acres, suitable for building a wide range of film sets, and also extended to a second lot of twenty-seven acres in the Valley, through which the River Dargle flowed.

A first-class crew was assembled to operate the studio, consisting of key personnel with many years' experience in the film industry abroad and having connections with all the major studios. Many Irish technicians were glad of the opportunity to return home. The company also had available a large pool of skilled craft workers plus make-up, hair-dressing, wardrobe and property men and all skills of the building trade.

Stages A and B in the studio were capable of accommodating major productions. The smaller Stage C was suitable for medium sized films. This was what Ardmore, one of the most modern studios in the world, with the newest equipment and latest techniques, had to offer the film-maker. The studio worked on a rental basis. The rental was £1,000 a week for one of the larger stages, with use of the workshops, dressing-rooms, projection theatres etc. and a certain allocation of equipment. Stage C rented at £500 per week.

The studio got off to an encouraging start with a series of traditional Irish films produced by Emmet Dalton, similar to those envisaged by Fred

Ardmore Studios

O'Donovan. The first film to take the floor was *Home is the Hero*, a screen adaptation of Walter Macken's stage success. Macken, one of Ireland's leading playwrights and novelists, played the title role opposite American star Arthur Kennedy. The supporting roles were cast from the ranks of the Abbey Theatre led by Máire O'Donnell and Harry Brogan. Veteran American Fielder Cooke directed. It had a typical National Theatre rural setting to which Macken returns after completing a prison sentence following the death of a man in a public house brawl. The story traced the consequences for his family and friends.

The pattern was similar to pre-Ardmore productions of 'from stage to screen' scenarios such as *Professor Tim* and *Boyd's Shop*. Much of the acting was exaggerated, with many of the cast not yet familiar with the intimacy of screen acting. However, these films were released as second features of approximately sixty minutes duration.

British director George Pollock must have been fascinated by Irish themes because he directed the next two films at the studio—two Abbey comedies, *The New Gossoon* by George Shiels, retitled *Sally's Irish Rogue* and *The Big Birthday* by Hugh Leonard, retitled *Broth of a Boy*. Pollock had been in the business for thirty years, having worked as assistant to directors like David Lean. His major break through came, after several small budget productions, with *Rooney*. Since then he had turned out some first-rate family entertainment. He had high praise for the Irish actors and stated that any type of film, from science-fiction to westerns, could be produced here.

Sally's Irish Rogue starred Julie Harris, a graduate of the Strasberg School of Acting, where class-mates had included Marlon Brando and Montgomery Clift. She captured beautifully the blarney of the country lass but Tim Seely, an English actor, was less convincing as the restless young man. The film was generally accepted although it showed no significant returns. Harry Brogan, Philip O'Flynn, Eddie Golden and Márie Kean played strong character roles. It described how a young man revolted against his family and friends a few days before he was to come into possession of his late father's farm. He even broke his promise to marry Sally, the daughter of a wily poacher. *Broth of a Boy* was a light comedy about a television producer who discovers the oldest man in the world in an Irish village and tries to entice him onto television. Tony Wright, as the English producer, was outshone by such players as Harry Brogan, Márie Kean and Dermot Kelly. Top honours again went to Barry Fitzgerald. Sadly, it was to be Barry's last film performance.

It was now becoming apparent that it was the producers' policy to use big star names in every film, whatever its size and budget, and to employ Irish actors in the lesser roles. This policy was understandable to a neutral observer who could see the desirability of a big name to make the product a commercial proposition but it did not please the Irish actors, who felt no more than 'glorified extras'.

These three films ironed out teething problems and opened the way for larger productions. Already, stories of the excellent design and equipment of the studio, coupled with the accessibility of suitable locations, had filtered through the industry. Dalton and Elliman went to America to sell studio space. As a result many leading producers came to see for themselves the high standard on offer. They were enthusiastic and began their bookings. Ardmore had completed its

A Black and Tans scene from
Shake Hands with the Devil

Michael Anderson (right) directs James Cagney in
Shake Hands with the Devil

running-in period and was ready for its first major
production in the autumn of 1958.

One subject which was always a reliable one
for a good action-packed film was the Black and
Tan era in Ireland. These films were to Ireland what
the westerns were to America, Roman epics to Italy
and costume dramas to England. Executive
producers George Glass and Walter Seltzer selected
one such subject for their big budget film to be
shot at Bray. It was *Shake Hands with the Devil*,
adapted from the novel by Reardon Conor. Young
British director Michael Anderson, with a number
of successes to his credit (including *The Dam
Busters, Around the World in Eighty Days* and *Yangtse
Incident*), was producer/ director. He was a stickler
for perfection and periodically, on the set, his
temper struck fear into the cast and crew. He
gathered quite an array of stars for this story of
Ireland's fight for freedom, led by James Cagney,
Don Murray, Dana Wynter, Glynis Johns, Cyril
Cusack, Dame Sybil Thorndike and Sir Michael
Redgrave.

The film centres on Kerry O'Shea, an Irish-
American, who is a medical student in Dublin at
the height of 'The Troubles' in 1921. Although

his father has been one of the early leaders in the
movement, Kerry refuses to become involved.
When an IRA classmate of his is killed, Kerry
discovers that his professor of surgery, Seán
Lenihan, is an IRA leader. Ultimately Kerry
changes his mind, joins the movement and helps
kidnap the daughter of a senior British officer and
hold her hostage.

The IRA general informs Lenihan that a
compromise peace treaty is to be signed, but
Lenihan will settle for nothing short of
unconditional victory and, in a frenzy of anger,
breaks with the movement. The death in prison of
Lady FitzHugh, for whom the IRA had hoped to
exchange their hostage, sends Lenihan, now an
unqualified fanatic, out to kill the English girl.
Kerry, who has fallen in love with her, reasons in
vain. In a final effort to halt the senseless killing
he draws his own gun. Both men fire
simultaneously, thus bringing the story to a violent
climax.

James Cagney, giving one of his best,
performances, played Lenihan, the IRA leader.

Dan O'Herlihy, Arthur Flynn and Robert Mitchum
on location for *A Terrible Beauty*

Don Murray was the young medical student torn between loyalty to his friends and to his country. He gave a brilliant performance as the strong-willed pacifist. Both American actors made a good fist of the Irish accent. Dana Wynter and Glynis Johns supplied the love interest. The old Irish reliables filled the minor roles, led by Cyril Cusack, Harry Brogan, Noel Purcell and Ray McAnally. Richard Harris, in another bit-part, went on to achieve international stardom. Sir Michael Redgrave played the small but nevertheless important, role of the General—thereby supporting Stanislavsky's theory that there are no small parts, only small actors. This black and white production used the contrast between the claustrophobic back streets of Dublin and the open, rugged landscapes of County Wicklow to exquisite effect.

While in Bray, Cagney was casual and relaxed and could often be spotted strolling with his wife along the promenade or on one of the many river walks. He took daily tap-dancing lessons, to keep himself fit, from a local dancing teacher, who also ran a fishmonger's. They became such good friends that Cagney insisted that all fish used in the studio during his stay was to be purchased in her shop.

Emmet Dalton chose yet another stage adaptation, *This Other Eden* by Louis D'Alton, for his next production. Emmet's daughter, Audrey, then gaining quite a reputation for herself in Hollywood, played the female lead opposite British comedian Leslie Phillips. It was reasonably well produced and showed the most fruitful returns so far from a medium budget film shot in Ireland. It

Control room in Ardmore Studios

presented motley ingredients of comedy and drama, with the shadow of a dead Irish hero of the Troubles looming in the background. Outstanding in his first big screen appearance was Norman Rodway from the Globe Theatre, playing an angry young man.

This was followed by a film of similar content and magnitude to *Shake Hands With the Devil* but not nearly so successful. It was Arthur Roth's *A Terrible Beauty* directed by veteran American, Tay Garnett and the first of a number of films to be shot by producer Raymond Stross at Ardmore over the next few years. The cast was headed by Robert Mitchum, Anne Heywood, Dan O'Herlihy and Richard Harris who was then climbing up the credits.

The film concerned the activities of the IRA in a border town in Ireland at the closing stages of World War II. Led by their club-footed leader (O'Herlihy) they intend to blow up the local RUC station. Mitchum, an undaunted patriot, on learning that the sergeant's wife and family are in the barracks, strongly objects. He threatens to expose the plot unless O'Herlihy and his colleagues rearrange their plans. Subsequently Mitchum is smeared as a coward and traitor. In a farcical ending the hero cum-pacifist sails to a self-imposed exile in England .

Robert Mitchum simply plays Robert Mitchum. Richard Harris's stature had increased remarkably since his Cagney film. At times he even upstaged Mitchum. Co-starring with the two hell-raisers was Dublin-born actor Dan O'Herlihy who was now appearing in numerous American television serials. Noel Purcell, Cyril Cusack, Joe Lynch and T.P. McKenna were also in the cast. The village of Rathdrum in County Wicklow was the focal point of the film. Although set in the same period and area as Reed's *Odd Man Out*, it would do a grave injustice to the latter to attempt a comparison. A remark by Richard Harris best summarises the film: 'It was one of the six worst films ever made'. On its release most of the people concerned with the project were totally disenchanted with it.

Irish actor Dan O'Herlihy

Chapter 7

British Thrillers

In the winter of 1960 the King Brothers' horror film *Gorgo*, starring Bill Travers, William Sylvester and Vincent Winter was shot at Coliemore Harbour in Dalkey, County Dublin. Eugene Lourie was director. MGM transferred tons of equipment from England to accommodate the crew on their one week's location.

Much of the proceedings were improvised and the Irish lines had to be written on the set with the assistance of some helpful locals, as the script-writer seemed unable to provide appropriate dialogue. The plot stretched credibility. It concerned a sea-monster which is captured off the west coast of Ireland and put on display in London - this much is credible enough - but then its parent comes after it to wreak havoc on the city. The ingenious special effects used so frequently through out the film completely outclassed the rest of the production.

On the last day's shooting the entire unit was marooned for several hours at the end of Dún Laoghaire pier, as a thunderstorm with mountainous waves lashed the coast and blocked their retreat. Fortunately the canteen was with them and the crew were consoled with a warm

Bill Travers on location for *Gorgo*

57

meal. It was late afternoon before the storm abated, making it possible for the cavalcade of trucks to move slowly to the shelter of the harbour.

A high proportion of the scenes shot during their stay in Dalkey were cut from the film. A tighter shooting schedule, preceded by a period of rehearsal, much favoured by the younger directors, would have largely avoided such extravagant expenditure. Old-time directors, such as John Ford, had a system of shooting their films strictly in sequence and by the script, thereby minimising wastage.

Up to this time Ardmore had produced films with a strictly Irish provenance, consisting of a natural story set locally. In 1961 that policy was to change. The English producers, Roy Baker and Monty Bergman wished to put the activities of the anarchist movement in London in 1911 on celluloid with *The Siege of Sydney Street,* which they co-directed. Starring in this non-fiction film were Donald Sinden, Nicole Berger, Kieron Moore and

Peter Wyngarde. Screenwriter Jimmy Sangster, bearing a striking resemblance to the young Winston Churchill, then Home Secretary, who personally supervised the final battle, made a walk-on appearance.

This film challenged the resources of the studio but also those of the producers who faced the problem of acquiring costumes and authentic props of the period. The production manager had quite an array of sites to choose from in Dublin, which were suitable because they resembled buildings where the action actually took place. Locations ranged from quaint narrow lane ways to terraces of Georgian houses. The main reason for not shooting in London was the fact that the East End haunts of Peter the Painter were now replaced by skyscrapers. An advantage Ireland had to offer foreign film-makers was the availability of exteriors dating to the latter half of the nineteenth century; another was its comparative freedom from air pollution and factory smog.

Action Scene from *The Siege of Sydney Street* in Wellington Street, Dublin

Equity turned out actors and extras by the score to fill the minor parts and crowd scenes. Major roles went to Godfrey Quigley, Joe Lynch, Christopher Casson and T.P. McKenna. Extras doubled as poorly clad Londoners, Scots Guardsmen and members of the London constabulary. The climax of the film is the siege, when the gang is trapped in a house by the police. It develops into one of the bloodiest battles it the annals of British crime. When this sequence was being re-enacted in Wellington Street in Dublin, a large crowd gathered and even the numerous gardai had quite a job controlling them. However, this portion of the film was executed brilliantly and showed the director's thorough research into the actual incident. The end result was an exciting, fast-moving thriller.

The Siege of Sydney Street was one of the first films to receive financial assistance from the Irish Film Corporation. This state-sponsored body, a wholly owned subsidiary of The Industrial Credit Company, was incorporated in 1960, when it became apparent that the absence in Ireland of an organisation to provide risk capital for producers wishing to film in Ardmore Studio retarded the development of the studio's facilities.

In 1960 a production company from the Bavarian Studio in Munich came to Ireland to make two feature films on the popular G.K. Chesterton character, 'Father Brown'. The company hired equipment from Ardmore but shot the films on location in Howth and Galway. The director and leading actors were German and the Irish members of the cast, although speaking in English, later had their voices dubbed into German. A German actor, Heinz Ruhman, popular in his native country for Fernandel style comedy, played the part of 'Father Brown'.

Bill Luckwell, producer of the successful *Maigret* television series, made four second-feature films at Bray in a two-year period: *Ambush in Leopard Street*, *Enter Inspector Duval*, *A Question of Suspense* and *Murder in Eden*. All were run-of-the mill thrillers with English settings which Max Varnell directed. They began on Ardmore's small Stage C but when the larger stages became available

they used them also. Luckwell had intended to make only one film, but when the opportunity of gaining priority in a top studio came, he grabbed it. Hence his films were churned out in rapid succession.

These films were disappointing when one considers his achievements with the Simenon series. They were more like episodes from the popular television series of the period such as *No Hiding Place* and *The Saint*. Although British actors such as Peter Reynolds, Bruce Seton and Anton Diffring played leading roles, these films did bring Irish actors to prominence, most notably Norman Rodway and Ray McAnally. In *Murder in Eden* McAnally gave a very creditable performance as a detective investigating an Art Gallery murder. These productions, with budgets ranging from £4,500 to £20,000 merely maintained employment at the studio.

Residents of Bray found these films amusing for what, to them, seemed a ridiculous lack of continuity. One instance, guaranteed to bring howls of laughter in local cinemas, was a scene where an actor walked down one street and turned into another, supposedly around the corner, but the link up shot was obviously filmed in an area miles away.

With film-making at an all-time high in England during the early sixties, Ardmore benefited from the overflow. One of the busiest periods was when three productions with star casts were in progress simultaneously. They were Nigel Patrick's *Johnny Nobody* with Patrick himself, Aldo Ray, William Bendix and Yvonne Mitchell; Terence Fisher's *Sword of Sherwood Forest* with Richard Greene, Peter Cushing and Sarah Branch; and, on location in Dublin, Richard Fleischer's *The Big Gamble*, starring Stephen Boyd, Juliette Greco and David Wayne.

Nigel Patrick's film was an off-beat thriller with the unusual story of an atheist writer being shot dead by a mysterious stranger in an Irish village and becoming famous as *Johnny Nobody*. The villagers claim the act to be a miracle. The local priest himself becomes a suspect and is pursued by the police. The village of Enniskerry was the focus of the story. Other important scenes were shot at the old disused railway line at Carrickmines, at Mountjoy Jail and in the Wicklow mountains. American actor Aldo Ray, who played the title role, persistently complained about the size of his role. He declared that it was the smallest part he had ever played, with only three short appearances, in the beginning, the middle and the end. Jimmy O'Dea made one of his rare film appearances as a postman. Other Irish actors in the cast included Noel Purcell, Eddie Byrne and Joe Lynch.

The Sword of Sherwood Forest had all the ingredients of the earlier Robin Hood films and the only touch of originality was in the choice of actors. Produced by Michael Carreras and directed by Terence Fisher for Hammer Films, it was the first costume drama to be shot at the studio. The landscapes and waterfall of Powerscourt again offered a picturesque backcloth. Richard Greene brought to the big screen the role he had played for several series on television. Following this film he went into semi-retirement in Wexford. Peter Cushing, taking a break from horror films, played the villainous Sheriff of Nottingham; Sarah Branch was Maid Marion; Nigel Greene, Little John and Niall McGinnis, Friar Tuck.

Peter Cushing in *The Sword of Sherwood Forest*

The Big Gamble, from a script by Irwin Shaw, told the story of an Irishman (Stephen Boyd), his wife (Juliette Greco) and a meek cousin (David Wayne) who sought their fortune on the Ivory Coast. The only memorable part of the film was the opening sequence which was shot from the bridge of a ship sailing up the Liffey. For the first time colour photography captured the red-bricked heart of the city to best advantage. Other Dublin scenes were shot on the quays and at an old house in Kilmainham. Stock Irish actors including Philip O'Flynn and Márie Kean played character roles.

Juliette Greco in Dublin for *The Big Gamble*

When the scene shifted to Africa the film developed into a second rate melodrama.

Up to this time Julie Harris was the only graduate of the Strasberg Acting School in New York to work in Ardmore. This academy was famous for its method style of acting. The second graduate to hit Ireland was cast in the lead role in the next Emmet Dalton production, *The Webster Boy* (or as it was called during production *The Middle of Nowhere*). This was the versatile actor/ director John Cassavetes who in later years achieved fame as one of America's most important and original directors. In this drama, he played an American who had been divorced many years before and returns to his ex-wife, now happily remarried with a growing son. She cannot resist

The Webster Boy
with David Farrar and Richard O'Sullivan

his charm and they fall in love again. Understandable friction erupts as the wife finds herself suddenly with two husbands. Her son, undergoing harsh treatment at boarding school, warmly admires the American. And so the plot progresses, knee-deep in sentimentality. Clients of the Royal Hotel in Bray were frequently treated to spontaneous rehearsals in the lounge. Other roles were played by Elizabeth Sellars, David Farrar, Seymour Cassel and Richard O'Sullivan; direction was by Don Chaffey.

Lies My Father Told Me, a second feature drama, came from the same group of Dalton and Chaffey. The story centred on a Dublin Jewish family and starred American actress Betsy Blair, making one of her rare film appearances. Harry Brogan led the supporting players. The film literally vanished after its initial screening at the Cork Film Festival where it received good notices. Most people who saw the film regarded the performance of Harry Brogan as the best of his film career. Harry told me that the film was regarded as anti Semitic in some quarters and that was the reason it was shelved. He found it to be not the least bit so.

Next on the floor at the Bray studio was another controversial film, *The Mark*, produced in 1961 by Raymond Stross with a star cast. Originally Richard Burton was to play the leading role as a man who seeks to re-establish himself in

society after a conviction for assaulting a young girl. He was replaced by rugged American actor Stuart Whitman. Rod Steiger was the Irish psychiatrist and Maria Schell played a young mother with whom Whitman falls in love. Donald Houston played the reporter who shadows the ex-convict, endeavouring to secure a sequel to his first story.

The film's strength lay in its remarkable duologues between Steiger and Whitman. Their scenes together were directed with great firmness by Guy Greene and acted with convincing sensitivity and good humour. The actors brought an uncommon depth and conviction to their roles.

Stuart Whitman on location in Dun Laoire for
The Mark

At first this director of contrasting themes hesitated to tackle *The Mark*. It was an extremely delicate subject and required a mature professional to ensure it did not go over the top.

Director Guy Greene had begun his career on the bottom rung as camera operator in Noel Coward and David Lean's *In Which We Serve*. Carol Reed made him his first cameraman on *The Way Ahead*. Among his other photographic successes were Oliver Twist and *Great Expectations*. His directing début came in 1954 with *River Beat,* but his breakthrough into the big time came with *The Angry Silence* starring Richard Attenborough. Greene believed the reason for that film's success was the remarkable teamwork of writer, director, cast and crew.

The Mark was generally cold-shouldered in England and received a limited showing. Not surprisingly, with its controversial subject-matter, it was banned in Ireland. In America, it was a top box-office draw and reviewers referred to it as 'a first rate psychological drama', 'a masterpiece' and 'an absorbing, memorable film'. *The Mark* was also to bring the first Academy Award nomination to a member of the cast of an Ardmore production, Stuart Whitman was nominated for the 1961 Oscar but lost out to Gregory Peck for his performance in *To Kill a Mockingbird.* The number of enquiries about the studio's availability increased.

The One Nighters was a documentary shot on a modest budget away from the studio in 1962 about the life of the Royal Showband from Waterford. It traced the day-to-day activities of the showband from the time they left home in the morning until they took the stage that night. The band with its lead vocalist, Brendan Bowyer, was then at the height of its popularity. It showed many interesting and original touches by its director Peter Collinson. Collinson who was working with Radio Telefís Éireann at the time, went on to a highly successful career as a director of major films until his untimely death.

The next three films shot at Ardmore did little to enhance the reputation of the studio. The first two were *Freedom to Die* and *Stork Talk,* both of which received grants from the Film Finance Corporation. The former, a second feature thriller directed by Francis Searle, was similar to the Luckwell series. The latter film brought Anne Heywood back to Bray to co-star with Tony Britton in this saucy comedy set in a hospital and directed by Michael Furlong. The film was banned in Ireland and little was heard of it elsewhere after its completion. The third film, made in 1962, was a mediocre thriller, *A Guy Called Caesar.* It was also

Anne Heywood and Raymond Stross

directed by Searle and starred Conrad Phillips, George Moon and Philip O'Flynn. In the film a policeman poses as a crook to join a gang of jewel thieves and unmask their leader. Former RTE newsreader Charles Mitchell featured as one of the crooks.

The same year an MGM unit under the direction of American Robert Stevens moved into the small village of Crookhaven in County Cork for a stint of location work on *I Thank a Fool.* It was an Antole de Grunwald production with a screenplay by John Mortimer, based on the best-selling novel of the same name by Audrey Erskine Lindop. The story tells of a doctor (Peter Finch) who employs a repentant murderer (Susan Hayward) as a companion for his mentally ill wife (Diane Cilento). While they are visiting the wife's drunken father (Cyril Cusack), she dies and the companion believes she has been set up. Cyril Cusack, in particular, was praised for his performance but the plot was dismissed as being too contrived and banal.

Chapter 8

Coppola and Low Budgets

The next large-scale production to take the floor at Ardmore was *Term of Trial*. At first it was announced that Hayley Mills would play opposite Laurence Olivier but she was later replaced by an unknown actress, Sarah Miles. At the helm were producer James Wolfe and director Peter Grenville. Oswald Morris was director of photography. Other members of the cast included Simone Signoret, Terence Stamp, Hugh Griffith and Thora Hird. No Irish actors featured prominently in the credits. The film was released in 1961.

Director Grenville was a versatile young man who had produced brilliant stage and screen productions of *The Prisoner*, Tennessee Williams's *Summer and Smoke* and *Becket*.

In *Term of Trial* Miss Miles played a fifteen-year-old school-girl infatuated with her middle-aged teacher (Olivier). At first it seems nothing more than a harmless adolescent attraction for an older man, but on a school outing to Paris she schemes to be alone with him and they tour the city together. Owing to an unfortunate delay on the return journey the party are forced to stay overnight at a London hotel where the girl's true motive is revealed when she tries to entice him to

make love to her. He maintains his fatherly pose and sends her back to her room. At home her obsession continues and, because of his degrading rebuke, she tells her parents he assaulted her.

The subplots are neatly interwoven with the main one - the master's nagging wife in whose eyes he must damn himself to regain her affection; the amorous mother who only has time for her male companion, and ignores her impressionable son; the bully who makes life unpleasant for all.

All shooting, with the exception of one week's location in Paris, was done in Ireland. The film-makers transformed Quinsboro Road in Bray into a street similar to Dublin's Moore Street, complete with stall-holders and fish-mongers. Various schools throughout the country supplied children for the classroom scenes. *Term of Trial* served as a spring-board to international stardom for two young unknowns — Sarah Miles and Terence Stamp, who played the young thug.

The Very Edge, a Raymond Stross production, was less sophisticated. Had it not been for its big-star names it could have come from the Luckwell stable in a television series. Areas of

County Dublin duplicated for an English town where the story was set. It told how a housewife (Anne Heywood) is menaced by a stranger who attacks her, causing her to have a miscarriage. He is arrested and jailed but to stretch the film to the customary ninety minutes he conveniently escapes. The second half of the film is almost a repetition of the first as he sets about his sinister deed again. The film concludes when he meets his end by falling from the top of a block of flats. The cast was sadly wasted. Anne Heywood wore appropriate expressions of shock and fear. Richard Todd as her husband displayed a constant frown, Jack Hedley was the plodding detective and Jeremy Brett was not the least bit menacing as the intruder. Cyril Frankel directed this insipid thriller.

Jack Hedley in Bray while filming for *The Very Edge*

It was inevitable that an enterprising producer would attempt to bring John M. Synge's *Playboy of the Western World* to the screen. In 1961 Brian Desmond Hurst directed a version with Siobhan McKenna as Pegeen Mike and Gary Raymond as Christy Mahon. Niall McGinnis and Liam Redmond played other leading roles. The actual plot, about a young stranger who becomes the idol of a small village, was less important than the soaring, poetic language of the play. McKenna gave a marvellous performance, although her age — she looked too old to be Gary Raymond's girlfriend — was a weakness in the production.

Two of the highlights of the film, which was principally shot on Inch Strand in County Kerry, were the score by Sean Ó Riada and the cinematography of Geoffrey Unsworth.

Within months of each other, two renowned directors of the old school — John Huston and Carol Reed, returned to Ireland for location work on their latest films, *The List of Adrian Messenger* and *The Running Man*, respectively. Both productions were modern-day thrillers, with Huston's winning by a short head, but curiously both failed to glow.

Huston's film, based on a novel by Philip MacDonald, opened with a writer handing a detective a list of twelve men who died accidentally during the previous five years. Later, he himself dies in a plane crash but manages to babble a few delirious words to the only survivor, a friend of the detective's. Patching together the clues, the detective — a retired intelligence officer — realises that the 'accidents' in fact were perfect crimes. Following many tense atmospheric scenes, the detective interprets the clues with almost Holmesian powers of deduction before apprehending the killer.

Each new venture of Huston's was a challenge. His film characterisations varied enormously, from the sadistic Captain Ahab to the young Yankee soldier's conflict in *The Red Badge of Courage* or the rugged portrayals of Bogart. One gathered the impression that Huston, after his rigorous experience earlier with *Freud*, was inclined to relax too much with this genial thriller. Yet his fox-hunting scenes will be long remembered, with the blazing red jackets and tally-ho of the gentlemanly riders on their sturdy mounts, attuning with the melodious yapping of the pack. Huston, who had been Master of the Galway Blazers, made a fleeting appearance during this sequence. George C. Scott and Dana Wynter were the stars. Many big names including Kirk Douglas, Robert Mitchum, Burt Lancaster, Tony Curtis and Frank Sinatra made guest appearances. Most of the Irish scenes were shot in the County Dublin area around Cabinteely. The film was made during Huston's love affair with Ireland when he had set up home in Craughwell, County Galway. He took every opportunity to do a stint of location work in Ireland even when the film did not warrant an Irish setting.

Carol Reed's *The Running Man* related how Rex and Stella Black defrauded an insurance company of £50,000. Rex, presumed killed in an air-crash, remains in hiding until the claim has been paid to his wife. He sets out to join Stella in Spain and stumbles across an insurance agent who has accidentally blundered into the situation and fallen in love with Stella. This lights the fuse on a chain of events that finally conclude in tragedy.

Reed shot his interiors at Ardmore, where a plane crash was simulated on the back lot. Locations were filmed at Bray, although Ireland was not an integral part of the plot. A further period was spent in Spain. His stars were Laurence Harvey, Lee Remick and Alan Bates. Irish actors such as Eddie Byrne, Noel Purcell and Joe Lynch filled undistinguished roles.

This production was low-key compared to the flamboyance of the Marlon Brando version of *Mutiny on the Bounty* that preceded it. Reed resigned midway through that production because of differences with Brando about the interpretation of the script. With *The Running Man*, it seemed as if the script had been mislaid and that the director had plodded on optimistically. The result was an artistically jagged production.

In the same year a British second-feature was made on location in Counties Dublin and Wicklow. It was *Dead Man's Evidence* directed by Francis Searle and starring Conrad Philips and Jane Griffith. It concerned a secret agent investigating the death of a frogman who is exposed as a traitor.

Brendan Behan was the first contemporary Irish literary figure to have his work produced at the Bray studio. It was his outstanding prison drama, *The Quare Fella*, which was based on his own prison experience. His play traces the final hours of a condemned man and the effects on the other prisoners. Fundamentally it was an anti-capital punishment statement. The film did not do justice to the original. The glorification of the new warder and the love affair between him and the condemned man's wife, were departures from Behan's text that diffused the impact of the whole.

The cast was headed by two British stars, Patrick McGoohan and Sylvia Syms, with Walter Macken, Pauline Delaney, Harry Brogan, T.P. McKenna and Dermot Kelly heading a large contingent of Irish players. The direction of the American Arthur Dreyfuss was evenly paced. Kilmainham Jail provided a perfectly dank environment. Vincent Corcoran made an impressive début in feature films with a documentary like introduction which was screened behind the credits.

A short film made at the studio at this time entitled *Meet the Quare Fellow* was a straight face to face interview between Eamonn Andrews and Brendan Behan. Although by no means as sensational as the Malcolm Muggeridge television interview, it did manage to convey a great deal of the warmth and humour of the Dublin writer. Fred O'Donovan directed the fifty minute film for the extraordinarily low figure of £500.

Another film unit found that Dublin's streets offered good period locations for another detective film about Conan Doyle's famous sleuth: *Sherlock Holmes and the Deadly Necklace*. It was a German-English production directed by Terence Fisher with Christopher Lee in the title role, supported by Senta Berger and Thorley Walters. Holmes and his faithful aide Watson were again locked in combat with the evil Moriarty, who was in pursuit of a valuable diamond necklace.

The last film under the Emmet Dalton banner to be made at Ardmore was *The Devil's Agent*. This was the most disappointing of Dalton's films. It concerned spying at the UN and was a complicated and wooden production. The story related how Draste meets his old friend, Von Straub, who subsequently invites him to his home for the weekend. He is tricked by Von Straub's sister into acting as a secret agent and from there is inveigled into becoming a double agent. John Cowley, a household name in *The Riordans*, played an important role. The unit had to move to Vienna for the concluding scenes because Trinity College refused permission to shoot within its grounds. The film was a waste of talent and did justice neither to director John Paddy Carstairs nor to such talented players as Peter Van Eyke, McDonald Carey and Christopher Lee.

Lack of capital was the main excuse given by Irish film-makers as to why feature films could not be successfully produced here.

In 1963 one small film made at Ardmore challenged this conventional notion. *The Haunted and the Hunted*, retitled *Dementia 13*, was made by an American company owned by producer-director Roger Corman. It was made quickly and cheaply, with a small cast and crew of nine and a minimum of sets. Francis Ford Coppola, a twenty-

Director Francis Ford Coppola

three-year-old American from the University of California film school, who had worked in other capacities on Corman films, was given his big chance with this claustrophobic horror story. He wrote the screenplay in three days and also directed.

The film was shot in three weeks, two weeks in the studio and one week on location in the village of Newtownmountkennedy in County Wicklow. The average shooting schedule on a film was between six weeks and two months. A crew of fourteen, ten of them Irish, worked on this production and cut the staffing of the unit by approximately fifty per cent.

The total budget for *Dementia* was only £30,000. On some films that amount would not even have covered the construction of sets. The entire studio work was done on the small Stage C at Ardmore. Before each scene Coppola gathered his artists and technicians and discussed the script in depth. The result was a minimum of takes on each sequence and of wasted film caused by faulty lighting or an actor fumbling his lines. This preserved-planning technique was favoured by some American directors and also by the New Wave *avant garde* French directors, most of whom had no other option because they worked on a shoe string budget. The technique was almost entirely boycotted by British studios.

The plot of *Dementia* was simple. The setting is a sinister Irish castle with a neurotic family dominated by a widowed mother, Lady Haloran. When one of her sons dies from a heart attack his

Rita Tushingham in *Girl with Green Eyes*

wife pretends he is still away on a business trip. To further this plan she decides to deceive the mother, but is hacked to death by a mysterious figure after a midnight swim. From then on it transformed into a real shocker. There were many similarities between *Dementia* and the later *Godfather*: the Haloran family share with the Corleones a boundless desire for power and a taste for violent solutions.

The acting of the cast, which included William Campbell, Laura Anders, Patrick Magee and Eithne Dunne, was only adequate. The production employed many gimmicky effects but also hinted at the originality behind *Godfather I* and *II* and *Apocalypse Now.*

Comparatively low budget films had been produced successfully for a number of years by the veteran American director Andrew Stone and by Woodfall Productions. Both companies made films in Ireland within a six-month period and both had, for the early sixties, a revolutionary method of operating: they worked entirely on location. Many established directors frowned on that style of filming but both Stone and Woodfall were justified by their list of credits—the former with *The Last Voyage* and *The Password is Courage* and the latter with *A Taste of Honey* and *The Loneliness of the Long Distance Runner*. Like the remainder of the films produced by Woodfall they were frank, provocative dramas, pioneering a new trend in realism.

Andrew Stone's reason for employing this style was that he could complete a film in a considerably shorter time and avoid the enormous overheads of hiring a studio and building a set. The long tedious job of loading and unloading trucks was also eliminated. Moreover, only a small crew of technicians was required. All his equipment was compactly stacked in a Volkeswagen van and erected on the spot in a matter of minutes.

Robert Stack, Dorothy Malone, George Sanders and Dirk Bogarde were typical of the names to be found in Stone's production. Woodfall gambled on casting unknowns in top roles. They had made stars of Albert Finney, Rita Tushingham and Tom Courtenay. Another difference between the two was that almost all Woodfall's films were adapted from novels or plays while the American co-wrote most of his original screenplays.

Woodfall's Irish ventures were very much true to formula. *Girl with Green Eyes* was adapted from Edna O'Brien's *The Lonely Girl* and starred Peter Finch, Rita Tushingham and Lynn Redgrave. It gave Desmond Davis, who had started at the age of sixteen as a clapperboy and worked as a

Peter Finch on location in Wicklow for
Girl with Green Eyes

Pat Boone filming *Never Put It In Writing* in Dublin

camera operator on all Tony Richardson's films since *A Taste of Honey*, the opportunity to direct his first film. The story concerned a quiet and rather philosophical English writer who drifts into a transitory love affair with an Irish girl much younger than himself. A memorable sequence, perfectly modulated by Davis, was their long conversation which sustained a logical train of thought while the visuals shifted from one setting to another — tea-shop, book shop, pub, and seashore - indicating a passage of time and a growing rapport. The device was not a new one in the cinema, but it had never been employed to better purpose. It was skilful and unusually touching. Davis said of the film: 'It was about illusion and the impermanence of relationships and love'. It was shot entirely on location in Dublin and Wicklow.

Character actor Harry Brogan

Stone's film, *Never Put it in Writing*, concerned the plight of a young executive who must retrieve a letter of resignation before it reaches his boss. American singing star Pat Boone played the young man, supported by Milo O'Shea and Fidelma Murphy. The scenes focused mainly on the trio rushing in and out of buildings in pursuit of the letter. The result was little more than a sub-standard slap-stick with few funny moments. It had a long cast of Irish supporting players including Colin Blakely, Eddie Golden and Harry Brogan.

Some misfortunes attended the shooting of both these films. On the first day's shooting of the Pat Boone film at Shannon Airport a small Proctor plane came into collision with the camera truck. Five members of the crew, including the director, were injured, though not seriously. At a later stage in the filming the producer was informed by the Department of Transport and Power that permission for further flying sequences over Dublin had been refused. Subsequently the unit had to transfer to London for concluding scenes. The Woodfall film was delayed for a week when Rita Tushingham became ill with a duodenal ulcer.

Girl with Green Eyes was part of a remarkable renaissance in the British cinema. This began in the late fifties with a return to films of reality. The cinema turned to successful new novels and plays of authentic regional and working-class life. Jack Clayton directed an adaptation of John Braine's novel *Room at the Top* and Tony Richardson brought John Osborne's *Look Back in Anger* to the screen. As these films proved a success, there was a rush to imitate them. For a number of years practically every British film director took his turn at 'kitchen-sink' drama.

Chapter 9

The Trials of Ardmore

A number of factors contributed to the onset of Ardmore's difficulties. They came under the headings of distribution, finance and industrial disputes. Independent producers, many of whom had received loans from the Irish Film Finance Corporation, experienced problems with the distribution of their films. After participating in the financing of fifteen films to the extent of £385,000 in the period 1960-62, the Corporation was reluctant to back any further projects. Many of these films had failed to recover their costs and the Corporation, therefore, incurred heavy losses which were only marginally offset by profits on a series of successful second features in which they participated. The main reason for the losses was the failure of the films to secure a release on either of the British circuits, J. Arthur Rank Organisation or ABC. In some cases this might have been due to the indifferent quality of the product but it was obvious that at that time (and the same is mainly true today) neither circuit was keen to take films by independent producers.

When Ardmore Studio was established no provision was made for the training and staffing of Irish film technicians and the resultant vacuum was quickly filled by British technicians. In fact Ardmore became an extension of the British film industry. Irish carpenters and plasterers, canteen and office staff were casually employed from the local work-force whenever the studio was in operation, but the crewing of film technicians was arranged in London by whatever company had hired the studio for its film. Also, by a quirk of film tradition, electricians were regarded as film technicians and it was at that level that one saw most clearly the paradox of British film employment at Ardmore. In 1962 a conflict flared between the Irish Electrical Trade Union—ETU (I) —and its British counterpart, which bedevilled the studio until the end of 1964.

The Irish union claimed that as it was Irish Government money which built Ardmore they should supply the electricians for productions there. The British union counter-claimed that as it was British Government money that subsidised films made at Ardmore it was they who should enjoy the employment opportunities. The British Federation of Film Unions closed ranks behind their electricians and threatened to stop all future productions at Ardmore. The arrangement,

Filming *Of Human Bondage* in Bray

resulting from long deliberations between the unions, was that a meeting would take place before each film to be shot at Ardmore to decide the ratio of English and Irish electricians employed on that particular film.

The next crux came when the ETU (I) claimed a breach of agreement on the crewing of the film, *Of Human Bondage*, which was also plagued by many other problems. They placed a picket on the studio which was passed by members of other Irish unions employed there and the filming proceeded without interruption with British electricians.

The behind-the-scenes antics during the Ardmore remake of Somerset Maugham's classic, *Of Human Bondage*, in 1963 had enough dramatic ingredients to warrant a film of its own. Laurence Harvey and Sophia Loren were originally cast as the stars but Kim Novak replaced Miss Loren before shooting began. There was the on going row between the British and Irish unions. Soon after filming commenced, Kim Novak had a row

with director Henry Hathaway over her characterisation and Hathaway resigned. Bryan Forbes, one of the cast, became temporary director until Ken Hughes took over as the third director.

Laurence Harvey in *Of Human Bondage*

Kim Novak had another disagreement and flew to Paris, refusing to finish the film. Elizabeth Taylor was one of those considered to replace her. Following consultations Miss Novak returned to work and filming resumed. Harvey and Novak held a Saint Patrick's Day party. When students

Bryan Forbes on location in Dublin for
Of Human Bondage

threatened to kidnap Kim as a rag-day prank she received a Garda escort. An American film unit flew in to make a film on this much publicised production. Actor Joe Lynch was replaced as Kim's husband. Bob Rooney took over as PRO from Ernie Anderson. Bryan Forbes had to leave the film owing to prior commitments and was replaced by Jack Hedley. His scenes had to be reshot.

The final scenes were shot on a sunny September day in the shadow of the gasometer behind Bray Harbour. The previous week carpenters had transformed the over grown field into a diminutive cemetery. Almost five months' collaboration for actors and crew had created a family-like atmosphere, but now the end was near.

Ken Hughes, the director, stood ready. The assistant director called for the onlookers to remain silent. The generator was humming, mighty arc lights played a strong beam on the actors. A last minute check was made on the light meter. Camera was focused on the cemetery gate, mike boom loomed overhead. In the foreground Nanette Newman stood tensely beside a cab. When directed, an old steam-engine shunted to and fro on the railway line above to add a period touch.

Laurence Harvey strolled from the cemetery of plaster and plywood tomb stones, towards the waiting cab. He paused for a few words with Nanette before boarding the cab. In the background some elegant grave-diggers, complete with top hats, filled in Mildred's (Kim Novak's) grave. With a deep sense of satisfaction Hughes said politely 'Cut! Just one more time please' — quite a contrast to his predecessor, Henry Hathaway, who bellowed at his actors. With a few additional directions to Harvey and Newman the scene was performed once more. By 7.30 that night he had shouted 'cut' for the final time on the set of *Of Human Bondage.*

For the next twelve months the stages of Ardmore lay idle. Potential customers were put off by the rows behind the Maugham remake. Finally in November 1963 William Sandys was appointed receiver. The studio closed and Justin Collins, the managing director resigned. An advertisement appeared in an English trade magazine saying the studio was for sale.

Later in the year, almost unnoticed, a major production slipped into Ardmore and was announced officially only a few days before shooting began. It was the straight acting début of American jazz musician Ray Charles in *Ballad*

Richard Burton and director Martin Ritt on set of
The Spy Who Came in from the Cold

in Blue. Paul Henreid, once a Hollywood heart throb himself, was chosen to direct this sentimental weepie. Charles's international co-stars included Tom Bell, Mary Peach, Dawn Addams and eight-year-old Piers Bishop.

Receiver Sandys was also responsible for enticing Paramount to Ardmore to film *The Spy Who Came In From the Cold* starring Richard Burton, Claire Bloom Oscar Werner and Peter Van Eyke, under producer/director Martin Ritt. Cyril Cusack filled the small, yet important, role of the chief of the secret service. A week's exterior work was completed in London prior to moving into the studio for a seven week schedule. After Ireland, the unit moved to Holland and Germany for concluding scenes. The overcast conditions which prevailed during the winter schedule ideally suited the film-makers, as they reflected the atmosphere of the plot.

Richard Burton took on one of the year's most demanding and coveted roles as Leamas, a seedy, cynical British agent in Paul Dehn's screenplay adaptation of John Le Carré's sensational world-wide best-seller. The story reveals how the spy (Burton) is recalled for one more mission in East Germany — to destroy the head of the espionage service there.

Martin Ritt, who was making the three million dollar film for his own company, Salem Films, (Paramount Films had made his reputation with films dealing with contemporary America), was no stranger to controversial themes. He spoke of his reasons for filming in Dublin:

It is because of the cold grey climate. The predominantly overcast sky was a particular asset, as a gloomy background was required throughout the film. Then the studio cost, with that of labour and materials, is considerably less than in Britain or the continent. Many of the Irish settings appeared more realistic than Berlin at the time of the action (1961).

Burton, too, spoke highly of the studio:

It's the best studio I've ever worked in. Only one major film can be produced here at one time and that company receives full priority. There are beautiful surroundings and peaceful seclusion. In Hollywood, films are churned out in factory style and people treated like machines. There are also too many distractions. You've got John Wayne strolling across one set and Sophia Loren across another.

Burton was a likeable and friendly man with a wry sense of humour. His performance earned him a well-deserved Oscar nomination but the award eluded him. The film itself lived up to

Ardmore Studios

expectations and was regarded as a masterpiece, receiving almost unanimous praise from the critics.

Even Dubliners found it difficult to identify the city locations which were so skilfully transformed into British and East German settings. The Checkpoint Charlie (the official crossing point between East Berlin and the American sector) set, erected at Smithfield, was built to the most exactingly authentic standards. A fifty man construction team spent a month building the set, which included West Berlin shops, barbed wire barriers and twenty-five foot high guard towers. Four hundred feet of seventeen foot high walls were pre-constructed of lathe plaster. Even a lane of sixteen specially made lamp posts was imported.

When 20th Century Fox set out to make *The Blue Max* (1965), they found that there was little similarity between how the site of the battle looked at the time of the First World War and how it looked in the mid-sixties: the skies were extremely smog-laden and crowded with commercial and private aircraft. They had to search for a film location similar to the Somme. In Kilpedder, County Wicklow, they found a perfect site. The unit was based at Ardmore and the aerial sequences were shot at Weston Aerodrome.

The production team, headed by executive producer Elmo Williams, producer Christian Ferry and director John Guillermin, recreated the era with painstaking authenticity. The nine fighter planes featured in the film were exact replicas of the World War I aircraft used by both the Germans and Allies. The planes were built in France and flown to Ireland. The Department of Defence permitted the film-makers to use several hundred troops in the battle scenes, the troops doubling as both Allied and German soldiers. The FCA's traditional opposition to the regular army made for such a high degree of realism in the battle scenes that there were several casualties, though happily no mortal ones. The producers assembled a top cast headed by George Peppard, James Mason, Ursula Andress and Jeremy Kemp.

The film depicts the evolution of air power during the Great War and the emergence of determined pilots whose field of honour was the sky and who fought and died by a gentlemen's code that was never to be known again. It centred on one such pilot, Bruno Stachel (Peppard), who combined all that was best and worst in that breed of men. It was glory rather than love he sought— the ultimate glory crystallised in a few inches of blue enamel and silver known as *The Blue Max* and achieved by shooting down twenty planes.

George Peppard, a rather passive actor, allowed the character's inner determination to be so deeply soured as to be barely visible, but he gave a competent performance in a difficult role. Bruno was far from being a hero and the film failed to bring him to life. Ursula Andress was not impressive as the Countess (wife of the German air commander - the James Mason character), a part developed out of box office consideration, but she made the most of a wooden character.

The Blue Max

During the shooting of the war scenes, seven tons of explosives were used each day. To unleash the power under strict control while simulating battle conditions with intensive gunfire and bombardment, twenty-five miles of electric charge wire and five two-way radio sets linked the sixty-man team. The result was one of the most realistic representations of battle ever filmed. The Irish locations, which included Christ Church, Trinity College and Powerscourt, were so meticulously camouflaged that they were almost impossible to identify. The film had some superb photography and the staged aerial battles were regarded as some of the best ever filmed.

Eamonn O'Higgins, Arthur Flynn and Richard Burton during filming of
The Spy Who Came in from the Cold in Phoenix Park, Dublin

Chapter 10

Joyce and the Cinema

James Joyce had had a keen interest in the progress of the cinema since its inception by the Lumière Brothers in Paris in February 1896. The medium had a strong influence on *Ulysses* and

James Joyce

even to a greater degree on *Finnegans Wake*. In 1930 he was visited in his Paris flat by the renowned Russian director, Sergei Eisenstein, best known for his *Battleship Potemkin*. The latter believed that cinema, and cinema only, could combine and synchronise the senses of sight and sound, yet he was so taken with *Ulysses* that he declared Joyce had done for literature what he (Eisenstein) was attempting to do for cinema. The two men formed a common bond: both were aspiring to create new forms of expressing the inner processes of thought and emotion, and Joyce hoped that if anyone was to film his work it would be the Russian. Joyce read passages of his work to Eisenstein and despite his growing blindness, expressed a desire to see *Battleship Potemkin*. In his Film School in Moscow, Eisenstein used to set his pupils passages from *Ulysses* to be turned into film format.

Eisenstein did, in fact, endeavour to set up a film of *Ulysses* but did not succeed. He was only the first of many film-makers, including John Huston and Hollywood producer Jerry Wald, who tried unsuccessfully to bring the complexities of the book to the screen. Wald, in fact, bought the film rights and went as far as coming to Dublin to scout for locations and a possible cast, but he was too preoccupied with his successful television series, *Peyton Place* to proceed with the filming. 20th Century Fox, the company in which Wald was involved, were plagued by financial difficulties, not least from the mounting expenditure on *Cleopatra* and such an ambitious project as *Ulysses* had to be shelved. It is worth noting that such names as Rod Steiger and Marilyn Monroe were mentioned for the parts of Leopold and Molly Bloom.

Director Joseph Strick

Then American director, Joseph Strick bought the film rights for $75,000 and planned to film *Ulysses* as a trilogy: the first part, the day of Stephen and Bloom; the second, every word of Nighttown; and the third, every word of Molly. The bankers were not enthusiastic and forced him to turn it into one film. He was turned down by most American and British producers before Walter Reade, who was associated with British Lion, decided to back him. Strick's next problem was discovering that the banks were insisting on Reade and himself putting up personal sureties of £50,000 as insurance against the film being turned down by the British censor. Determined to make the film, Strick raised some of the cash by directing a play, *Gallows Humour* by Jack Richardson, at the

Olympia Theatre for the Dublin Theatre Festival and making a documentary on the British General Election for the BBC.

Eventually, after surmounting most of the problems, the film went into production on a budget of $450,000. Strick had a ground rule that there would be no new writing, no additions or corrections, and no play narrative. Every pound of expenditure had to be examined closely. On occasions they were fortunate, as when they procured a circus free of charge. He directed the film entirely on location in Dublin, in many of the places depicted in Joyce's classic: the Irish House, Martello Tower, Sandymount Strand and Howth Head. He gathered a fine cast, albeit virtually unknown outside Ireland, headed by Milo O'Shea as Bloom, Barbara Jefford as Molly, Maurice Roeves as Stephen Dedalus, T.P. McKenna as Buck Mulligan and Joe Lynch, Fionnula Flanagan, Martin Dempsey and Anna Manahan. None of the crew or actors were paid more than £100 per week but everyone received a percentage of the profits.

Overall the film was disappointing but Strick did manage to convey some interesting images. The main criticism was that the period was transferred from its original 1904 to present day (1965) and Strick was forced to agree with this but argued that he could not afford a period film. In technical terms some extremely old-fashioned techniques were employed and a number of the performances were inadequate while others were exaggerated. Although the film was to establish Milo O'Shea as an international star, many interpreted his portrayal as nothing more than the antics of a dirty old man. Barbara Jefford beautifully delivered Molly's soliloquy in language hitherto unheard in cinemas in the British Isles.

Even before its release, *Ulysses* had a stormy passage. In Britain, Strick had many confrontations with the Board of Censors and its Secretary John Trevelyan, both while scripting and on completion of filming. The censor demanded cuts amounting to two scenes and four hundred words. The film was banned from some cinemas in Britain but it did enjoy a long run in the West End of London. In America it opened simultaneously, uncut, in a hundred and fifty cinemas from coast to coast for a limited run of three days and was acclaimed by public and critics alike. Back in Joyce's native Dublin, the then Lord Mayor, Seán Moore, wanted it made known publicly who had financed the film.

Strick, by now obsessed with the works of Joyce, returned to Dublin to film *Portrait of the Artist as a Young Man* in 1975. This chronicled the childhood memories and emerging manhood of Stephen Dedalus, Joyce's alter ego, and examined the struggle of the artist in relation to himself and his culture in the Dublin of the 1890s. The story follows Stephen Dedalus through many segments of his life - the famous Christmas dinner scene, life at Clongowes Wood College and later Belvedere and University College, and his gradual disenchantment with religious and political life in Ireland. Again Strick shot on location in Dublin, this time in period costume, and used an almost entirely Irish cast headed by Bosco Hogan in the title role. Supporting him were T.P. McKenna, Maureen Potter and Rosaleen Linehan, the latter

two playing very much out of character. Sir John Gielgud made an impressive cameo appearance as the preacher who delivers the hell-fire sermon. The production, less complex than *Ulysses*, captured more successfully the essential elements of the book and its characters and lent itself more satisfactorily to treatment on film. *Portrait* fared better with the censor and was released in Ireland.

Strick's ultimate goal was to film all of Joyce's major works. Joyce himself during his lifetime cherished the thought that if by some act of the fate the city of Dublin was destroyed it could be rebuilt simply by reference to his books. Many buildings, filmed by Strick for *Ulysses*, have since been demolished and this film may well serve as a pictorial record of the places so beloved of the writer.

In 1964 Joyce's *Finnegans Wake* was skilfully brought to the screen by Mary Ellen Bute in a black and white adaptation of the Mary Manning play on which it was based. It took seven years to get the film off the ground and it was finally made

Volta Cinema, Mary Street, Dublin

only by a subvention from the University of Minnesota. The budget was a modest £85,000. The film was shot in a small New York studio and on location in Dublin. Miss Bute, in consideration of the non Joycean student, included subtitles — a most unusual practice for an English speaking film shown to an English - speaking audience! The cast of twenty-three Irish and Irish-Americans included Martin J. Kelly as Finnegan, Jane Reilly, Peter Heskell, Page Johnson, John V. Kelleher and Ray Flanagan. Before filming began, many of the cast had just finished a run of Behan's *The Hostage* on Broadway.

The film concerns a Dublin publican, Finnegan, who as he lies asleep dreams of a legendary Irish hero named Finn McCool and of his own wake when his friends rouse him from the coffin with whiskey. The dream is crammed with images and experiences from Joyce's own life expressed in a richly allusive dream-language that Joyce himself described as 'a mess of mottage'.

Director Bute and cameraman Ted Nemeth successfully overcame the difficulty of attempting to transcribe Joyce's words onto the screen. The film never received widespread release and was screened only in art houses.

Joyce was fully aware of the powerful potential of the cinema imagery and it is unfortunate that he died some twenty-five years before the first of his major works was brought to the screen, thus missing the opportunity to assess the various interpretations.

Milo O'Shea in the film *Ulysses*

Chapter 11

On Location

Producer Harry Alan Towers bought the film rights to Sax Rohmer's novels of the exploits of Fu Manchu and announced that he would make five films about the oriental menace with Christopher Lee, most noted for his portrayals in Hammer Films, cast in the title role. The first Fu Manchu story was written in 1911 by Rohmer, pseudo name for Fleet Street journalist Arthur Sarsfield Ward. Between 1915 and 1935, four feature films were made with Warner Oland and Boris Karloff playing the 'plotter-of-evil'. In the first of the new productions, *Face of Fu Manchu* (1964), Tsai Chin played his daughter, Howard Marion Crawford was the British Home Office pathologist and Nigel Green was Fu's stalwart adversary, Nayland Smith.

'A most unconventional film-maker ' was how producer Towers had been described. In a two-year period he made twelve films on location in such varied places as South West Africa, Mozambique, Marrakesh, Beirut, England and Ireland. Most of his films had been made as co-productions with German companies and featured a mixture of German, English and American actors.

He chose Ireland to film *Face of Fu Manchu*

although the plot was set in China and rural England. Kenure House in Rush was the main location. Other scenes were shot in Skerries, the Dublin docks and Kilmainham Jail. There was an excellent sense of atmosphere which period cars, horse-drawn carts and cobbled streets helped to create. Under Don Sharp's direction the film became a fast-moving thriller.

Immediately on its completion, Towers started another film in Ireland with relatively no advance publicity. It was based on an Agatha Christie thriller, *Ten Little Niggers*, discreetly retitled *Ten Little Indians*. It had been filmed some years previously with Barry Fitzgerald and called *And Then There Were None*, but this second mounting lacked the suspense of the Rene Clair version. Towers assembled a top-line cast including Hugh O'Brian, Shirley Eaton, Stanley Holloway, Wilfred Hyde White, Fabian, Dennis Price and Leo Genn. George Pollock directed the entire film at Kenure House. Valuable props, insured for £40,000, were shipped from England to add authenticity to the set. They included Edwardian ornaments, Tudor furniture, glittering suits of armour and valuable paintings.

Shirley Eaton on set of *Ten Little Indians*

The action takes place in a large house in the Austrian Alps, cut off by a raging blizzard. The only access is a cable railway which has been wrecked, severing all means of escape. Ten people are forced to take shelter in the eerie atmosphere of the mansion. One by one they are murdered, with everyone held under suspicion. Finally, there are only two people left and at that point the audience are given an intermission to puzzle it out for themselves.

Dennis Price on set - *Ten Little Indians*

Towers explained why he had been so keen to make a second film in Ireland:

I'm so pleased with conditions in Ireland that I intend to make many more films here. We can film in the heart of Dublin and still nor cause much disruption to traffic. This is utterly impossible in London where one has enormous problems working away from the studio. The only minor difficulty we have encountered here so far is that outdoor locations attract large crowds. At times this can become annoying. Film-making is still a novelty here and people travel miles to watch a film in production.

The next film to go before the cameras was John Ford's *Young Cassidy*, his third project in Ireland. It was shot entirely on location in Dublin with the exception of two weeks' interior work at MGM's Elstree Studio. John Whiting wrote the screenplay based on Seán O'Casey's autobiography, *Pictures in the Hallway*. O'Casey's permission for this film had been given because he was friendly with the film's two producers—Robert Graff and Robert Emmett Ginna. Graff had previously directed a television film for NBC called *A Conversation with Seán O'Casey* and Ginna, with Gjon Mili, had done a feature for *Life* entitled 'The World of Seán O'Casey'.

For the title role of the rebel playwright several big names were considered, including Richard Harris and Peter O'Toole. Eventually Sean Connery was cast as the young O'Casey, but before the film commenced, Connery was asked to play the secret agent James Bond in *Dr. No,* which set him on his way to becoming an international star. He was replaced by Australian actor, Rod Taylor. Two actresses, who were later to become international stars, were cast as the loves of his life, Julie Christie as the Dublin girl, Daisy Battles, and Maggie Smith as Nora, a book shop assistant. Others in the distinguished cast included Flora Robson as his mother, Sian Philips as his sister, Dame Edith Evans as Lady Gregory and Sir Michael Redgrave as W.B. Yeats. Irish actors appearing were Philip O'Flynn, Jack McGowran, Pauline Delaney, Donal Donnelly, T.P. McKenna and Joe Lynch. Almost every actor and extra on Equity's books was on the film's payroll.

Rod Taylor on location for *Young Cassidy*

The story begins in Dublin in 1911 where Johnny Cassidy, a working class boy, works as a navvy. He writes and distributes propaganda sheets and during a riot between strikers and police he rescues young Daisy Battles. When the Easter Rising of 1916 erupts, Johnny is a member of the Irish Citizen Army. With the collapse of the Rebellion he escapes capture. The joy when his first book is accepted by a publisher is short-lived as his mother dies soon afterwards. Later he falls in love with Nora but she recognises the rebel and dreamer in him. Although his first play is rejected by the Abbey Theatre, he perseveres and eventually they accept his play *The Shadow of a Gunman*. It is a moderate success and Johnny is befriended by Lady Gregory and W.B. Yeats. Soon afterwards another of his plays, *The Plough and the Stars,* causes a riot at the theatre. After a row with his friend Mick (Philip O'Flynn) he leaves Nora and sets out for England.

Ford (who was paid $50,000) and the producers had a difference of opinion as to how the film should be approached. The producers felt that the Dublin of 1964 bore little resemblance to that of 1911, and wanted to work in a less-developed provincial town. Ford insisted that if they were to make the film in Ireland it must be Dublin. Filming began in mid July 1964 at the King's Inns on Henrietta Street in Dublin. During the course of shooting several accidents befell the unit. Blow number one was when Rod Taylor and several other actors were thrown heavily from a sidecar and could resume work only after medical attention. The next misfortune was when Julie Christie was rushed to hospital to undergo an emergency operation for acute appendicitis. She returned to the set after a few days' convalescence. The greatest misfortune, however, came after thirteen working days when John Ford fell seriously ill with viral pneumonia. Lord Killanin's wife, Sheila, nursed him. He was advised by his doctor to retire from the film and was flown back to Los Angeles for hospital treatment. He lost thirty-eight pounds during his illness. Shooting came to a standstill for several days while a substitute was sought. Ford had already shot the first twenty minutes, as he preferred to shoot in sequence. Jack Cardiff flew to Dublin to take over as his successor.

Cardiff made an even greater effort to capture the colour and flavour of Dublin. He had tried for many years to secure support for a film on the most celebrated of all literary records of

Flora Robson and Rod Taylor in a scene from
Young Cassidy

Sarah Miles and Sean Caffrey in a scene from
I Was Happy Here

Dublin life, *Ulysses*. Having failed to obtain the necessary financing for the latter, he was determined to put Dublin on film with *Young Cassidy* and succeeded remarkably well, although it did tend to be marred by its episodic nature. Rod Taylor felt it was one of the most important films of his career.

The next production in Ireland saw the return of Desmond Davis and Woodfall Productions to produce *I Was Happy Here*. It had a great deal in common with his previous Irish venture, *Girl with Green Eyes*. Both had Irish settings with young girls as the central characters and both were adaptations from the works of Irish novelist Edna O'Brien. His new production was based on her short story *Passage of Love* and starred Sarah Miles, Cyril Cusack, Sean Caffrey and Julian Glover. It was produced by Ray Millichop and photographed by Manny Wynn. The film was the first to be financed under the new National Film Finance Corporation and the Rank financing scheme for independent producers.

The heroine (Sarah Miles) comes from her Irish village to a London bedsitter and marries a Wimbledon doctor (Julian Glover) who seeks to mould her to his upper middle-class ways. Fleeing from a marital quarrel, she returns to her village and the fisherman she once loved (Sean Caffrey). There she realises she now fits neither world and must painfully work out her own salvation The theme reflected the social change occurring in the conservative society of the times.

The love scenes on Ireland's Atlantic coastline in midwinter were powerfully evocative. Photography and editing were a delight for the student of the cinema: tracking shots into tracking

Arthur Flynn and Burl Ives during filming
Rocket to the Moon

shots, jump-cuts that far from simply jumping had a clear editorial continuity - a seagull's provocative cry that jumps to a shot of brakes screeching in a loud street - and a virtuoso 6 x 360° hand-held shot of Sarah Miles cycling around a London courtyard. If her playing occasionally hovered between winning innocence and King's Road frivolity, one was gradually impressed by the deepening of her character. Both the male characters were seen through the girl's eyes and accordingly were less rounded, though the character of the spoiled doctor was established with deft, strong strokes. Cyril Cusack was the quiet, sensitive, cagey Irish publican whose presence dominated some scenes, which were to win him international fame.

Harry Alan Towers returned to Ireland in

1966 to shoot his next film, *Rocket to the Moon*. Dave Freeman wrote the screenplay, inspired by the writings of Jules Verne. Don Sharp was again assigned to direct the three million dollar comedy featuring some of the most talented international stars. From America came Burl Ives and Troy Donohue, from Germany came Gert Frobe, from Israel Daliah Lavi and from Britain Terry Thomas, Lionel Jeffries, Dennis Price and Jimmy Clitheroe. The cameras began to roll in Kenure House, Towers's improvised film studio. Later, the unit moved into a variety of picturesque and historic locations, including Dublin Castle, the Botanic Gardens, Avoca, Brittas Bay and the Curragh. At least eighty per cent of the film was shot out-of-doors. Once again it proved that Irish locations could substitute for countries as diverse as Germany, England and France.

The story was an amusing piece of Victorian science-fiction about the launching in 1875 of a moon-bound spaceship. A strange assortment of characters were involved. Leading the adventure was Phineas T. Barnum (Ives), assisted by Tom Thumb (Clitheroe), a French balloonist, some rival inventors, a dim-witted lord, Queen Victoria and a few delectable girls. It was, in fact, a pedestrian piece with more than its fair share of tedious segments. Its numerous cast literally tripped over each other as they made their entrances and exits. Many talented actors were totally wasted.

It was inevitable that a film would be made about the Great Train Robbery of 1963 and three years later Stanley Baker starred in, and produced, *Robbery*, based on the subject. His co-stars were Joanna Pettit and James Booth. Although it out lined in great detail the planning and execution of the raid on the London night mail-train, it also examined carefully the personal lives of the gang. This distracted from the central theme. A German film on the same subject was far more successful. Most of the Baker film was shot in England but the prison sequences, involving a daring jail-break, were filmed at Kilmainham and Arbour Hill jails. The film will be best remembered not so much for its robberies — there were two, a £75,000 jewel heist to finance the big one — as for its exciting

car chase at the beginning, forerunner to director Peter Yates's high powered car chase in *Bullitt*.

The next offering from Ardmore was the *Viking Queen*, an action adventure in colour and wide screen, starring Don Murray, back in Bray in a greatly diminished part, with new discovery Carita, his co-star. Others in the cast included Donald Houston, Andrew Keir, Niall McGinnis and Adrienne Corri. It was produced by John Temple-Smith and directed by Don Chaffey, an Ardmore regular. Exteriors were shot in a variety of locations in the Wicklow Mountains with vast crowds of extras. A large contingent of the Irish Army worked in the big-scale action scenes in Powerscourt. The *Viking Queen* is the story of a Boadicea-like queen of ancient Britain (Cariu) who is forced to take arms against the Roman occupation forces commanded by the man she loves (Murray). The successful team of producer Harry Alan Towers, director Sharp and stars Christopher Lee and Tsai Chin returned to make another Sax Rohmer yarn, *The Vengeance of Fu Manchu*. They did a short stint at the studio and Dublin's back streets. Don Sharp was notable in that he tried, whenever possible, to introduce new faces in his Fu Manchu films, including many Irish actors:

I think that goes back to my days as an actor of being given opportunities by people and also when I was directing in the theatre working with completely new people. I find it very exciting. I don't think you can mix too many new people in the film and you can't always give a person new to film techniques a prominent role. You can have somebody with all the natural characteristics in himself that the character requires but because of a lack of film technique he may not be able to bring these characteristics out as clearly as you would wish.

The Irish stage and screen actor Míchael MacLiammóir

Chapter 12

Huston's Initiative

John Huston found in Ireland a tranquillity that recharged his batteries between the rigours of film-making. He lived in St. Clerans, a Georgian mansion at Craughwell, County Galway, for almost twenty years. The house was adorned with mementoes of his travels to film locations in many continents. He entertained, in his Irish home, many celebrities, from Arthur Miller to Marlon Brando and Montgomery Clift. He became so immersed in the Irish way of life, as country squire, Master of the Galway Blazers, recipient of an honorary degree from Trinity College, that he became an Irish citizen in 1964.

One long-term ambition of Huston's was to produce a film on the most dramatic few days in modern Irish history — the Easter Rising of 1916. He began preliminary work and assigned writer Gerald Hanley to adapt Thomas M. Coffey's novel *The Agony at Easter* for the screen. He received the Government's backing and their commitment to allow him all facilities and the use of several hundred troops. Even the rebuilding of Nelson's Pillar was on the agenda. Unfortunately, owing to the escalating Northern troubles and the sensitive nature of the subject, the production had

to be postponed. Despite this, the number of films Huston wholly or partially shot in Ireland during the period of his residency here increased substantially.

One of these was *Casino Royale* (1966), a lavish, big budget spoof on the James Bond spy adventures, produced by Charles K. Feldman. Wolf Mankowitz wrote the screenplay from the novel in which Ian Fleming introduced the original Bond character. The £4 million film, which took ten months to shoot, was divided among five directors — John Huston (38 minutes), Val Guest (26 minutes), Joseph McGrath (26 minutes), Robert Parrish (20 minutes), and Ken Hughes (25 minutes), though a substantial amount of footage was shot by the 'action director', seventy-year-old Richard Talmedge. A host of stars including Orson Welles, George Raft, Peter Sellers, Woody Allen, Peter O'Toole, Charles Boyer and William Holden added their lustre to the extravaganza.

Even though the film had no Irish connection, Huston came to Ireland to shoot part of his quota. He brought David Niven, Deborah Kerr and a bevy of beauties to romp around the wilds of Glencree and Killeen Castle. Huston tried to persuade Charlie Chaplin to take the role of 'M', Bond's boss, and when Chaplin declined, he played the cameo role himself, with a carroty red wig, fated to be blown to kingdom come. Deborah Kerr played Mimi, a lusty secret agent, masquerading as Lady Fiona McTarry, a Scottish chieftain who planned to seduce Niven (James Bond) and failed. She got uproariously drunk and set her teenage daughters to accomplish the task which had proved beyond her. She then renounced the world and entered a convent. She reappeared at the end in a wimple to give Niven a valuable clue (and a wink which implied that the holy lady had not entirely forgotten her early self). The sequence was an endearing touch of Huston at his most irreverent.

The plot and continuity of the film were a disaster: the film looked as though it was the product of several different scripts that got mixed up. It might not have been a bad idea if Huston had blown up the other directors and most of the stars and let Niven and Kerr get on with the film! One of the most impressive aspects of the film was the sets designed by Michael Stringer. Originally assigned to design thirty sets he ended up, as new ideas were incorporated, designing over fifty, constructed at three different studios. At one point the film had three units filming simultaneously. Another redeeming facet of the production was the special effects. Also, the gambling finale in the casino of the title was well staged.

Not long after the Bond fiasco, Huston was back in Ireland for his next production, *Sinful Davey*, the story of Davey Haggard, the son of Scotland's most notorious highwayman. His cast was headed by John Hurt, Pamela Franklin, Nigel Davenport and Robert Morley. In 1821 Haggard deserts the King's army and sets out to outdo his father's legend, at first pick pocketing, then robbing graves for which he is thrown in jail. He endears himself to the Duke of Argyle (Morley) and during a grand ball he robs the Duke's guests of all their jewellery. He is caught and sentenced to hang but of course he escapes.

Unfortunately, the film turned out to be nothing more than a romp in the Walt Disney

John Huston directing Pamela Franklin in *Sinful Davey*

tradition. One expected more from a Huston film but it was redeemed some what by the performance of John Hurt in the title role. He tumbled, fought, robbed, made love and generally charmed his way through the film, making the most of his cardboard character. The best feature was the photography of Ted Scaife, who had already worked here on *Young Cassidy*. He captured magnificently the soft lights and dewy mountains of County Wicklow. The craftsmen did a skilful job of transforming Glencree Reformatory into the period Scottish village of Stirling. The sets, costumes and locations were chosen with great care and were a joy to watch. There was a strong Irish contingent amongst the supporting players, including Fidelma Murphy, Donal McCann, Eddie Byrne, Mickser Reid and Niall McGinnis.

During the course of filming *Sinful Davey*, Huston took the opportunity of expressing his opinion on the need for an Irish film industry which he had advocated for some time. In July 1967 he invited the then Taoiseach, Jack Lynch, and some of his ministers to the location at Glencree where he expounded his views. He pointed out to them that the only reason this film was being made in Ireland was that he himself liked to work here and his associates, who realised this, humoured him.

Jack Lynch with Fred Astaire and Charlotte Rampling during a break in shooting at Ardmore Studio

Huston suggested that a Board be set up to get the ball rolling. It should decide on a programme of six modest budget films. The aim should be higher than purely commercial targets: creative and artistic values and the education of young Irish people in the film business must be a priority. The type of pictures he had in mind would be financed partly by the Government, partly by cinema owners and partly by private capital. Each would have a budget a quarter of that of his present film and could be made with a handful of technicians—as in Sweden where, he added, technicians got higher salaries than those in any other place, not excepting Hollywood itself. He also put forward the value of films in promoting trade and tourism as well as representing Ireland and things Irish abroad; but it was for the employment of Ireland's great resevoir of artistic talent that a native film industry was most important.

In November 1967 the Government took up Huston's suggestion and the Minister for Industry and Commerce set up a committee to examine the problems involved in the establishment of an Irish film industry and to advise him on how they could be solved. Naturally Huston himself was appointed chairman. Included on the committee were Dermot Breen, Patrick Carey, Dermot Doolin, Wilfred Eades, Lord Killanin and Louis Marcus. When the Committee finished its work (in June 1968) it produced a sixty-one page Report of the Film Industry Committee.

Louis Marcus

They drew up recommendations on how an Irish film industry could be established and, more importantly, how it could function.

Some examples of film-making practices in other countries were listed:

The present artistic and commercial success of countries such as France, Poland and Czechoslovakia in low budget feature films stems directly from the short story films of these countries. Their technicians such as French cameraman Raoul Couterd, the Polish director Roman Polanski and the Czech director Jan Nemac all began as makers of short fiction films. As the skills and techniques required for this type of short film are similar to those required for features there is obviously no better training ground and no clearer indication as to the feature-making potential of the various sectors involved.

On the question of finance the Committee recommended:

That the Government should establish a Film Board which should have the positive function of furthering and encouraging the development of an Irish feature film industry. The Board should not itself engage in the production of feature films; its role should be the creation of conditions in which others interested would be likely to do this and the stimulation of those interested to undertake the task.

The Board should be empowered to make loans up to the full cost of production to Irish producers who can show that they are professionally qualified and who submit acceptable proposals for the making with predominantly Irish personnel of Irish feature films costing not more than £50,000 each. A loan would of course be authorised only where there was merit in the proposal and evidence that the proposers had the necessary professional ability and were likely to make a film that would be exhibited in Ireland and abroad. These loans would be repayable with interest out of receipts from the showing of the films. The power to make them should lapse after six such films had been made and the position should then be reviewed in the light of the experience gained. Where films of the kind dealt with in this paragraph are made in the Irish language they obviously must be dubbed, subtitled or shot in double version to be successfully distributed abroad. The Board should be empowered to make special loans in addition to what would normally be provided under the recommended scheme to cover these extra costs.

The Board should be empowered to make loans up to a maximum of £10,000 to producers of international repute who submit acceptable proposals for the making of Irish feature films. These loans would be intended to cover pre-production costs only and would be repayable with interest if the film went into production. The Film Board should review the sources of film finance available to producers of feature films and should take such steps as it considered appropriate to facilitate the provision of such finance by commercial interests.

The Board should engage in the following activities:

(a) DISTRIBUTION AGREEMENTS to advise on or assist producers in the making of arrangements for the marketing of films.

(b) CO-PRODUCTION AGREEMENTS to assist in negotiating arrangements between Irish film makers and those of other countries with a view to the sharing of resources and facilities in specific ventures.

(c) TRAINING FACILITIES to provide the opportunity and financial assistance to writers, musicians, directors, artists, designers, craftsmen and technicians to be trained in film making either at home or abroad.

(d) THE PROVISION OF OTHER FACILITIES NECESSARY FOR FILM PRODUCTION to provide to any producer contemplating the making of a film in Ireland advice on location, technicians, extras and any aspect of film Imaking in Ireland including finance.

(e) To make recommendations from time to time to the Government which it might consider necessary to advance the Irish film industry .

(f) NATIONAL FILM ARCHIVE to establish a national archive.

These were the main proposals that the Government and other interested bodies had to consider.

Chapter 13

From O'Toole to Dunne

While the backroom boys sat down to talk about Huston's proposals, Ardmore was kept busy. When it was decided to bring James Goldman's excellent Broadway play *The Lion In Winter*, to the screen, one man was an obvious choice for the role of Henry II — Peter O'Toole. For O'Toole, who had already excelled himself in *Becket* opposite Richard Burton, it was his first film, not only in Ardmore but in Ireland and it was at his suggestion that the film moved into the Bray studio. The interiors were filmed on the sound stages at Ardmore and location work was done in France. The executive producer was Joseph E. Levine, the producer Martin Poll and the director Anthony Harvey who was making his second film. In support of O'Toole a top-line cast was signed up including Katherine Hepburn as Eleanor of Aquitaine, Jane Morrow, Anthony Hopkins, John Castle and Timothy Dalton. John Barry wrote the musical score. The film takes a look at politics in the Middle Ages and examines the ruthless power play among England's royal family — and their three sons — in choosing a successor to the crown. It is set at Christmas 1183 when Eleanor visits her husband, Henry. The luminous Rosemary Harris

had dominated the Broadway stage-show. In this screen version Miss Hepburn put in a performance for which she was nominated for an Academy Award. She was popular with the locals in Bray as she cycled around the town and swam daily in the wintry sea. During the course of this production they employed a system very agreeable to late risers — they did not commence work each day until ten o'clock.

Joseph McGrath, one of the *Casino Royale* directors, came to Dublin to film a segment of *30 is a Dangerous Age, Cynthia* in 1967. Heading his cast were Dudley Moore, Suzy Kendall, Patricia Routledge and Eddie Foy, Jr. The film concerned the efforts of a piano player (Moore) to attain success and marriage by his thirtieth birthday — in six weeks' time. Moore, one of the English-speaking theatre's most inventive comedians, gave this uneven production moments of inspired lunacy with his virtuoso musical parodies. Moore came to Ireland to research his subject. He was seen walking through many picturesque locations in Dublin, running around the gasometer and doing weird things on Sandymount Strand. There was a disappointing cameo featuring Mícheál

Patrick Dawson in *Guns in the Heather*

MacLiammóir telling a story as he lies in a four-poster bed in a Martello tower.

Kilkenny was chosen as the location for eighteenth century London in *Lock Up Your Daughters*. The film was a rehash of the stage play *Rape Upon Rape* by Henry Fielding which became a stage musical and finally the basis for a screenplay by Keith Waterhouse and Willis Hall. It had a confused plot about lusty sailors whose amorous pursuits entangled them with Lord Foppington and Sir Tunbelly Clumsey and his daughter Hoyden. Director Peter Coe orchestrated an amusing custard-pie throwing battle. Some difficulty arose when the film-makers were unable to persuade local girls to play buxom wenches in low-cut gowns and had to bring some in from England. It is surprising that this farcical theme was able to attract such an all-star cast as Christopher Plummer, Susannah York, Ian Bannen, Glynis Johns, Tom Bell and Roy Kinnear.

Counties Clare and Galway saw a considerable amount of filming during the summer of 1968. One film was *Guns in the Heather*, a £500,000 Walt Disney production. It was a quintessential Disney yarn about two boys, one American, one Irish, who become involved in mystery and intrigue and are chased by a gang of crooks along the west coast. The boys were played by Kurt Russell, a regular in Disney films, and Bray boy Patrick Dawson. The crooks were played by Peter Vaughan, Alfred Burke and Godfrey Quigley. The script did not call for any of the actors to overtax themselves but it was a piece of clean

escapist entertainment. It was directed by Robert Butler.

Filming at the same time in Galway, on a much longer shooting schedule, was MGM's *Alfred the Great,* an epic tale that told of the bloody battles between the Viking invaders of Britain and the settled Saxons, and studied the character of the king who tried to impose order not only on his country but also on himself. British actor David Hemmings played King Alfred and was supported by Michael York, Prunella Ransome and Colin Blakely. Clive Donner, whose past work included *Nothing but the Best* and *Here We Go Round the Mulberry Bush*, directed what was his first outdoor epic. Areas of County Galway around Loughrea represented Alfred's Wessex and replicas of Viking ships sailed up the River Shannon. Local farmers and students were hired by the hundreds for the summer months and were required to grow their hair long and sprout beards. The producers built their own studio close to the area in which they were filming. They were too far from Ardmore, and, moreover, Irish weather conditions being so unreliable, it was sensible to have a base nearby where they could construct sets and store their equipment.

Also shooting that summer was *The Prince and the Pauper*, produced by Professional Films of New York. Director Elliott Geisinger and producer Ronnie Saland brought a cast of unknowns to an old farm in Navan which was the main location

Julie Andrews filming *Darling Lili*

for this Mark Twain yarn. A film made strictly for children, it was to be released nationwide in America for afternoon showing.

In 1967 Ardmore Studio changed hands and was bought by an English Company, New Brighton Enterprises. Lee Davis, an Englishman, became the new studio chief. He was the nearest thing to a Hollywood mogul that the studio had ever seen and seemed to imagine himself taking over the mantle of Louis B. Mayer. Davis went to America to sell the studio's services and brought back some big contracts, including *Darling Lili* and *The Violent Enemy*. To the flamboyant Davis, money seemed to be no object. He had his office panelled in expensive wood, with concealed lighting, sumptuous seating and a huge desk. He drove a Jaguar with a crest on the door, the letters A.S. for Ardmore Studio and L.D. for his own initials. *Darling Lili* brought to Dublin the combined talents of Julie Andrews and Rock Hudson under the direction of Blake Edwards, who had made such films as *The Pink Panther* and *Days of Wine and Roses*. It was a return to Ireland for Hudson who had made *Captain Lightfoot* here some fourteen years previously. This was a high budget, glossy comedy in which Julie Andrews played a seductive singer who was also a spy and who moved in glittering social circles during World War I. Her previous film, *Star*, had not been the huge success that had been predicted, so everybody kept their fingers crossed for this production. It turned out to be no more than a moderate success.

The opening sequence was shot in Dublin's Gaiety Theatre. The audience of socialites, with a sprinkling of khaki-clad soldiers on leave from Mons and Cambrai, are enjoying themselves at a show given by Julie when suddenly air-raid sirens sound and the audience jump to their feet. She begins singing some rousing songs of the period, such as 'It's a long way to Tipperary' and the entire audience, forgetting the danger, join in the singing. Other Irish locations included Heuston Station, Carton House and Trinity College. The many flying sequences were filmed near Weston Airport with the producers able to utilise the planes and flyers from *The Blue Max*. In fact this latter film had served as a dummy run and a lot of the difficulties had been ironed out.

For the film *Where's Jack?* director James Clavell set about transforming the old Glencree Reformatory once again from the remains of Huston's Scottish village into a slice of Hogarth's London. The film tells the tale of Jack Sheppard, a locksmith's apprentice in eighteenth century London, whose only crime is that of poverty. He meets with Jonathan Wild, a notorious and unscrupulous thieftaker (bounty hunter). Wild, however, tricks Jack into crime. Eventually he breaks free of Wild and, spurred on by his love for Edgeworth Bess, he rampages through London, looting. His fame reaches the royal court and the king himself. He becomes the darling of society and soon it is fashionable to be robbed by him.

This film had a good deal in common with *Sinful Davey* but was far superior. Clavell's direction was crisp, full of action and colour, and he sought to pack every frame with details from Hogarth's paintings. The inn scenes, in particular, were alive with movement and atmosphere. Singing star Tommy Steele was toothily heroic as the hero, Stanley Baker (who also produced) was treacherously villainous as Wild and Fiona Lewis was decorative as the buxom wench. Noel Purcell, minus his beard, played a mute.

The *Italian Job* film unit came to Dublin to work at Arbour Hill and Kilmainham Jail. Kilmainham was receiving so many visits from film-makers that it could have doubled as a film studio. Both jails figured prominently in the film as Sir Noel Coward, who was incarcerated within, was master mind of a number of highly successful robberies. The leading crook on the outside was played by Michael Caine. It was an amusing, exciting film with most of the acting honours going to Coward but even his performance was overshadowed by the stunt drivers who did some spectacular driving in the Italian locations. The film brought back to Ireland Peter Collinson who had worked with Radio Telefís Éireann in its early days and by now had carved out quite a lucrative career for himself as an international director.

In the same year, 1968, Wilfred Eades, studio manager at Ardmore, produced a taut little thriller, *The Violent Enemy*, at the studio with exteriors around Dublin. A regular visitor to Ireland, Don Sharp, again directed. English actor Tom Bell, whose acting ability was often under estimated, played the main role of an IRA man who breaks jail, as his expertise in explosives is needed in Ireland. Veteran American actor, Ed Begley co-starred and Susan Hampshire, from the television series, *The Forsythe Saga*, switched to modern dress to supply the love interest. Noel Purcell and Philip O'Flynn were well placed in supporting roles.

Over the next few years, several works of Dublin best-selling author Lee Dunne were filmed. First came a screenplay in which he was co-author titled, during production, *I Can't, I Can't,* but released as *Wedding Night.* It was directed by Piers Haggard and starred Dennis Waterman and Tessa Wyatt with Eddie Byrne and Márie O'Donnell in support. The drama revolved around the difficulties of a young married couple. Lee Davis said of the film, 'This was a low budget film which recouped its production costs in America alone.'

Next followed a short film, *The Girl with the Pale Face*, in which Dunne was closely involved — he wrote much of it and also played a small part as a bus-conductor. It concerned a young man who meets a girl at a dance and takes her off to a lonely beach, hoping to have his way with her. It starred Fidelma Murphy and Donal McCann. In almost every respect this film was, to put it mildly, hammy and contrived, badly acted, directed, written, and technically it left a lot to be desired. It was directed by Paul Gallico Jr.

Dunne's third film, *Paddy*, was the most ambitious of all his projects. It was the screen adaptation of his best-selling novel *Goodbye to the Hill,* and followed the trial and tribulations of young Paddy Maguire from a Dublin slum, and his sexual pursuit of various females. It gave young Abbey actor, Des Cave, his first screen role as the active youth. Two of the females in his life were played by Maureen Toal and Dearbhla Molloy. The film was shot entirely on location in and around Dublin with a small crew and on a $100,000 budget. Director Daniel Haller had intended to make an Irish version of the classic French film, *A Man and a Woman.* To achieve this end the same French camera crew worked on this film, but they fell short of their goal. As expected, the film was banned in Ireland.

Underground was the first of two World War II films to be shot at Ardmore, with exteriors in the surrounding counties, by producers Jules Levy and Arthur Gardner. It was the first subject on that war to be shot in Ireland. It is the story of a group of French Resistance fighters and the guerrilla warfare they waged against the Germans. The County Wexford town of Enniscorthy, with a little camouflaging, served quite well as a French town of the period. The film was directed by Arthur Nadel and starred American singing star Robert Goulet, Daniele Gaubert and Joachim Hansen. It maintained a fast rate of action and was average for this genre.

The second Levy-Gardner production was the *McKenzie Break* which gave a new twist to the prisoner-of-war theme, with German prisoners in a British camp in Scotland who were the ones seeking to escape. The film-makers built a complete prison camp, consisting of huts, guard towers and barbed wire, at Ballymoney, County Wicklow. Members of the Irish Army, who by now were something of experts at the game, acted as both British and German troops. The film will be remembered for the rugged performance by American actor Brian Keith as one of the camp's officers. He was well supported by Ian Hendry as the camp commander and the leading German actors, Helmut Griem and Horst Janson, who gave first class performances.

Also in 1969, Peter O'Toole took a break from epics to bring another film into Ardmore. It was *Country Dance*, an unusual love story set in Scotland. This MGM production was produced by Robert Emmet Gina and directed by J. Lee Thompson from a screenplay by James Kennaway. Susannah York played O'Toole's sister and Michael Craig her husband in a three cornered relationship, O'Toole having more than brotherly feelings towards his sister. He played the part of an eccentric land owner of a stately mansion in the Highlands quite sensitively. Other important roles were played by Cyril Cusack and Harry Andrews.

Chapter 14

David Lean's Ireland

One of the biggest films to be shot in Ireland, on a par with John Ford's *The Quiet Man*, was *Ryan's Daughter* (1969). It was directed by David Lean as an epic spectacle, entirely on the Dingle Peninsula in County Kerry, except for a short sequence done in South Africa, in the same meticulous style that had made his previous films such as *Dr. Zhivago*, *Bridge on the River Kwai* and *Laurence of Arabia* so memorable. The shooting of the film in Panavision 70 took an entire year. Lean again teamed up with Robert Bolt, who had scripted his two previous films. Bolt wrote an original screenplay set in a remote coastal village on the west coast of Ireland just after the 1916 Rising. It was about a local girl who deserts the village schoolteacher to whom she is married for a British officer, and the local reaction that arises from her act. As in all Lean's films, a top-line cast was assembled, headed by Robert Mitchum, Sarah Miles, John Mills, Trevor Howard, Leo McKern, Christopher Jones and Barry Foster. Mitchum took some persuading before he accepted the role of the gentle schoolteacher. The gamble of the tough guy playing against type paid off. The role of the unfaithful wife was specially written by Bolt for his wife, Sarah Miles. Sarah, who had got her first break at Ardmore seven years before, was now an international star.

The West Kerry region, particularly around Dingle, reaped the benefits from the protracted visit of the film-makers. Every available room in the hotels, guest houses, and farm houses was completely booked out for the duration of filming. All aspects of local trade and industry felt the generosity of the big spenders from Hollywood. Locals were employed as extras and in many other capacities. Tradesmen were engaged in set-building which included an extensive one of an entire village. Equity members were employed as 'special extras' earning £50 a week in what amounted to non-stop employment. Leading actors and actresses for the Dublin Theatre Festival that year were extremely scarce as players such as Márie Kean, Arthur O'Sullivan, Des Keogh, Niall Tóibín and Emmet Bergin were contracted on the film. Author Bryan McMahon was assigned as technical advisor for the school sequences but unfortunately broke his leg the night before filming commenced and had to withdraw.

Sarah Miles and Robert Mitchum in *Ryan's Daughter*

share of atrocious weather throughout the winter but when a storm was needed it did not materialise. Lean had to wait almost a year until he got a storm ferocious enough for his liking and then it was in Kilkee, County Clare, some distance up the coast. The actors who participated in this sequence, which was marvellously executed, should have been awarded the Blue Max. The film won two Academy Awards, although nominated for four - one went to Freddie Young for his magnificent photography and the other to John Mills for his faultless performance as the village fool. One unfortunate aspect was that only a few seconds of cloud effect behind the credits was all that remained of the work of Irish director Patrick Carey who had spent many months shooting thousands of feet of second unit footage.

One of the biggest delays Lean encountered was waiting for a storm for the dramatic climax to the film. The west coast, particularly the Dingle Peninsula, is noted for having more than its fair

Ryan's Daughter can best be summed up in the words of Robert Mitchum:

I loved every minute of it. Robert Bolt had written an excellent, literate script. The film emerged as David Lean's love affair with Ireland. A costly love affair it might be added - fourteen million bucks worth. I felt for him at times. The trouble with David

David Lean (right) directing Márie Kean, Sarah Miles and Gladys Sheehan in a scene in *Ryan's Daughter*

Director David Lean on location for *Ryan's Daughter*

is that he shoots four versions of a film and then chooses the best.

The music of Maurice Jarre, whose association with the Lean films, *Lawrence of Arabia* and *Dr. Zhivago*, had earned him Academy Awards, was most effective, particularly 'Rosy's Theme' where the haunting score seemed to glide over the windswept beaches.

A film with the strange title *Quackser Fortune has a Cousin in the Bronx* was completed in Dublin in one-tenth of the time it took to shoot the Lean epic. It was produced on a shoestring budget and starred two then unknown Americans - Gene Wilder and Margot Kidder. The strong Irish supporting cast headed by May Ollis, Seamus

Forde, David Kelly and Martin Crosby were overshadowed by Wilder's likeable personality. His Dublin accent was surprisingly authentic and far more true to life than attempts made by other stars in the past. He was ably supported by Miss Kidder who played an American student at Trinity College. Hardly a street or place of note in the city was omitted from Quackser's wanderings. Next to *Young Cassidy* this film best captured the flavour and character of Dublin. Director Warris Hussein managed his actors and actresses to the best advantage.

Quackser tells the tale of a Dublin man from a working-class background and his fight against the establishment. Instead of taking a conventional job in the foundry he tours the streets of the city, with his barrow, collecting horse manure and selling it to the ladies for their gardens and window boxes. He meets an American girl, and she introduces him to a whole new middle-class world where he feels out of place. Although a simple idea, it was a humorous film with sharp moral overtones.

The film which was well received, particularly in America, where it built up a cult following, served to illustrate just how effectively an Irish film industry might function. It was a wholly Irish tale with a simple story line. The entire film was shot on location apart from a small number of interiors filmed on the barest set at Ardmore. But how many Irish actors could have filled the title role? What was to prevent an Irish crew from making a similar film?

American actor Cliff Robertson, who had won an Oscar for his performance in *Charly*, spent two weeks at Weston Airport using their World War I fighter planes for a spoof film he was trying to get off the ground, entitled *Where Were You the Night the Baron Was Shot Down?* Robertson was both star and director of this comedy. When the Irish sequences were completed Robertson put the film into cold storage, as he sought backing to finish it. It emerged some time later as *Ace Eli and Rodgers of the Skies.*

The play *Philadelphia, Here I Come* by Brian Friel was first staged at the Dublin Theatre Festival in 1965 and later moved to Broadway where it played to packed houses and won worldwide acclaim. It was inevitable that it would be brought to the screen. This happened in 1970. The stars of the stage production, Donal Donnelly and Patrick Bedford, were replaced in the film version by Donal McCann and Des Cave, both graduates of the Abbey Theatre. Others in the cast included Siobhan McKenna, David Kelly and Eamonn Morrissey. The story of *Philadelphia* concerns the last night at home of a young man about to emigrate to America from a small town in Donegal. True to the stage play the script was wise, witty and full of compassion.

The producers took a gamble and gave Englishman John Quested his directional début. He had proved his ability as assistant director on several films made in Ireland and was well-known around Ardmore. It was a difficult film to translate to the screen as the bulk of the action took place in one setting. It would have been easy to bore an audience with the succession of similar shots and angles and this tested the versatility of the director. Quested, however, managed to be flexible with his cameras and opened out the story from its claustrophobic setting, with the town of Baltinglass

in County Wicklow standing in for the Donegal setting. Friel had used the theatrical device of an inner and outer self and here Quested could have taken a little liberty with the original and allowed one actor to play both parts — it would have been more effective. Donal McCann gave a brilliant performance as the outer self and Des Cave was only a shade behind with his subdued portrayal.

The film was made entirely by Irish people with the exception of the director and cameraman. After its completion it encountered some distribution difficulties and it was not until 1974 at the Cork Film Festival that it was screened publicly.

Powerscourt and Ardmore saw a few weeks' activity with yet another remake of Anna Sewell's classic tale, *Black Beauty*, from the screenplay by Wolf Mankowitz. It was filmed in Ireland and Spain by director James Hill, noted for his animal films (in particular *Born Free*). Some of the film's best moments were the work of the second unit executed by Patrick Carey. The film starred *Oliver* star Mark Lester, Walter Stezack, Patrick Mower and Ushi Glass.

Jack Wild in a scene from *Flight of the Doves*

Also shooting around the same time was *The Sky is Blue* which was no more than a suitcase French production starring Alexander Stewart and French actor Frederico Du Pasquale. It told of a bitter-sweet romance set in Ireland of a girl working in the American Embassy in Dublin who meets a French sports journalist covering the Ireland-France International rugby match. Scenes for the film were shot during an international match between the two countries.

Two films by top American directors were shot simultaneously in Ireland during the summer of 1970. The first was *Flight of the Doves* under the control of producer/ director Ralph Nelson. It moved into Ardmore at a critical stage in the life of the studio. It was the first feature film to be shot there that year. This lean period followed several bumper years. Nelson's film, his first outside America, was based on the book of the same name by author and playwright Walter Macken and was made entirely in this country, covering many counties from Dublin to Galway.

It brought together such talented performers as Ron Moody and Jack Wild (Fagin and the Artful Dodger respectively in the hit musical Oliver), the satirist William Rushton, American actress Dorothy McGuire, star of many Hollywood films of the forties and fifties, and the grand old man of the English stage, Stanley Holloway. The supporting cast of Irish players was led by Noel Purcell, Tom Hickey, John Molloy, Brendan O'Reilly, Barry Keegan, and making her screen début as a tinker girl was Dana, Ireland's Eurovision Song Contest winner.

The second film was *The Red Baron* directed by horror film director, Roger Corman. This was his most ambitious project to date and he painstakingly recreated the exploits and ultimate fiery death of Germany's fabled World War I flying ace, Baron Von Richthofen. John Philip Law played the ace and Don Stroud the pilot in the British Air Force who shoots him down. Other

John Philip Law in *The Red Baron* at Powerscourt, Co. Wicklow

important roles were played by Corin Redgrave, Tom Adams and David Weston. In contrast to the Nelson film, few Irish actors were employed; among these were Des Nealon and Martin Dempsey.

The main shooting for the film, which was referred to as a mini *Blue Max* with a budget of a mere million dollars, took place at Weston aerodrome, which doubled for both the German and British airstrips. Some of Ireland's most scenic locations were secured for additional scenes with parts of Powerscourt House used as the German officers' club. Other sites included Leinster House, George's Hill, Baldonnel and the drawing-rooms of Dublin Castle.

Roger Corman spoke of his reasons for choosing Ireland:

Well, firstly, because the planes were here and they were incapable of flying across the Irish Sea. All of the pilots had gained tremendous experience flying them in the two previous films and they knew exactly what we wanted from them. Then there is such a wide range of locations and all within easy reach of the aerodrome . I'm very pleased with the way things have been going in Ireland and with the facilities accorded us, and I intend to film here again.

This film is running for an eight weeks' schedule and is the longest I've ever made. My shortest was a film with Boris Karloff called The Terror which I shot in two days but this was done as a gag even though it was a success. I'll never again let a film run this length as short schedules keep interest stimulated.

Only a matter of days before the completion of filming a British stunt pilot was killed at Weston. Ten planes in all were engaged in the scene when one of the planes spun to the ground, hitting a truck. The pilot, Christopher Boddington, had only arrived at the location the previous day to take part in the dog-fight sequences. When another less serious accident occurred the next day involving Don Stroud, Corman called off the rest of the aerial scenes.

Another film with a World War I setting, *Zeppelin*, was also struck by tragedy as it was shooting dog-fights off Wicklow Harbour between

five bi-planes. The scene was being shot from a helicopter and four dummy runs had already been made to get the timing right. One plane was being chased by the other four, it swept below the helicopter and when it rose out of the dive it struck the helicopter at a thousand feet. Both craft fell into the sea and four men died. The bulk of *Zeppelin* was filmed in England and only the aerial

American director Roger Corman

scenes shot in Ireland. It was a variation of the war theme seen through German eyes with the introduction of the Zeppelin—their new flying machine. It was directed by Etienne Perier and starred Michael York, Elke Sommer, Anton Diffring and Andrew Keir.

Sitting Target, the next production shot in Ireland, was a fast-moving thriller about a convict who breaks jail in order to kill his wife for her infidelity. Oliver Reed played the vengeful husband with his usual brooding expression and Jill St. John looked decorative as his wife. They were supported by Ian McShane and Edward Woodward. The director was Douglas Hickox. Kilmainham Jail and Arbour Hill were the locations for the prison scenes.

Chapter 15

Altman and more Receivers

American director Robert Altman, who made his reputation with the smash hit film *M.A.S.H.*, came to Ireland in 1971 to film *Images*. With the exception of a few days filming at an isolated house in Wicklow and at Powerscourt, the film was confined to the stages of Ardmore. Susannah York, in one of the highlights of her screen career, played a woman gradually deteriorating into madness. It was a film of shadows that trembled on the uncertain line between fact and fantasy. It worked as much through John Williams's remarkable musical score as it did through the fractured pictures Altman created.

The plot concerned Cathryn (York) and her husband Hugh, who divide their life between a luxurious city apartment and a house in the country. She confuses Hugh with a previous lover, Rene, now dead, and talks to him, mocks him and finally eliminates him from her memory. Her confusion is heightened when a friend of her husband's, Marcel, visits their country house with his daughter Susannah who bears a striking resemblance to Cathryn. She finds reality frightening as characters become interchangeable and does not know whether she is speaking to her husband, her dead lover or the friend, her would-be lover.

A disturbing film, it hinged almost entirely on Susannah York's performance which was first-rate. There were no Irish actors in the cast which was comprised mainly of unknowns — Rene Auberjonis, Marcel Bozzuffi, Hugh Millias and Cathryn Harrison. An unusual aspect was that, the characters used their own christian names for their screen roles. The film was entered as Ireland's first official entry at the Cannes Film Festival and won for Susannah York the Best Actress Award. The cinematography of Vilmas Zsigmond was also highly praised.

Italian director Sergio Leone was the best non-American interpreter of westerns — having found a successful formula which produced such box-office hits as *A Fistful of Dollars, The Good, the Bad and the Ugly* and *Once Upon a Time in the West*. Leone, a beefy, bearded man with a strong aversion to violence, although violence figured prominently in his work, came to Ireland for a short spell of location work on his film *Duck, you Sucker*, retitled *A Fistful of Dynamite*, with his crew

Director Robert Altman

and two stars, James Coburn and Rod Steiger. He chose Glendalough and some rich pastures in County Wicklow for his Irish segment which was effective in the finished film.

For *A Fistful of Dynamite* the Italian director switched from a straight western to a turn-of-the-century revolutionary story. Coburn played an exiled IRA man whose knack with explosives almost wins the Mexican Revolution for Pancho Villa. Leone said of his work:

Movie making is my life, my hobby and my food. It never bores me. My fascination with physical violence and the philosophy behind it will always play an important part in my work. In this film the violence is not a personal one between individuals but rather between the individuals and the state.

A strange film called *Act Without Words*, assembled by producer Richard Denypont, brought Rod Steiger back to Dublin to star in what was to be a one-man feature film based on a mime work by Samuel Beckett. Originally the film was to be shot entirely in the Eamonn Andrews Studio

under the direction of Tom Blevins but problems arose over insurance. The equipment was being flown in from Britain and the insurance company stipulated that it could be insured for £1,000 a week in Belfast but would cost £5,000 per day in Dublin. The reverse would have been easier to understand. Despite guarantees from Fred O'Donovan of the Eamonn Andrews Studio that the equipment would be under strict security at all times, the figure remained. The film, therefore, transferred to Ardmore but soon afterwards the production broke up — and the film has never been finished. There was an unconfirmed report that a row had developed between Steiger and Denypont.

The tenure of New Brighton Enterprises and Lee Davis, one of the most colourful characters ever to operate the studio, lasted until 1971 when another Receiver, Alex Spain, was appointed. In July 1972 the studio was again put up for sale and there was keen interest shown in it. A group headed by George O'Reilly were the highest bidders at £265,000 and became the new owners. O'Reilly became chairman and general manager. On the board of directors were such notables as John Huston, Bing Crosby, John E. Nolan and Thomas Farmer. O'Reilly went abroad to sell studio space at Ardmore and in the intervening weeks he lined up quite a number of films, but they were never to materialise. The new owners began to fall out over policy and several resigned from the board. It was not long before O'Reilly was left as the only director. The group was in business no longer than four months before another Receiver, Thomas Kelly, was appointed.

It was a costly gamble for O'Reilly:

I lost my home and my money over Ardmore. I had a vision of the studio as a really top-class international centre to make films. But I did not get the time to realise my dreams. The trend was toward doing films on location in the streets of San Francisco or New York using the natural backdrop. This was bad for studios throughout the world. My plan was to make not only major films at Ardmore but to cash in on the rapidly growing television film market.

I discussed my ambitions with two very good

friends of mine, John Huston and Bing Crosby. They felt so strongly about it that they loaned their name to the project. I went to the Cannes Film Festival and held a reception for producers and directors. It was very successful and I stayed for a week. I made some trips to America and was promised work to keep the studio going.

Unfortunately I wasn't given a chance. In the film business it takes between six months and a year from the time of arranging a film to the date it actually commences. I wasn't able to keep going that long because financial backing was withdrawn and the receiver stepped in. Ardmore practically ruined me. Luckily, many of my friends and former staff stood by me.

The formation of the Dublin Film Co-operative was the first really practical step taken to set up an entirely Irish-made film. The co-operative embraced many who had gained experience at home and abroad. The members intended to work for a nominal wage and take a share of the profits when production costs had been recouped. Their first film, *The Hebrew Lesson*, ran for only half an hour and was intended as a pilot for a series which they hoped to sell world-wide. But the series did not materialise.

Behind the camera it was literally a one man show as it was written, produced and directed by veteran film-maker Wolf Mankowitz. He had settled in Cork and had taken a keen interest in trying to foster a film industry in this country. The film was shot in ten days on a small set at Ardmore. The story was set in Cork in 1921 and starred Milo O'Shea and Patrick Dawson. O'Shea played an old Jew who sheltered Dawson, an idealistic young IRA man on the run from the Black and Tans. The film related the interplay between the two as they expounded their philosophies of life. Playwright Alun Owen made a fleeting appearance as a Black and Tan.

A new idea in film-making, which originated in America, was the telemovie. Films in this category fell somewhere between a television series and a full length feature film. This meant that the end product could be screened on either medium. The first of these to be made in Ireland was *Alive,*

Alive O which later became *And No One Could Save Her*. It starred American actress Lee Remick and Milo O'Shea. Miss Remick spends the duration of the film trying to trace her missing husband, played by Frank Grimes, an unlikely choice to begin with. O'Shea played a stage-Irish solicitor and the supporting cast included a host of Irish actors.

Director Kevin Billington produced a film aimed at pleasing the Irish-American market. He appeared to do no more than position his actors in front of some famous city landmarks and have them spout their lines. A cedar-wood bungalow built over looking Brittas Bay was the setting for the American sequence of the film. It was a below-standard thriller.

A film with the strange sounding title of *Mother Mafia's Loving Fold* was one of a series of Italian films which chose, rather surprisingly, Dublin as their central location. Little was known about the Italian group except that they gave work to a handful of Irish actors including Liam O'Callaghan and Arthur O'Sullivan. They merely appeared in a street with the minimum of equipment, usually two minibuses holding their entire stock, and set up their camera and two small arc lamps. They held a quick rehearsal and then shot the scene and moved to the next location. *Mother Mafia's Loving Fold* was one of the cheap imitations that hoped to cash in on the success of *The Godfather*. It was a tale of the Mafia in the New York of the 1920s and the producers felt they could best reproduce the New York of the period in the dock-side streets of Dublin. The film makers caused something of a furore when they attempted to import prop guns - and had a good deal of explaining to do to the Customs officials at Dublin Airport before the matter was resolved. Later there was some question of harassment because the film company pulled out of Dublin with their film unfinished.

John Huston found yet another opportunity to bring a big production into Ireland in 1973 with *The Mackintosh Man,* but this time with good reason, for a section of the plot was actually set in this country. Other locations included Malta and

England. American actor Paul Newman starred and co-produced with John Foreman. Others in the cast list were James Mason as a British MP, Dominique Sanda, Harry Andrews, Ian Bannen, and Nigel Patrick. In one pub scene, set in Roundstone in Connemara, almost every Irish actor was present as a customer—amongst them Noel Purcell, Eddie Byrne, Joe Lynch, Joe Cahill and Donal McCann. The almost mandatory car chase also came in the Irish segment — across the bogs and along the rugged roads of Connemara, ending in a spectacular crash with a Mercedes hurtling down the Cliffs of Moher.

The Mackintosh Man was a complex spy thriller—Mackintosh of the title (Harry Andrews) is a mystery man who hires Reardon (Paul Newman) to stage a diamond robbery. Following an anonymous telephone call, Reardon is arrested and sentenced to twenty years imprisonment. Here, for the umpteenth time, Kilmainham Jail doubles as an English prison. Also in prison is a convicted Russian spy named Slade, played by Ian Bannen. For a large sum of money, both men are freed, and are smuggled out of England to Ireland where the plot thickens. Although not a Huston classic, the film did manage to keep the action and suspense well balanced. Newman's performance was rather wooden and disappointing throughout.

A telemovie produced in Ireland by Harlech Television, entitled *Catholics*, was based on the

Leading Irish screen and stage actor Cyril Cusack

102

novel by Brian Moore. The setting was a remote island off the coast of Ireland where an order of monks defy the Vatican and retain the Tridentine Mass. The story tells how a young priest (Martin Sheen) is sent from Rome to rectify the matter. A strong cast was headed by Trevor Howard, giving one of his best performances, Cyril Cusack and Raf Vallone, and also included a host of Irish character actors. It was directed by Jack Gold at an even pace with a balance of humour and pathos.

Two films set against the Northern Troubles were shot secretly in Dublin, within a year of each other. The two production companies maintained a low profile during their spell in the capital, and neither was prepared to talk to the press. In fact, neither revealed its true theme until much later.

The first, by an American company under the direction of George Schaffer, was *A War of Children*, with many Dublin streets standing in for areas of Belfast, as the producers felt it would be too dangerous to shoot in the strife-torn Northern capital. The original report — that it was a story of the relationship of two children — was far from the truth as it depicts a tale of bigotry and hatred between the two sections of the community. Some on-lookers did become suspicious when they saw a British Army saracen and British Tommies running along Camden Street in the early hours of the morning, but the film makers managed to get in and out without any interference. It was difficult for Dubliners to credit that such recognisable places as Westland Row and Blackrock College could be passed off as areas of Belfast, even CIE buses were passed off as Ulsterbus vehicles. British actresses Jenny Agutter and Vivien Merchant headed the cast and among the Irish names were Aideen O'Kelly and Patrick Dawson. Although it caused more raised eyebrows in Ireland when it was first shown at the Cork Film Festival, it was a runaway hit in America and won an Emmy Award.

A year later, in 1973, the second company, from Canada, slipped into Dublin to film 'a television film'. It was not until they returned to Toronto that they announced they had produced a cinema feature film against the background of the Northern Troubles. It was called *A Quiet Day in Belfast* and once again areas of Dublin, particularly around Smithfield, doubled for Belfast. The producers claimed it was non-political and non-partisan, a dubious claim since the hero is a British soldier killed in the street by an IRA sniper. The stars, Barry Foster and Margot Kidder, were no strangers to film-making in Ireland — Foster now playing a British soldier had had a contrasting role as the IRA leader in *Ryan's Daughter*. Canadian actress Margot Kidder had previously been seen as the lively young American student who fell in love with *'Quackser Fortune'*. The story line was kept so secret that even the two dozen Irish actors and actresses employed on the set were unaware of its true purpose. During the filming of one scene, where Margot Kidder, tarred and feathered, is thrown from a moving car, local women came to her assistance with tea and blankets, unaware that it was a scene from a film. The director was Milad Basada.

A film with the strange title of *Steve McQueen . . . I am not* and also called *Horowitz of Dublin Castle,* was a medium-budget thriller set in Dublin — a cops and robbers drama with touches of humour. It starred American actor Harvey Lembeck whose main claim to fame was his appearance in the popular *Sergeant Bilko* television series. Here he played an American cop who comes to Ireland and becomes involved with crooks, finally solving the crime more, by accident than design. His performance was in the same mould as *Columbo*. He was ably supported by Cyril Cusack, his daughter Sinead and Martin Dempsey. Writer Michael Judge recalls how unorthodox the production was. He was put into a hotel room and told to write a few pages of dialogue. Then at the end of each day they would take the pages and give him a handful of money. The film was directed by William Kronick.

Veteran screen and television actor Noel Purcell

Chapter 16

Exit Mr Kubrick

Early in the summer of 1973 one of the greatest masters of the craft of film-making, Stanley Kubrick, arrived in Ireland to scout locations for his next film, *Barry Lyndon*. He chose Ireland because he feared interference from pressure groups following a UK High Court judge's opinion that his last film, the highly controversial *A Clockwork Orange*, had inspired two killings. He set up base in a Waterford hotel and inspected areas in Killarney, Cork and Waterford itself. Kubrick, a self made genius, was reluctant to talk about his work to the press but gradually information about the film leaked out — the film was tentatively titled *The Luck of Barry Lyndon* and based on a novel by William Makepiece Thackeray. If Kubrick remained true to form, this was expected to be one of the most significant films ever made in Ireland. Besides *A Clockwork Orange*, he had an impressive list of films to his credit, including *Lolita, Spartacus, Dr. Strangelove, Paths of Glory* and *2001, A Space Odyssey*. Each film differed completely in content but had the Kubrick stamp.

For *Barry Lyndon*, which he was making for Warner Brothers, he cast the star of *Love Story*, Ryan O'Neal, as the Irish rogue, gambler and womaniser,

and amongst the ladies was Marisa Berenson, who had previously appeared in *The Damned and Cabaret*. A German actor, Hardy Kruger, co-starred. Irish members of the cast included Godfrey Quigley, Patrick Magee, Márie Kean, Arthur O'Sullivan and Patrick Dawson. The story, set in Ireland, England and Europe in the eighteenth century, features Lyndon as a seducer, bully, liar and card-shark who regards gambling as the highest occupation man can have. He likes to dress flamboyantly, to wear a sword with grace, to carry away his plunder with affected indifference, to be agreeable to women and look like a gentleman. These, according to Lyndon, are life's main objectives.

Ryan O'Neal said of Kubrick:

Stanley is an amazing man. He uses his camera like an old gunfighter with his six-shooter . . . I'm too tired when I get back to the hotel I don't even eat dinner, but it's worth it working with someone like Stanley Kubrick. Even if he did make me do a scene forty-eight times, in which I had to carry a man up some stairs, and at the end said 'It doesn't work, we'll scrap it.'

Filming commenced in mid-autumn in the

Waterford area amidst a veil of secrecy. There was quite an amount of employment given locally and those involved found Kubrick to be a hard taskmaster. Kubrick, a stocky man with a bushy beard, in an oversized waterproof supervised every aspect of the production, even choosing the extras himself from their photographs. He chose the actors from video-tape auditions. To ensure absolute control, Kubrick had as few people around him as possible, and then only those he trusted implicitly. He overshadowed every inch of the film personally — from the casting and selection of locations, right through the shooting, deciding the musical score (provided by the Chieftains), to the final editing. He wrote the screenplay himself which he changed and rewrote constantly during the filming. Many scenes were improvised in his caravan on the set on the actual morning of shooting. Entire sections of completed film were scrapped and new characters were written into the script while others were written out. There were many sackings on the set and this inevitably led to bad feeling. Even at meal times there was an air of uneasiness as Kubrick dined apart from the remainder of the stage hands.

In another innovation, Kubrick lit most of his interior scenes entirely by candlelight — thousands of candles replaced the artificial lighting. On more than one occasion Kubrick left the set because he was not entirely happy with the location — some small detail irked him. He wanted total perfection and would settle for nothing less. When the unit moved to Dublin he encountered a major snag — they were to film in some stately homes but the families concerned were not too happy at the film makers taking over their homes at Christmas. So it was not until January that the cameras rolled again in such picturesque settings as Powerscourt House, Dublin Castle and Carton House, which had been transformed into gaming houses.

On the day when Dublin was hit by a spate of bomb hoaxes the unit was lining up a shot with a carriage in the Phoenix Park. Kubrick heard the news on the radio and immediately left the set, returned to his house in Leixlip and refused to leave. It was late afternoon before he could be persuaded by his associates to return to a new location at Dublin Castle but not until he got a garda escort and an assurance that civil war had not broken out. He had constant fears of the IRA and wanted armed guards on the set. It was reported that he kept a double-barrelled shotgun and boxes of ammunition in his bedroom. It is ironic that a man who had depicted so many violent scenes in his films would seem to recoil from the reality of violence.

The rumours began filtering through that the film was encountering major problems. Ryan O'Neal was reported to have had a row with Kubrick after he had appeared on The Late, Late Show to discuss the film: Kubrick always frowned on publicity. Another report was that Kubrick was running over budget and Warner Brothers were extremely concerned. These reports were denied by some faceless executives but matters soon came to a head when Kubrick suddenly pulled the unit out of Ireland at a few hours' notice.

During the Wednesday lunch-break at Dublin Castle the cast had waited in vain to be recalled to the set but Kubrick had slipped quietly unannounced into the traffic in Dame Street and headed back to Leixlip. It was reported that an anonymous phone call had been received earlier that day and one of the film personnel had recognised the voice as that of an extra who had been dismissed the previous day. Other sources suggested that there may have been other calls of a more sinister nature, and that the IRA had ordered him to leave the country or else. A press release from the film company denied these reports and stated that the reason for his departure was that he had completed his shooting schedule in Ireland and was finishing the film in rural England.

For whatever reason, he left many puzzled faces and at least five more weeks filming in hand, including two large ball-room scenes to be filmed at Powerscourt, which would have employed five hundred extras at about £10 a day. Also cancelled was the wedding scene of Barry in the chapel of the disused King's College School at Blackhall Place which workmen had transformed into a London church. Kubrick did not appear behind the camera again until the following Tuesday in Salisbury, England.

Chapter 17

Enter John Boorman

One director who has always been a good friend to Ardmore is John Boorman. He has been living with his family in Wicklow since the end of the sixties. His first encounter with Ardmore came in 1969 when he was engaged in post-production work on *Leo the Last*. In the Wicklow countryside he found a retreat from the rat-race of film-making. When casually one day he wandered into an auction in Dublin and bought himself an old rectory in Annamoe, County Wicklow, his Irish sojourn began. It was not long before he, like Huston, became committed to the realisation of an Irish film industry.

When others were avoiding the Bray Studio, he set about bringing in an extraordinary film, *Zardoz* (1973), with a futuristic setting in the year 2293. He was familiar with the studios, having done post production work there on several of his previous films including *Deliverance*. Behind the camera, it was virtually a one-man show with Boorman serving as writer, producer and director. He had conceived the idea, brought it through the planning stages and into production in barren Ardmore, then in the hands of the Receiver. Everything was against him — the equipment was

run down and badly in need of overhauling, there were very few of the permanent staff still in residence — yet he persevered.

Since his departure from the BBC as a producer, he had made a number of important films, each distinct in style and content, including *Catch Us If You Can, Hell in the Pacific, Point Blank* and *Leo the Last*. They culminated in the highly praised *Deliverance*, which had been nominated for an Academy Award. On the crest of his success with this latter work, he went to Warner Bros. for backing for *Zardoz*. He gave them a ten-minute synopsis, but not the script, demanded a free hand at all stages of production from casting to final editing, and gave them one hour in which to make up their minds. They turned him down. So did Columbia. 20th Century Fox accepted the offer and Boorman returned to Bray to set the wheels in motion.

On the matter of finance Boorman said:

I get my financial backing from America and can make my films anywhere I choose. I would prefer if possible to make them in Ireland. But for a film-maker who looks for finance here, there is simply no

Director John Boorman

structure of film finance. Whom do I ask? To whom do you go?

American actor Burt Reynolds, one of the stars of *Deliverance*, was set for the leading role but was struck down with a double hernia shortly before filming began. Boorman's second choice was Sean Connery, whom he located on a Spanish golf course; he asked him to fly back and read the script. Connery read it and accepted immediately. Soon the other main roles were filled by Charlotte Rampling, Sara Kestleman, John Alderton and Irish actor Niall Buggy. Behind the camera he assembled a strong team, led by director of photography Geoffrey Unsworth who had won an Oscar for his work on *Cabaret*.

The interior scenes were shot on some elaborate, highly imaginative sets at Ardmore and the exteriors were filmed in Glencree and the rugged surrounding countryside. Boorman even used the grounds of his own house at Annamoe for some sequences. The title *Zardoz* was derived from The Wizard of Oz. The story goes that in

the year 2293 we find that the world as we know it has disappeared but a small group made up of scientists, intellectuals, the rich and powerful, have formed a new perfect society. They call their new world 'The Vortex' and their aim is to protect the knowledge and treasures of civilisation from the ravages of the outside world. During their three hundred years of development they have evolved a self-supporting life system and a machine called The Eternaliser which, if any member is killed or attempts suicide, can rebuild him with all his past memories and experiences intact.

In the Outlands beyond the sheltered cocoon live the remnants of the war-torn, polluted old world and from that chaos emerges a new breed of man, physically perfect, to launch nature's counter-attack. When their leader Zed (Sean Connery) invades the ordered world of the Vortex there is a dramatic and resounding clash. Boorman's wife, Christel, who was costume designer, said she based her designs on 'pure intuition' using as a guideline the fact that the Vortex community could manufacture silk from silk worms and velvet from flax.

Boorman, who brought the film in for about a million and a half dollars, said:

In Hollywood they just couldn't believe this. The experts there felt it must have cost five or six million dollars. It proved the point that I've been trying to prove for a long time about Ardmore — that international film-makers can make the films there economically. Something else that astounded them in Hollywood was the film's locations — all that wild scenery within a few miles of the studio. Nowhere else in the world can you drive twenty minutes from a studio and discover vast landscapes, without pylons or telegraph poles, with lakes, beaches, mountains, old houses — you name it.

He admitted the film had taken its toll on him:

It was two years of slavery and hard labour. Since Zardoz is set in the future I had to create an entirely new world for my characters. And once you've invented that world you have to live with it. It is an immensely complex and sophisticated film, as sophisticated as you'll find.

The film received mixed notices in London, New York and Paris but one thing is certain, it was not ignored. John Boorman had done a first-rate PR job and was now showing the world the amenities that Ireland, and particularly Ardmore, had to offer.

The finance Boorman spoke about had been sought since 1970 when then Minister George Colley introduced a Film Industry Bill in the Dail but the Government was in no hurry to implement the Huston Report. Then a General Election intervened and brought the Coalition Government to power. Colley was replaced by Justin Keating who was more committed to establishing a native film industry.

When Receiver Thomas Kelly put Ardmore up for auction in July 1973, a new group calling themselves 'The Irish Film Workers Association' was formed. The members of the association covered every aspect of the film industry and included such people as Robert Monks and Kieran Hickey. They petitioned the Minister to save Ardmore and to encourage and promote the growth of the film industry. They argued that the studio was a viable proposition — not only would it provide employment for members within the industry but it would attract enormous amounts of money into the country by encouraging feature films to be made here. At this time building speculators were showing a keen interest in the prime building land at Ardmore and there were great fears that the property would become a shopping centre or housing estate.

On the first day of the auction, 25th July, in a surprise move, RTE on behalf of the Government bought Ardmore Studio for £390,000. RTE were

Sean Connery in *Zardox*

to manage the studio in a caretaker capacity pending the establishment of a body to be set up by the Minister for Industry and Commerce. The Government's intention was to safeguard the employment of skilled Irish personnel and to ensure the continued existence of those facilities for the Irish film industry. It was also their wish to set up a film school, in association with the studio, to train Irish technicians.

In the interim the studio was managed by Dermot O'Sullivan of RTE whose first task was to give the camera and lighting equipment a badly needed overhaul. Much of the equipment was by then obsolete. In the first six months the studio showed a profit of £22,000. which primarily accrued from the production of commercials and the short visit from Stanley Kubrick.

Following a degree of re-structuring, a new Board was appointed and Ardmore became a state-sponsored company known as the National Film Studios of Ireland, with John Boorman as chairman and senior RTE producer Sheamus Smith as managing director. Other members of the Board included film director Vincent Corcoran and trade union chief Ruairi Roberts. Boorman reiterated the Government's dual intention of maintaining both an on-going film centre and a film school.

Justin Keating had hoped to re-introduce the Film Bill but a General Election resulted in the defeat of the Coalition Government and Fianna Fail returned to power. There were numerous calls both inside and out side the Dail for the introduction of a Film Bill but that did not happen for another six years. During the intervening years animosity grew between two groups —the NFSI and the Irish independent film makers who claimed they constituted the core of an Irish film industry and that any finance available should be channelled in their direction.

Chapter 18

Uncertainty

There followed a depressed period in film production worldwide, particularly in Britain where the decline was drastic. This naturally had an adverse effect on Ireland which depended so much on its neighbour's fortune. The reasons for the decline were manifold: escalating film budgets (some far exceeding $30,000,000), the ever-present influence of multi-channel television and the growing threat of the video. Some major studios were forced to close and the property was sold. Those remaining were utilised to a greater degree by American companies; the completed films were classed as 'American' and the profits remitted to the USA. Two prime examples of this were *Star Wars* and *Superman*. The output of actual British films fell to an all-time low, with producers relying almost entirely on film versions of successful television series or soft-porn comedies.

Rumours concerning Kubrick's sudden departure and the bombs in Dublin in May 1974, together with the continuing Northern conflict and anti-British slogans, also contributed to a fall-off in film-making in Ireland. Amongst the losses was a John Huston film which he insisted should be made here, but the producers were resolute and said no. There was a strong possibility that the screen version of the internationally acclaimed play *Equus* by Peter Shaffer would be produced at the Bray Studio but producers Lester Persky and Elliot Kastner shied away and transferred to Canada. It had an impressive cast list which Ireland could ill afford to lose: Richard Burton, Peter Firth and Jenny Agutter, under the direction of the highly rated Sidney Lumet.

Despite the recession, films continued to be shot here, albeit at irregular intervals. Some productions maintained a low profile and it was only following their departure that their visit was publicised. One such example was *McVicar* starring Roger Daltry and Adam Faith. Arbour Hill and Kilmainham Jail were in constant demand by the film-makers, because it was virtually impossible to obtain permission to film inside a British prison. Kilmainham Jail Restoration Fund was greatly boosted by the revenue that accrued. The inconsistencies of film settings, as exemplified in *McVicar*, proved amusing for Dublin audiences — the opening sequence showed a police escort leaving St. Patrick's Institution, North Circular Road, and travelling what was supposedly several hundred miles before entering the gates of Mountjoy Prison, a mere hundred yards from its starting point.

Other films of the mid-seventies included the umpteenth remake of Mary Shelley's classic *Frankenstein*. This Swedish version, directed by Calvin Floyd and starring Per Oscarsson and Leon Vitali, was filmed in many atmospheric locales. *Seamarks*, a ninety-minute tele-film, directed by Ron Maxwell, was also made at the National Film Studio. Ireland was one of a variety of world-wide locations for a four million dollar oil thriller, *The Next Man*. Director Richard Sarafian brought stars Cornelia Sharpe and a bearded Sean Connery, as a peace-making Arab, to the National Stud and Castletown House before moving to such exotic destinations as Nassau, Austria, London, Munich, Nice, New York and Morocco.

On location in Kenmare, Co. Kerry for *Purple Taxi*

Two very contrasting star-studded films went into production almost simultaneously during 1976. They were Yves Boisset's *Purple Taxi* and Marty Feldman's *The Last Remake of Beau Geste*. Boisset's film was based on the book by French author Michel Deon and featured Charlotte Rampling, Peter Ustinov, Fred Astaire and Philippe Noiret. The aging Astaire, as the village doctor, drives the brightly-painted London taxi of the title, manipulating the fate of everyone around him. The

Marty Feldman - *The Last Remake of Beau Geste*

unit travelled about 2,000 miles, covering counties Dublin, Wicklow, Galway, Kerry and Mayo during its long twelve-week schedule. The film served as a perfect showcase for the windswept scenery of the West.

For the first time the National Film Studio agreed to provide facilities, personnel and finance (to a maximum cost of £270,926) There have been conflicting estimates of the proportion of this figure that has since been recovered.

Yves Boisset said of the film:

It's not specifically a story of love or great action, It's about justice, man's search for the true meaning of his life. His relationship with others is a universal theme. It reflects a slice of life.

Different in every respect was funny man Feldman's re-telling of the Wren classic, as he explained:

My original intent was to make The Four Features but I inadvertently gave the wrong title and was stuck with it. I wanted a simple low-budget film and they gave me millions and a string of stars. They told me Hollywood was too expensive and I was to film in Spain and Ireland. So here I am.

And what an array of stars — Ann Margaret, Peter Ustinov, Trevor Howard, Michael York, and Spike Milligan. The only Irish name to feature

Sean Connery and Gladys Sheehan in
The First Great Train Robbery

prominently in the credits was Sinead Cusack. Following a country-wide search for a look-alike, Feldman signed Dublin boy Michael McConkey to play Beau Geste as a child. The two major locations used were the house and grounds of Adare Manor in County Limerick and, once again, Kilmainham Jail for the prison sequence.

Nineteen seventy-eight proved to be an eventful year with several diverse styles of film going into production. The most prestigious of these was *The First Great Train Robbery*, based at the National Film Studio and filmed at various other locations throughout the country. Michael Crichton directed from his own novel and screen play, this seven million dollar production for Dino de Laurentis Productions. It starred Sean Connery as the brains behind the robbery, Lesley Ann Down as his mistress and Donald Sutherland as a pick

pocket. It told the story of the robbery of gold bullion bound for the Crimea.

Producer John Foreman, who had such successes as *Butch Cassidy and the Sundance Kid* to his credit said that Dublin had been chosen because it possessed some of the best preserved Georgian and period style buildings anywhere in the world, which made it ideal for any film set in the nineteenth century. Several coaches were constructed for the Victorian train laid on the wheels of CIE rolling stock and pulled by the famous '184' steam engine from the Transport Museum at a cost of $250,000.

Stunts were an important feature of the film, ranging from a roof-top escape from Glencree Recreation Centre to scaling the exterior wall of Heuston Station. The most spectacular stunts were performed by Connery for the hair-raising climax on top of the moving train. The star used no stuntmen for this sequence which was filmed around Moate, County Westmeath. The train reportedly had a maximum speed of 35 m.p.h. but the pilot of the helicopter from which the scene was being filmed stated that it was travelling at 55 m.p.h. Connery and Crichton went to the engine and discovered that there was no speedometer. They asked the driver how he judged the speed and he replied 'we just count the poles'.

A disillusioned Vietnam veteran of Irish descent who comes to Belfast to join the Provisional

A location scene in Ringsend for *The Outsider*

IRA of the 1970s was the subject of *The Outsider*. It was produced by a Dutch company and based on the book, *The Heritage*, by Colin Leinster. Unable to film in the North, the producers reached an agreement with a residents' association to take over an area of Ringsend in Dublin and transform it into a working-class district of Belfast. Peace-lines, political slogans, a red postbox and bombed buildings were erected; and large crowds flocked to see director Tony Luraschi at work. Interiors were filmed at Ardmore. Stars were Craig Wasson, Patricia Quinn, Niall Tóibín, and J.G. Devlin, with Sterling Hayden in a cameo role.

Producer Corman, who had filmed *The Red Baron* in Ireland some years previous, returned with a cast headed by Lee Marvin, Mark Hamill and Robert Carradine to make *The Big Red One*, written and directed by Hollywood veteran Samuel Fuller. The main location for this World War II drama was Israel with a two-week stint in a variety of Irish stately homes including Trim Castle and Carton House.

It was only a matter of time before the movie-makers saw the enormous box-office possibilities of North Sea oil. Screen writer Jack Davies wrote an inventive story involving a gang of terrorists who hijack an oil rig and hold the British Government to ransom for £25 million.

Producer Morgan O'Sullivan

The film was *North Sea Hijack* directed by Andrew McLaglen, son of the great character actor, Victor. Andrew had last worked in Ireland some twenty eight years earlier when he was John Ford's assistant on *The Quiet Man*. He assembled a strong cast headed by Roger Moore, James Mason and Anthony Perkins and spent five weeks filming in the Galway Bay area.

Joanne Pettet and Rod Taylor in
Cry of the Innocent

McLaglen explained his reason for coming to Ireland:

We needed to simulate a port so we came to Galway which was just big enough for what we wanted. We put up Norwegian signs on the dock and local warehouses, while other scenes were shot on the decks of ships being loaded up. We filmed right up to the Aran Islands on the way to the actual oil rigs in the North Sea. The weather was appalling and we experienced some incredible gales. For five weeks we filmed in the hills and dales of Galway (which also stood in for Scotland) without losing the spirit of the story. Everything we wanted was right there within a few miles, from the sea to castles.

Filming simultaneously in County Clare was *Tristan and Isolt* with Richard Burton and Kate Mulgrew as the ill-fated pair, under the direction of Tom Donovan. Other leading roles were taken by Cyril Cusack and Niall Tóibín. The producer had high hopes for the film and had tentative plans to follow it with a production based on the life of Countess Markievicz. Unfortunately on its screening at the Cork Film Festival *Tristan and Isolt* was harshly reviewed by the critics. As a result it experienced distribution difficulties and to date has not received a commercial screening.

During the seventies the National Film Studios were utilised for other purposes besides film production. Commercials proved the main source of income. Other projects included Boorman's post-production work on *Heretic, Exorcist 11,* Blake Edward's second-unit material for *The Pink Panther Strikes Again* and the editing of *Teardrops,* which was shot in Turkey, and the dubbing of it into English using Irish actors and actresses exclusively for the English language version (incidentally the music for the film was arranged and performed by traditional musician, Donal Lunny).

The late seventies also saw the emergence of a new Irish film company, Tara Films, the brainchild of radio and TV personality Morgan O'Sullivan. He approached best selling author Frederick Forsyth, then living in Enniskerry, to write a film treatment which he in due course presented to NBC Television in New York. With dogged perseverance he began to assemble the pieces of his package. Michael O'Herlihy, the American-based Irish director, agreed to direct. Rod Taylor, Joanna Pettit and Cyril Cusack were cast. Finally O'Sullivan signed a deal with NBC and the million dollar *Cry of the Innocent* went into production. Although there was a small crew, 80 per cent of the people working on it were Irish. O'Sullivan had instigated a system, in conjunction with AnCO (the Industrial Training Authority) whereby a number of newcomers were trained in the techniques of film-making. This authority is now defunct and has been replaced by FÁS.

O'Herlihy worked fast and completed the film in twenty-three days. It was a thriller in which Rod Taylor is bent on tracking down the killers who planted a bomb in a plane which crashed into his house and killed his family. The film enjoyed both a cinema and television release and in America it filled the prestigious Film of the Week spot. It attracted good reviews from the American media, a typical comment designating it several cuts above the average TV movie. O'Herlihy returned within a year to direct a screen version of one of Barbara Cartland's phenomenally successful novels, *The Flame is Love*. The story was set in France but O'Herlihy persuaded NBC and producer Ed Friendly to shoot it here. The stars were Linda Purl and Timothy Dalton. Dublin's Georgian buildings and Bray's period style railway station were major locations.

The same station, a mere mile from the film studios, also featured prominently in *The Hard Way*. Young film makers Richard F. Tombleson and Kevin Grogan approached John Boorman with their initial script and he allowed them the facilities of the studio to shape it into a working scenario. Tombleson was assigned to direct and Michael Dryhurst to produce this thriller with an Irish setting. Boorman acted as executive producer. The casting teamed the slit-eyed gunman of so many westerns, Lee Van Cleef, with rugged Patrick McGoohan, the star of many thrillers; but most surprising of all was the casting of novelist Edna O'Brien as McGoohan's wife. The film experienced a number of problems, not least the fact that the director was replaced by Dryhurst after only a week's shooting. The final result was a routine body-strewn thriller.

Richard Burton and Kate Mulgrew in *Tristan and Isolt,* filmed in County Clare

Chapter 19

Excalibur and After

A life-long ambition of John Boorman's was to make a film based on the legend of King Arthur and Camelot. From time to time he had presented characters and symbols from the Arthurian period in other guises in his films, such as *Deliverance*, *Zardoz* and *Point Blank*. One of the most noticeable of these was the hand emerging from the water in *Deliverance*. In 1975 he wrote a draft script which would run for about four hours and then handed the text over to Rospo Pallenberg who helped him shape it into the final screenplay. The project, which went through several name changes, including Merlin and Knights, eventually became *Excalibur* after its completion. The huge success of *Star Wars* led indirectly to Excalibur going into production in 1980: the studios that had previously rejected the idea now regarded fantasy as good box-office.

The National Film Studio received a major boost when Boorman decided to shoot the eleven and a half million dollar production there (even though tempting offers had been made by several other countries). Directly and indirectly the film ploughed a considerable amount of cash into Ireland. Of the 280 technicians, over 200 were Irish

and an average of 260 Irish extras per week were employed. Boorman insisted that Irish film apprentices were employed in all departments and the young Irish writer, Neil Jordan, was accorded facilities to make a documentary on the shooting of the film.

Boorman's belief was that the NFSI should be involved in producing films themselves but was wary of the Government providing cash as this would have left them open to interference. His hope was for greater participation by Irish business interests and he sought to realise this with *Excalibur*. Through the Allied Irish Investment Bank, Boorman put forward a proposal to a consortium of Irish companies to put up three million dollars towards the making of the film. In short, they would own the negative for one year, share in the profits and hopefully would gain some tax advantages. He received commitments from all the interested bodies that the scheme would be allowed to operate, but the Allied Irish Investment Bank demanded written confirmation from the Revenue Commissioners. This was not forthcoming and after a year's negotiation a frustrated Boorman went to Hollywood for

Nigel Terry (above and right) in scenes from
Excalibur

finance. Orion, one of the largest Hollywood film companies, then fully financed the film. In its opening week in America *Excalibur* grossed over $35,000,000 and its final income was expected to be in excess of $200,000,000. On these figures the Irish companies would have had a substantial return for their investment.

Excalibur, the biggest undertaking ever mounted by the NFSI, was based on a mixture of historical fact and romantic fiction which was most vividly recounted in Thomas Malory's *Morte d'Arthur*. Boorman did not take a fee as producer, director or writer but settled for a percentage of the profits. He had an immense number of problems to contend with on the production — budget, schedule, weather and technical hitches. During the shooting schedule Ireland experienced one of its worst ever summers, with rain practically every day. This inevitably caused the film to run over schedule and therefore over budget. The working day was not the conventional 8 a.m. to 5 p.m. but varied between all-night shooting and a 1 p.m. - 9 p.m. schedule. The studio stages had to be extended to facilitate some of the major interior scenes.

Whereas for the demanding role of Merlin Boorman cast internationally famous actor Nicol Williamson, the remainder of the cast consisted mainly of performers from the London stage: Helen Mirren as the evil temptress Morgana; Cherie Lunghi as the Queen Guinevere; Nicholas Clay as Sir Lancelot and Nigel Terry playing Arthur from young man to elderly King; Irish actors featured prominently in the cast and included Liam Neeson, Gabriel Byrne, Niall O'Brien and Eamonn Kelly. Boorman set the story in the landscapes he knew so well: the bleak bogs of Sally Gap, Sugar Loaf Mountain, the Norman Cahir Castle in County Tipperary and the rich forests and mist-

capped mountains of County Wicklow. The splendour of Camelot was erected on the back lot at Ardmore.

The story begins as an idyllic young Arthur releases the enchanted Sword Excalibur from the stone and goes on to build the empire of Camelot, marry Guinevere and establish the Knights of the Round Table. Merlin, the mysterious magician and King Arthur's counsellor, observes and influences developments. Their solitude and contentment begin to crumble when Arthur's Knight, Lancelot, becomes Guinevere's lover and Arthur's evil half-sister, Morgana, tricks both Merlin and the King — posing as Guinevere she conceives a son by Arthur. Their son, Mordred, is raised with one purpose: to kill his father and claim the throne. As Camelot disintegrates the Knights of the Round Table are sent in search of the Holy Grail and Arthur goes into battle with his son.

Boorman used light and shade for atmospheric effect. Music and colour changed dramatically with the rise and fall of Camelot. One is left with the memory of the thundering music as the Knights rode into battle through the

Director John Boorman

blossoming orchard. The director centred the film around the character that had most fascinated him — that of Merlin, the sorcerer. *Excalibur* was one of the high-points at the Cannes Film Festival and was awarded a prize for its artistic contribution, although many favoured it for the Grand Prize. The film also featured amongst the award winners in the British and American Academy Awards.

Three other very contrasting films were produced in Ireland that same year. The first was a German/Irish production with an English sound

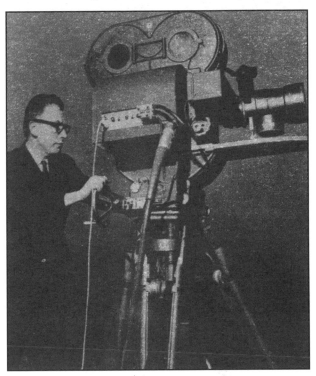

Swiss director Alain Tanner

track entitled *Fire and Sword*, directed by Veith Von Fuerstenberg and starring Peter Firth and Leigh Lawson. This version of the *Tristan and Isolde* legend was filmed in a variety of locations from the Cliffs of Moher in County Clare and Achill Island to Glendalough, where an entire medieval village was re-created. The highly talented Swiss director, Alain Tanner, moved his small unit into the isolation of Letterfrack in Connemara to film *L'Années Lumières* (English title *Light Years Away*), a mystical fable set in the year 2000. It was a Swiss/French production starring Trevor Howard and Mick Ford. The hero was Jonah (Ford), presumably the same figure of Tanner's earliest film, *Jonah*

Laurence Olivier filming *Inchon* in Ardmore Studios

Who Will Be 25 In The Year 2000, who becomes an apprentice to eccentric recluse Yoshka (Howard). Gradually Jonah discovers the ultimate aim of Yoshka's obsessive study - to discover the secret of flight. A number of Irish actors appeared in small parts. The film won the Jury Special Award at the Cannes Film Festival.

A section of one of the most expensive film flops of all time was filmed in Ardmore Studio. It was the $48,000,000 *Inchon*, funded by the Moonies and starring Laurence Olivier, Jacqueline Bisset and Ben Gazzara. When Reverend Sun Myung Moon decided to enter the film business he chose the most heroic episodes of the Korean War and General Douglas MacArthur's surprise landing at Inchon as the subject-matter. One of his leading disciples, Japanese newspaper publisher Mitsuharu Ishii, took charge of the project. The original budget was set at $18,000,000 with Andrew McLaglen as director but there followed a succession of problems as a result of which

McLaglen resigned and was replaced by Terence Young. An all-star cast headed by Olivier as MacArthur went into production in Korea in January 1979. The production was plagued by problems, from typhoons and an earthquake, which demolished sets, to the Government's reluctance to grant permits, as well as a major blunder in which 300 ships turned right instead of left, out of camera range.

The film's final sequence featured a victory parade in Seoul after MacArthur's successful campaign. The General waved from his limousine, then stepped into Government House, where he was greeted by a cheering crowd. This triumphal conclusion — lasting only three minutes on screen — had to be shot over the course of four months in three different countries, and then edited at great expense. Moon himself created most of the difficulties. He felt there were not enough people in the original scene and asked Ishii to try again. This involved bringing the entire crew back to Korea at a total cost of nearly one million dollars. The resulting footage pleased Rev Moon, but the larger number of people in the new sequence failed to match the previously filmed view of MacArthur in his limousine. Since Olivier had already returned to England and declined to make another trip to Korea for this single shot, the Moonies had to satisfy themselves with transporting their star to Ireland. They rented Ardmore Studio and placed Olivier in a stationary car, then filmed him against a back projection of the cheering throngs. Sean Kinsella of the Mirabeau Restaurant was hired as Olivier's private chef. He liquidised the star's meals, which had to be consumed through a straw to avoid disturbing his make-up.

Until then it was one of the most expensive films ever made and gained some of the 'Most Vicious Reviews Ever Penned'. Included in the chorus of condemnation were judgments such as: 'The Worst Movie ever made . . . A turkey the size of Godzilla . . .' *(Newsweek)*. 'A near total loss as well as a laugh . . .' *(Playboy)*. 'As military spectacles go, one of the sorriest in movie history' *(Time)*. It surpassed even *Cleopatra* and *Heaven's Gate* as one of the most expensive flops in movie history.

The Motion Picture Company of Ireland was set up by John Boorman and Sheamus Smith to produce low-budget films in Ireland. Their production, *Angel* (1981), was the first film to receive a grant (£100,000) from the Irish Film Board. The balance of the budget, £400,000, was put up by the new British independent television service, Channel Four. The day-to-day filming operations were in the hands of two relatively unknowns, Barry Blackmore as producer and author Neil Jordan as director and screen-writer. The two men had previously worked on *Excalibur*. The film, shot in six weeks in the Bray and Dublin areas, was set in Northern Ireland and centred on a disillusioned saxophonist (Stephen Rea) who witnesses the murder of his manager and a young girl and sets out on a trail of revenge. Others in the all-Irish cast included Honor Heffernan, Ray McAnally, Márie Kean and Donal McCann. It was retitled *Danny Boy* in America to avoid confusion with a soft-porn film of the same name.

The project caused a degree of controversy as the Association of Independent Producers, who were not represented on the Film Board, were suspicious of its intention. They voiced their anger when the film received the first grant from the Board, which had only three members, including Boorman, appointed, and four places left vacant. In reality, when the project came up for consideration Boorman declared his involvement and withdrew. *Angel* seemed the ideal vehicle to pioneer the intentions of the Film Board with only four of the forty-seven people credited not based here in Ireland. The film attracted considerable interest when it was screened at the Cannes Film Festival. It was the critical hit of the year in Britain with Chris Menges's photography and Honor Heffernan's performance receiving particular praise. Jordan then directed *The Company of Wolves* with Stephen Rea and Angela Lansbury at Shepperton Studios, which Los Angeles critics described as 'the most exciting British film of 1984'. He next wrote and directed *Mona Lisa* with Michael Caine and Bob Hoskins in London in 1985.

Stephen Rea in *Angel,* directed by Neil Jordan

Screen and stage actor Peter O'Toole

Chapter 20

The Film Board

When the National Film Studio was established in 1974 the board was given the studio but no money to operate it. This lack of capital injection by the Government led to serious losses at Ardmore as the re-equipping and modernisation had to come from bank loans. Even studio chairman John Boorman did not take his annual remuneration of £1,000. In the late seventies there was a dramatic fall-off in the number of days given over to the shooting of commercials, the main source of income for the studio. Sheamus Smith attributed this to the recession, which led to Irish companies using old television and cinema commercials.

The Coalition Government had planned to reconstruct and refinance the studio. Originally when the NFSI was set up the then Minister, Justin Keating, had ordered that some of the surplus land around the studio be sold off and the money ploughed back to improve its financial position. The order was later rescinded after pressure from the Board. As a result of further suggestions by a later Minister, Des O'Malley, tentative plans were drawn up to develop part of the land. Boorman had architect Jeremy Williams design draft plans to develop the surplus land in a crescent-shaped scheme of eighteenth century town houses, which would preserve the studio as a unique and highly specialised employment industry. Bray Urban District Council refused planning permission for the scheme on the grounds that the area involved was zoned 'residential'.

In spite of being used in the production of the enormously successful *Excalibur*, Ardmore again had substantial losses — the studio had no stake in that film's box office success. Michael O'Leary, then Minister for Industry and Commerce, expressed concern at the financial state of the company and undertook to keep it in operation. The expected increase in business following the success of *Excalibur* did not materialise and a big budget television series based on Walter Scott's *Ivanhoe* went to an English studio after Ardmore had been considered.

Frequently, NFSI Board member Vincent Corcoran voiced criticism concerning the activities of the Board:

Excalibur tied up the studio for nine months and only yielded rental payment of £65,000. They

Director Vincent Corcoran

had a Cecil B. de Mille complex, concentrating on attracting big foreign productions, where they should have put more effort into getting independent finance for Irish films.

The Government should sell the studio if they are unable to ensure that it would continue to be used for film production.

Towards the end of 1981 numerous official and unofficial approaches were made to purchase the studio and proposals were put to the Department of Industry and Commerce. In December that year a consortium, headed by Vincent Donoghue, a prominent businessman, made a bid to purchase the studio for £1,500,000 and gave guarantees of additional employment. Another Hollywood film consortium, headed by Jack Conrad, proposed a £20,000,000 film investment package and envisaged two thousand film industry workers being employed. The Department accepted none of the offers.

On Friday, 2nd April 1982, John Boorman resigned as chairman and board member of the NFSI and as a board member of the Irish Film Board. The following day the then Minister for Industry and Energy, Albert Reynolds, in a surprise move announced that the NFSI was to close. He convened a special board meeting of the operating company and stated that a liquidator would shortly be appointed. He was confident that people from a related industry - video manufacturer or small budget film makers - would purchase the studio. The Government decision to close the studios was based on the fact that its average annual loss was half a million pounds, an aggregate loss of two and a half million pounds since they were set up by statute. The Minister declared they were no longer a viable proposition and would be auctioned off in two lots—the studio and five acres of surrounding land in one parcel, and the remaining twenty acres for development.

John Boorman was not notified in advance of the Minister's decision nor was managing director Sheamus Smith or any other member of the board. Mr. Smith claimed that the studio had difficulty offering competitive rates to foreign film producers and its closure would seriously damage Ireland's chances of attracting big budget feature films in future.

Even before Michael McNulty was appointed liquidator, the forty-six strong studio work-force organised a very effective action group and lobbied the Government and Opposition parties. Their spokesman, Eamonn O'Higgins, said:

The workers want Ardmore retained by the state for three reasons - firstly the guarantee of our jobs secondly as a service to the Irish film industry and thirdly as an important section of the Irish economy. No one would see the Government closing RTE or The Abbey and Ardmore Studios are in a similar position.

Ironically the studio was closed at the very time that the Film Board was finally being established. The Bill which had been recommended by the Huston Report in the early seventies was not introduced by the Government until December 1979. Then followed the slow parliamentary process of debating the provisions of the Bill. The proposed legislation provided for the setting up of a Film Board which would disburse a fund of £4.1 million over a four-year period by way of investment, grant or loan to cover all or part of the costs of productions wholly or partly made in the state. The Bill caused a considerable amount of concern among independent film producers and Irish film workers. As a result the Association of Independent Producers of Ireland (AIPI) was formed to offer a united front in opposition to the Bill. In 1980 the Minister, Des O'Malley, introduced the Film Bill in the Dail. It provided for an Irish Film Board to promote and develop an Irish film industry. The only film to receive a grant the first year was the controversial *Angel*. The remaining fund was returned to the Exchequer. The funding of *Angel* by the Film Board angered the AIPI because Boorman was both a Film Board member and the film's executive producer.

Muiris Mac Conghail, Head of Television Features at RTE, was appointed chairman of the Irish Film Board and Michael Algar, chairman of the Irish Film and Television Guild, was appointed chief executive. AIPI ended their boycott of the Board when their chairman, Tiernan McBride, was appointed a member. The Board stated that their objective was to assist in the making of totally Irish films, i.e. films that used Irish writers, Irish directors, Irish production companies, Irish technicians, Irish post-production facilities and Irish distribution. In 1982 the Board considered eighty proposals, from which they selected twenty-two to receive aid.

Following the closure of Ardmore, several multi-million pound films were lost to the country. One was the Michael Caine/ Laurence Olivier thriller, *The Jigsaw Man*, under director Terence Young which had to transfer to England. The film version of Willy Russell's successful play, *Educating Rita*, again starring Caine, was to be made at Ardmore but had to move to Paris for studio work. Location shooting for this film, which re-united Caine and his *Alfie* director Lewis Gilbert, did go ahead in Dublin, principally at Trinity College. For their roles Caine and his co-star Julie Walters, were nominated for Hollywood Oscars. A disillusioned John Boorman cancelled plans to make a £4 million film, *Little Nemo*, for Channel Four at Bray. He did express a desire to work in Ireland again if suitable facilities were available. The biggest loss was the James Bond film, *Never Say Never Again*, which was to have utilised Ardmore for studio work.

Five months after its closure by the Government, Ardmore Studio was purchased for £1,100,000 by Ardmore Completion Communications, headed by Vincent Donohoe, who had made two earlier unsuccessful bids. Donohoe's partners in the new company included Peter Sprague, chairman of the billion dollar National Semiconductor Corporation, Rex Pyke, a London-based film producer whose credits included *Akenfield*, and American director Doug Trumbutt who made *Silent Running* and was responsible for the special effects on *2001: A Space Odyssey*. The new company intended to continue operating Ardmore as a film production centre as well as a film processing laboratory and to use it to manufacture the special photographic equipment for Showscan. Donohue was forced to withdraw from the deal when he was unable to secure financial backing. Several other potential purchasers opened discussions with the liquidator but no deal went ahead. In April 1983, after paying out over £2 million to meet Ardmore's debts, the then Minister for Industry and Commerce, John Bruton, set up a review body to examine the viability of the studio on the assumption it should not cost the Exchequer any more money. The group consisted of representatives of the Irish Film Board and the Departments of Industry, Finance and Arts. They submitted their report to the Minister three months later. Under a Government covenant the lands surrounding Ardmore were exclusively zoned for film-making purposes until October 1987.

While the future of Ardmore was being decided, a small feature film was being shot, not in Bray but in Cloghane, in the Dingle Peninsula. The Kerry village was chosen as the location for *Sense of Wonder*, a £400,000 film, by Argentine director, Martin Donovan. Of one hundred and fifty local people employed on the film, twenty-eight had speaking parts and three of the Kerry voices had to be dubbed for the international market. The film also starred Anne Chaplin, the youngest daughter of Charlie, in her film début. During the twenty-one days' filming, the sixty-strong crew took up every available bed in the village. It was the first feature film by the thirty-two year old director who also wrote the screenplay based on the death of his seventeen year old brother in a car crash. He changed the script on numerous occasions, moving the action outdoors to avail himself of the magnificent scenery. The film had its first public showing in Dingle's Phoenix Cinema in 1984.

In July 1984, following months of negotiations, Ardmore was sold to Mahmond Sipra, a Pakistan-born, American-based film-maker and businessman for £994,000 under an Irish registered company, Bondly Ltd. Forty-one year old Sipra agreed to the clause that the studio was to be retained as a film-making centre. He had only entered the film business two years before when he came to the rescue of the Terence Young film, *The Jigsaw Man*, which ran out of money at a crucial stage with barely ten days' shooting left. After seeing footage, Sipra stepped in with the eight million dollars needed to clear all debts and guarantee completion. He injected £100,000 into the company to enable it to commence operation. The company announced several major productions which were to use the studio in the coming months. There was an adventure film, *Khyber Horseman*, and *Gun Bus*, to be followed by *Buried Alive* starring Peter O'Toole. Fears were again expressed when all the films were deferred. By October news had broken that Sipra's companies were facing financial problems and there were doubts about the studio's future. Soon the electricity supply was cut off owing to non-payment of the ESB bill and the security staff were made redundant. Worse was to come when in January 1985 Justice Barrington appointed Robert Stewart as provisional liquidator. Again the studio was put up for sale.

Over the following months many inquiries and inspections of the premises were made by potential purchasers. Towards the end of the year

Mary Tyler Moore Enterprises made an agreement to acquire Ardmore if the American television network NBC agreed to 'pick up' a new series they were planning. MTM Enterprises, the producers of such highly successful series as *Hill Street Blues*, *Lou Grant* and *Remington Steele* had filmed a pilot programme, *92 Grosvenor Square* and if it succeeded the thirteen-part series, at one million dollars per episode, would be filmed at Ardmore. The pilot, with David McCallum and Hal Holbrook, dealing with intelligence work during World War II, was screened on both sides of the Atlantic in December and a final decision expected in January was postponed. In March 1986 when a definite decision was not forthcoming on the proposed series MTM Enterprises requested a further extension from the liquidator but this was refused and the deal collapsed. The studio was once again put on the market.

Following many months of uncertainty and additional bidders, in September 1986 Justice Lardner in the High Court made a judgment approving the sale of Ardmore Studio to a consortium, comprising Mary Tyler Moore Enterprises, Morgan O'Sullivan's Tara Productions and the National Development Corporation for £975,000 a twenty-five per cent deposit having already been paid. Within two months, three episodes of MTM's series, *Remington Steele*, were filmed at the studio. There followed enquiries from many leading directors and producers including Neil Jordan, Robert Altman and Michael Cimino for his proposed film on the life of Michael Collins. Managing director Morgan O'Sullivan attended the Cannes Film Festival, promoting the studio while a million pounds was spent refurbishing the property and building a large new stage.

Chapter 21

Irish Film Makers

Although from the beginning of film-making history international producers have always enlisted the best of the Irish acting talent, they largely ignored Irish directing talent. Despite the fact that directors of Irish ancestry have reached the pinnacle of success in Hollywood, until fifteen years ago there had only been two outstanding native directors — Rex Ingram and Michael O'Herlihy. Ingram, a Dubliner, gained his reputation in Hollywood during the silent era and will be best remembered for the masterly *Four Horsemen of the Apocalypse* and his discovery of Rudolph Valentino.

O'Herlihy, born in Dun Laoire, Co. Dublin, served his apprenticeship with Hilton Edwards and Mícheál MacLiammóir and worked with them as a designer at the Gate Theatre in the early fifties. Running parallel with his love for the theatre was his love for the sea and he sailed from Ireland in a yacht across the Atlantic, with the ambition of finding a job in the American film industry. Following a difficult period, he eventually got a job with Warner Bros. where he learned the craft of film-making. While serving as a 'technical advisor' on *Darby O 'Gill and the Little People*, he established a friendship with Walt Disney which led to his making several films for Disney, including *The Fighting Prince of Donegal*. He combined his film work with television and soon established himself as one of the foremost television directors in Hollywood, directing such shows as *Hawaii Five-O*, *The Man from U.N.C.L.E.* and *The A Team*. When he returned to Ireland in the late seventies to shoot two television films, Frederick Forsyth's *Cry of the Innocent* and Barbara Cartland's *The Flame is Love*, he expressed a desire to produce more films here and to assist in the formation of a native film industry.

From as far back as 1896 the only form of film-making to run at a consistently high level in Ireland was the documentary. From shaky views of trains and fire engines this medium began to capture the historical events at the beginning of the century and evolved slowly into a unique art form. Norman Whitton of Central Film Supply compiled a large library of film stock covering a variety of scenic and topical items during the twenties. Some of these were incorporated into other films, thus providing a forerunner to the services of a second-unit. Also during the twenties

Director Patrick Carey

Norris Davidson made a series of short films on various aspects of life in Ireland at the time. This form of film-making was not officially termed documentary until the 1930s. This decade also gave us the unique *Man of Aran* from Robert Flaherty.

George Morrison

The thirties saw many fine documentaries from Richard Hayward, including *Lough Corrib* and *In West Kerry*. Hayward alternated his documentary work with feature films.

The biggest successes in the film of the documentary have been Gael Linn's two epic historical reconstructions *Mise Éire* and *Saoirse?*, assembled by George Morrison with an impressive music score by Seán Ó Riada. They each ran for approximately ninety minutes and were exceptionally well received by the public. They remain the two definitive films depicting important developments in Irish history. Morrison also directed over twenty short films covering a range of Irish life and culture. In the early sixties Gael Linn also filmed a weekly newsreel in Irish for cinemas. It was produced by Jim Mulkerns and Colm O'Laoghaire and ran for 267 editions until it fell a victim to television.

The survival of the documentary is due in no small way to the work of a dedicated group of directors that included Patrick Carey, Bob Quinn, Louis Marcus, George Morrison, Vincent Corcoran and Eamonn de Buitléar. For many years this small band struggled to find finance for each new production. These short films were sponsored in the main by commercial companies but occasionally a government department would commission a film on a particular subject, such as road safety or hygiene. Only in that way was money forthcoming directly from an official source. Few documentaries are a commercial proposition and are normally shown in support of feature films, though to a lesser degree in recent years, with television serving a similar market. The output of these producers of about half a dozen films a year has been of a remarkably high quality and has won them many international awards. Amongst those of outstanding merit have been Patrick Carey's *Yeats's Country, Waves and Errigal*; Colm O'Laoghaire's *Water Wisdom and Irish Gossamer*; Louis Marcus's *Peil* and *Rhapsody of a River*; Vincent Corcoran's *Ireland*; Kieran Hickey's *The Light of Other Days* and *Faithful Departed*, based on the Lawrence Collection of late nineteenth and early twentieth century photographs in the National Gallery of Ireland; Eamonn de Buitléar's many wildlife studies and George Morrison's *The Easter Rising* and *Look to the Sea*.

In 1976 an inventive scheme was launched by the Arts Council in the form of a Film Script Award which was to be presented annually. It took the form of an open competition in which film-makers born or resident in Ireland could submit original scripts for consideration.

The scheme aimed to attract directors with a background in commercials, many of whom were to tackle ambitious short features. The first award went to *Poitín* which was co-written by Colm Bairead and Bob Quinn, who also directed it. This 16 mm colour film received a further £5,000 from the Department of the Gaeltacht and assistance from RTE, the NFSI, Ireland Fund and Gaeltarra. It was made with the involvement of the local people in Connemara and traced the antics of a poitín maker (Cyril Cusack) and his accomplices (Donal McCann and Niall Tóibín). The film which had Irish dialogue and English sub-titles was premiered in Carraroe. Some years previous Quinn made another important film *Caoineadh Airt Uí Laoire*. It has a complex narrative structure which looks at a modern theatrical presentation of the eighteenth century poem about the death of a

Wendy Hiller as *Attracta*

Film director and writer Kieran Hickey

Gaelic aristocrat and mixes scenes of the rehearsal with cinematic account. The film with Seán Bán Breathnach and Caithlín Ní Donnchu also had Irish dialogue and English sub-titles. Bob Quinn has since written and directed the series *Atlantean*.

Tom McArdle, an RTE producer, made his directorial début with *The Kinkisha*, written by his twin brother John, who also starred. The film, which they financed privately, deals with the effects of superstition on a Galway marriage. *It's Handy When People Don't Die*, set in Wexford during the 1798 Rising, was the second feature directed by Tom McArdle in 1980. The happenings are seen through the eyes of Art, a simple village youth who listens to stories and myths as events unravel around him. The film was superbly shot on location with a reliable cast headed by Garrett Keogh, Brendan Caldwell and Bob Carlile.

Kieran Hickey, whose first venture as a short feature director was *A Child's Voice*, a ghost story written by David Thompson and starring T.P. McKenna, won the second Arts Council Film Script Award which had now doubled to £12,000 for Exposure. Set in a rural hotel, the film described an encounter between three surveyors and a French woman-photographer and featured Catherine Schell, T.P. McKenna, Bosco Hogan and Niall O'Brien. It was a forty-eight minute feature shot on 16 mm and achieved on a small budget. Hickey followed this with *Criminal Conversations*, another short feature. His most ambitious undertaking was the screen version of William Trevor's short story *Attracta* which was adapted for the screen by the author. The film received a grant of £104,000 from the Film Board. Wendy Hiller, the veteran stage and screen actress, who won an Academy Award for her performance in the 1958 film *Separate Tables*, was signed on to play the role of the spinster teacher whose visit to the grave of a Belfast victim of violence evokes memories of her own experiences. The strong supporting cast also included Kate Thompson, John Kavanagh and Deirdre Donnolly. It was photographed by Sean Corcoran on a three weeks' shooting schedule. The film won a Drama Award at the Celtic Film and Television Festival in Glasgow. Corcoran was also responsible for the photography on *At the Cinema*

Sheila Flitton and Maeve Germaine in
The Country Girls

Palace, a documentary on the work of Liam O'Leary, the Irish film historian, directed by Donald Taylor Black.

The late seventies brought a number of significant short features and documentaries from Irish directors. Another Arts Council Script Award winner, Neville Presho, directed *Desecration* which depicts the clash of cultures when a valuable find is discovered under an archaeological site which is deemed a national monument. In the cast are Tony Hickey, John Murphy and Eamonn Kane. Tiernan MacBride directed a notable short film *Christmas Morning* in 1978. It was a visualisation of the old Irish ballad 'Arthur McBride', played and sung by Paul Brady. The film, which starred Godfrey Quigley and Paul Bennett, was Ireland's entry in the short film competition at the Cannes Film

Festival. Tim Booth made an ambitious animated short, *The Prisoner*, based on W.B. Yeats's poem with music supplied by Gary Moore and Phil Lynott. A short feature, *John, Love*, written and directed by John Davis, was set on the First Communion day of a young boy in the Dublin of the fifties.

Another young film-maker to produce an important short feature was Joe Comerford with a 16 mm film, *Down the Corner*, which was based on Noel McFarlene's book of the same name. It was set and filmed in Ballyfermot, a working class district of Dublin, and featured local youths in the main roles. The modest budget of £20,000 included £7,000 from the British Film Institute. Comerford was to follow this with *Travellers* from a script by Neil Jordan, about the life of two young itinerants. With the initial funding from the Film Board, film production commenced at an encouraging rate. The films were in the main by Irish producers and directors, dealing with Irish themes.

The first major investment by the Film Board was the grant for *Angel*. The next notable Irish feature film of the eighties was based on

Brid Brennan in *Anne Devlin*

Robert Wynne Simmons's Art Council award winning script, *The Outcasts*. The film, set in rural Ireland before the Famine, was directed by Wynne Simmons with financial assistance from the Film Board of £47,000 and Channel Four. It starred Cyril Cusack, Mick Lally and Mary Ryan. The central characters are Scarf Michael (Lally) and Maura O'Donnell (Ryan) and looks at a time of poverty and superstition when the power of magic is accepted everywhere. Scarf Michael is a wedding fiddler, but he has become a social outcast because his magic is said to bring unhappiness and even death. Maura, an introverted girl, is regarded as backward by the community until she comes under the influence of Michael. The film was screened at the Moscow Film Festival and won an award at the Brussels Fantasy Film Festival. A further £25,000 was forth coming from the Film Board for blow-up from 16 mm to 35 mm and for promotional costs.

Twenty years after producing Edna O'Brien's *Girl with Green Eyes*, Desmond Davis returned to Counties Wicklow and Dublin to film the earlier adventures of Babs and Kate with *The Country Girls*. Sam Neill played the Mr. Gentleman role and the two girls rebelling against a convent education were sensitively played by Maeve Germaine and Jill Doyle. Others in the cast included John Kavanagh, Niall Tóibín, Sheila Flitton and Agnes Bernelle. The Film Board made a £75,000 investment in the film, 10% of the total budget, which was also financed by Channel Four. It attracted excellent business in Irish cinemas and at the date of screening had the second highest viewing rate of any film or programme shown on Channel Four.

In 1982 two films by enterprising young Irish directors went into production simultaneously. Shooting on location in Strokestown, County Roscommon and Kilmainham Jail was *Anne Devlin*, directed by Pat Murphy and produced by Tom Hayes. Brid Brennan, who played a key role in Maeve, was cast as Robert Emmet's devoted servant with Bosco Hogan as Emmet. A native of Dublin, Pat Murphy moved to Belfast with her family in 1966. While studying art at Hornsby in London, she made a short film, *Rituals of Memory*. At film school she met John Davies and Robert Smith with whom she made her feature début, *Maeve*, for the British Film Institute. The budget for *Anne Devlin* was £600,000 with the Film Board providing £200,000. Cathal Black, the award-winning film-maker of *Wheels and Our Boys*, directed *Pigs*, a feature film on location in Dublin. The title referred to the lifestyle of a group of people in a squat in inner city Dublin. James Brennan who wrote the screenplay starred as the central character, drop-out Jimmy. The squat attracts a sad assortment of characters; George (George Shane) a broken middle-aged man, Tom (Maurice O'Donoghue) a gibbering unfortunate, Ronnie (Liam Halligan) a pusher, Orwell (Kwesi Kay) a Jamaican and Mary (Mary Harper) a prostitute. The dirge-like score by Roger Doyle was most effective in capturing the despairing atmosphere. The film was produced by David Collins; with the

Film Board putting up £90,500. One of the most outstanding aspects of both films was the excellent photography of Thaddeus O'Sullivan. Both films made a vital breakthrough when their producers managed to attract significant private investment in Ireland. *Anne Devlin* received a private investment of £250,000. Unfortunately these two films only received a limited release and failed to register significantly with critics and audience.

Cal was the first feature film by the ex RTE director, Pat O'Connor, who in March 1984 won the prestigious BAFTA award for his direction of the RTE/BBC co-production, *The Ballroom of Romance,* which was named best television drama of the year in England. O'Connor's experience in television drama and current affairs served him well in making *Cal*, a sensitive, moving film. Until now the troubles in Northern Ireland had not attracted many film-makers. The film was produced by David Puttnam, the Oscar-winning producer of

Brenda Fricker and Bob Hoskins in *The Woman Who Married Clark Gable*

Chariots of Fire for Goldcrest Films and was based on a screenplay by Bernard MacLaverty from his original novel. The film, with substantial American backing, was filmed entirely on location in Counties Kildare and Wicklow . It is the story of a nineteen year old unemployed Catholic, Cal McCluskey, who lives with his father (Donal McCann) in a working class housing estate near Belfast. He is on the fringe of the IRA and wants out. When their home is burned by the Protestant UVF, Cal takes refuge in a cottage on a farm where he works. Here he is attracted to Marcella (Helen Mirren), the Catholic widow of a RUC man murdered by the IRA. Cal was the driver for the assassination squad. Their love affair drifts to an inevitable tragic conclusion. Cal was widely acclaimed at the Cannes Film Festival, with Helen Mirren winning the Best Actress Award. Others in the cast included a young unknown, John

Catherine Byrne and Stephen Brennan in
Eat the Peach

Director Thaddeus O'Sullivan

Lynch, as Cal, Ray McAnally, Tom Hickey and John Kavanagh.

Despite the fact that not a single feature film was produced in Ireland in 1984 there existed a strong core of eager young film makers with no shortage of experience and ideas. With Film Board assistance they are striving to produce films identifiable with the cultural heritage of Ireland and the social and moral climate of the present. An indication of their number is evident from the list of eighty projects initially submitted to the Film Board for consideration. With this amount of

activity it would appear that the long-awaited Irish film industry was finally taking off.

The highly speculative nature of the film business makes banks and private enterprise reluctant to invest. Only a small percentage of films are an overwhelming financial success of the kind enjoyed by Steven Spielberg with *E.T.* and *Jurassic Park*. Films in the main take years to recoup their production costs. A high percentage are financial flops. The most seasoned directors are unable to predict what productions with constantly changing trends will succeed at the box-office. One of the earliest producers to entice private companies to invest in a film was John Boorman with *Excalibur*, but his elaborate plans collapsed owing to complications with the bank. Among Irish films which have secured significant private investment in recent years are Cathal Black's *Pigs* and Pat Murphy's *Anne Devlin*. Despite their artistic achievements these films failed to receive wide spread cinema release in Ireland and abroad and consequently were not an incentive to future investors. However, the efforts of Channel Four should be noted. They have encouraged film-makers to make low-budget films and have formulated a policy of investing in worthy projects. Several Irish-made productions, already mentioned, received generous funding from them.

Considerable interest was shown in Thaddeus O'Sullivan's first short feature, *On A Paving Stone Mounted,* which concerned emigration and starred Maureen Toal and Paul Bennett. O'Sullivan, who was highly praised for his cinematography on *Pigs* and *Anne Devlin,* chose a short story by Sean O'Faolain, *The Woman Who Married Clark Gable,* as the basis for his next production. The short black and white film, shot on a tight schedule on location in Dublin, featured Bob Hoskins, a highly regarded British actor, and Brenda Fricker in the leads. It received good critical reviews, winning the Sunday Independent Film Award and was nominated for a BAFTA as the best short film.

In February 1985 a new film company, Strongbow Film and Television Productions, was launched, headed by Oliver Maloney, John Kelleher and David Collins. They intend to avail themselves of the Business Development Scheme introduced in the Finance Act 1984 whereby investors could gain tax relief for investments of between £500 and £25,000. Their ambitious package of Irish feature films and television series began with a feature film, *Eat the Peach,* directed by Peter Ormrod. The company raised £1 million from individual and group investors, and further finance was received from the Irish Film Board and Channel Four. *Eat the Peach,* which went into production in July, deals with the realisation of one man's dream — to build a motorcycle 'wall of death' in his own back-yard. The unusual extension to his house provokes the hostility of his friends and neighbours. The idea for the film had come to director Peter Ormrod from a real life incident where a County Longford man had built his own 'wall of death'. Shooting of the £1,700,000 film took place at Allenwood, Wicklow, Meath and Dublin. The film's central characters are played by Stephen Brennan and Eamon Morrissey. Others in the cast include Niall Tóibín, Catherine Byrne and Joe Lynch. The film's title *Eat the Peach,* is taken from 'The Love-Song of J. Alfred Prufrock' by

T.S. Eliot, in which the anti hero asks himself, 'Do I Dare to Eat the Peach'. The film was distributed widely and was a box-office hit in Ireland. Strongbow Productions followed its success with a £2 million four-part television series, *When Reason Sleeps.*

In 1985 television and radio personality Mike Murphy became involved in three production companies. In Emdee Productions, which he set up with cameraman, Seamus Deasy, the concentration was to be on television productions. In Little Bird Productions he was joined on the board of directors by James Mitchell who had made *The Irish R.M.,* and Michael Colgan of the Gate Theatre. Their first project was to be a four-hour television film, *Troubles,* based on the novel by J.G. Farrell. In New Irish Film Productions, for which Murphy had raised a good deal of the £1.8 million budget for their first film, *The Fantasist,* he was involved as executive producer. One of his main roles was to inspire confidence in projects and raise development capital. With his high profile, Murphy was able to speak directly to the people controlling the purse-strings. *The Fantasist* is a modern-day thriller, based on the novel *Goosestep* by Patrick McGinley, under the direction of Robin Hardy, with American star Timothy Bottoms, Moira Harris, and Irish actors John Kavanagh and Liam O'Callaghan. It went into production on location in Dublin in November 1985. At an early stage there was ill-feeling when Cyril Cusack was replaced by Mick Lally, the popular actor from the Glenroe television series. Mike Murphy indicated that the film was aimed at an international market and would prove the viability of the Irish film industry. Unfortunately the film did not live up to expectations and was roasted by the critics.

Another Irish film, *The End of the World Man,* directed by Bill Miskelly and produced by Marie Jackson, won two of the three awards in the children's section of the 1986 International Berlin Film Festival. The film won the UNICEF award and the Berlin Children's Jury Award. The citation for the first award stated that the film 'shows children in an accessible way that they can take action and influence social circumstances'.

The first film to go into production in 1986 was *Rawhead X,* an Anglo-Irish co-production by Paradise and Alpine Pictures. This £1,000,000 horror film, directed by George Pavlow, was co-produced by David Collins, Kevin Attew and Don Hawkins. Two Americans, David Dukes and Kelly Piper, took the lead roles with the strong supporting cast headed by Niall Tóibín, Ronan Wilmot, Sheila Flitton and Derry Power. The film was shot in various locations in County Wicklow. The story concerns a man who digs up a huge stone which lay in a field for hundreds of years and releases a monster.

That same year two veteran Irish film makers, Vincent Corcoran and Bob Quinn were to produce new works. Corcoran's documentary was a long-cherished project entitled *Ireland - A Writer's Island,* about the lives of the country's best-known poets, playwrights and novelists. The film which cost £50,000 and took two years to make - dealt with such notables as John Millington Synge, Oscar Wilde, James Joyce and Sean O'Casey. It was directed by twenty-five year old, Paul Moore.

Quinn's film, *Budawanny,* was adapted from a novel *Súil Le Breith* by Connemara priest Father Pádraic Standúin. This low budget feature film concerns a priest who made his housekeeper pregnant and the ramifications of the situation. Independent film-maker Bob Quinn shot the film on Clare Island, off the Mayo coast, with Donal McCann and Margaret Fegan in the leading roles. Quinn did not invite any of the Irish critics to its first showing in Galway because he felt that film-making should be an art form, rather than a hype steeped business.

The College of Commerce in Rathmines Communications course was responsible for turning out a number of young graduates who made impressive first films, including Siobhan Twomey and Fergus Tighe. Siobhan Twomey, a twenty-three year old Dubliner, wrote and directed *Boom Babies* on a budget of £18,000 with assistance from the Film Board, RTE and an investment by an Irish businessman. The film, set in contemporary Dublin parallels the lives of two young people from opposite sides of the city, Aisling Toibin and Andrew Connolly. They meet when Connolly and his mates steal her Humber car on Dollymount beach.

Clash of the Ash was Fergus Tighe's directorial début, filmed in his native Fermoy in County Cork. The fifty-minute film, produced by Jane Grogan, charted the conflict of a Leaving Cert student and promising hurler (Liam Heffernan) 'as his search for identity in the confines of a small town leads to his disillusionment and ultimate departure.'

Other notable productions from young film-makers during the mid-eighties included Yellow Asylum's film of Samuel Beckett's *Eh Joe,* directed by Alan Gilsenan and starring Tom Hickey, with the voice of Siobhan McKenna. Another Dublin-based company, City Vision, made an impressive short, *Sometime City,* directed by Joe Lee and Frank Deasy and produced by Hilary McLoughlin. It was well received by audiences and critics at festivals in London, Edinburgh, Cork and Dublin. City Vision made the breakthrough into feature films with *The Courier,* a thriller set against the drug scene in Dublin. The film starred Gabriel Byrne as the villain and two newcomers, Padraig O'Loinsigh and Cait O'Riordan.

In the 1940s John Huston had been unsuccessful in his bid to bring James Joyce's *Ulysses* to the screen but forty years later, at the age of eighty, he fulfilled a life-long ambition when he filmed Joyce's short story *The Dead.* It was a family affair for the Hustons, with his Oscar winning daughter, Anjelica, playing the female lead in a screenplay by his son Tony. The original plan was to shoot the film in Ireland but John Huston was too ill to travel and interiors were filmed in America by Huston from his wheelchair. Producers Wieland Schulz and Chris Sievernich travelled to Dublin to audition Irish actors and the cast consisted almost entirely of Irish players headed by Donal McCann, Dan O'Herlihy, Donal Donnelly, Catherine Delaney and tenor Frank Patterson. Huston was deeply disappointed that he could not come to Dublin but a second unit under Seamus Byrne shot link-up scenes in Dublin and Wicklow, including Number 15, Usher's Island, which featured in the actual story.

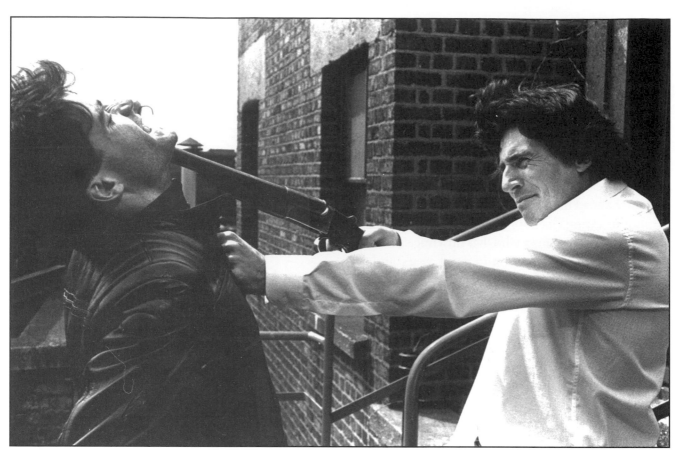

Padraig O'Loingsigh and Gabriel Byrne in *The Courier*

Maeve Germaine and Jill Doyle in *The Country Girls,* from the novel by Edna O'Brien

Chapter 22

Film Board Axed

The first feature film to fully utilise the facilities of MTM Studio was an Irish gangster thriller, *Taffin,* with Pierce Brosnan in the title role. He played a professional debt collector who is recruited by a local community to prevent corrupt businessmen from building a chemical plant in the town. Francis Megahy directed the five million dollar production in a variety of Wicklow and Dublin locations with a large Irish cast headed by Ray McAnally, Alison Doody, Alan Stanford and Jonathan Ryan. The film was a co-production with Metro Goldwyn Mayer and received substantial Irish investment.

By the autumn of 1987 Ireland was experiencing one of its busiest periods in over a decade of major film and television series in production or post-production. In Galway Joe Comerford was completing *Reefer and the Model,* his West coast thriller. The film, produced by Lelia Doolin, was initiated with an Arts Council script award in 1983. Ian McElhinney played a trawler captain who teamed up with Carole Scanlan, Ray McBride and Sean Lawlor to rob a mobile bank. A critic at the Berlin Film Festival termed it an Irish western with undertones of Bonnie and Clyde. The film went on to the Europa Prize of £150,000 at the Barcelona Film Festival. In Dublin, City Vision were editing *The Courier* for a spring release. Many familiar Dublin landmarks also featured in Jack Clayton's production of *The Lonely Passion of Judith Hearn,* based on the novel

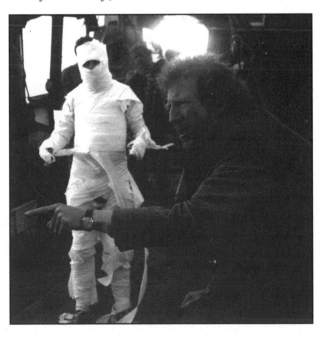

Joe Comerford directing a bandaged Ray McBride on location in *Reefer and the Model*

Doreen Hepburn and Barnard Hughes filming *Da*

by Brian Moore and starring Bob Hoskins and Maggie Smith as the middle-aged spinster. The setting of the original novel was transferred from Belfast to Dublin of the 1950s.

Within the space of a week in September, five important productions began shooting: - *Da, Now I Know, Troubles, Echoes* and *The Dawning*. Dalkey, County Dublin was the setting for a feature film based on Hugh Leonard's award-winning play, *Da* and his autobiographical book *Home Before Night*. The film directed by Matt Clark had Martin Sheen and Barnard Hughes adopting 'Irish' accents to play son and father respectively. The son, Charlie was played by three actors - as a young boy by Hugh O'Connor, in his late teens by Karl Hayden (an impressive début), and by Sheen as an adult. Following four weeks in Atlanta, Georgia, Strongbow Productions began location work in Dublin on *Now I Know* with Mathew Modine and Maeve Germaine. This humorous love story was written and directed by Robert Pappas. James Mitchell's much publicised *Troubles*, adapted from the novel by J.G. Farrell began a shoot in Greystones and Killala, County Mayo by the Irish company Little Bird for London Weekend Television. After an initial delay and re-casting the leading roles were played by Ian Charleson, Ian Richardson and Emer Gillespie. Dunmore East, County Waterford was the principal location for a television mini-series based on Maeve Binchy's best-selling novel *Echoes*, with Geraldine James,

Alison Doody and John Kavanagh. Jennifer Johnston's novel *The Old Jest*, adapted for the screen by Moira Williams and re-titled *The Dawning*, set in County Wicklow in 1920 was filmed in counties Cork and Wicklow with Anthony Hopkins, Jean Simmons and Trevor Howard.

Following the phenomenal success of his first three films Neil Jordan went into production on *High Spirits* in late 1987. He filmed exteriors for this twelve million dollar black comedy, based on his own screenplay, at Dromore Castle in County Limerick and exteriors on an elaborate set of Castle Plunkett at Shepperton Studio. His international cast was headed by Peter O'Toole, Daryl Hannah and Steve Guttenburg and counter balanced from Ireland by Donal McCann, Ray McAnally and Tom Hickey. Singer Mary Coughlan made her acting début. Derek Meddings who made Superman fly and created many of the effects in James Bond was in charge of special effects as they were an important factor in a film in which ghosts could fly. The film was set in Castle Plunkett, whose owner attracts American tourists by advertising ghosts and banshees but they get a rude awakening as they encounter many real ghosts. Jordan found the same reluctance as did John Boorman previously of encouraging Irish companies to invest in the film and had to raise finance in America.

Within the space of a week in June 1987 two contrasting Government decisions were to have serious implications for the future of film making in Ireland. The first move was an amendment to the 1987 Finance Bill by then Finance Minister, Ray MacSharry making provision for companies to obtain a tax write-off against profits for annual investments of up to £100,000 in Irish film production companies. These companies who had to be incorporated in Ireland and be tax residents here provided up to 60% of the cost of a film by means of this new incentive. A week later the Taoiseach, Charles Haughey announced that the Film Board was being wound up and the Arts Council, who already had a statutory function to promote the arts, 'including the cinema', would be responsible for future

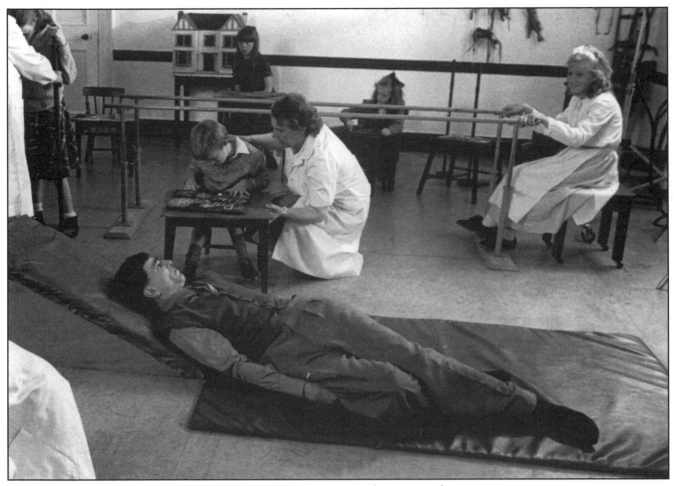

Daniel Day-Lewis in a scene from *My Left Foot*

funding. There was widespread condemnation of the Board's abolition from all quarters by native and foreign film-makers. Despite this set back a new breed of Irish film-makers continues to achieve international acclaim with an impressive list of high quality films.

The year 1988 saw the directorial début of two more Irish directors, Aisling Walsh and Jim Sheridan. Twenty nine year old Walsh, from Navan was determined to make a career in films. She studied at the National Film and Television School in London and from the time she first developed the original story for *Joyriders* she hustled until she raised the finance, from Granada Film Productions. The contemporary theme told of a young battered wife, who deserts her children and runs away with a joyrider on a voyage of mutual self-discovery in Clare. Patricia Kerrigan and Andrew Connolly played the young couple. English actress, Billie Whitelaw played a cameo role as a country and western singer working in a run-down hotel.

Veteran character actor David Kelly stole the film as a farmer.

A project which obsessed producer Noel Pearson for many years was to bring the life of the disabled writer Christy Brown, who could write and paint with his left foot, to the screen. While Jim Sheridan was working on the script with Shane Connaughton based on Christy's book *My Left Foot* he became desperate to direct it. Sheridan had not directed a film before but Pearson had enough confidence in him to put him in charge of the £1,700,000 film. The central role was played by Daniel Day-Lewis who spent months in preparation and remained in character throughout the entire production, impressing everybody by his absorption in the part. Hugh O'Connor played Christy as a boy. The film, which was shot in seven weeks in Ardmore and the Bray area, also starred Ray McAnally and Brenda Fricker as his parents with Cyril Cusack in a cameo role. Following its opening in Dublin the film broke box-office records and received rave reviews.

A real coup for MTM was attracting *Three of a Kind* the first major American network show to be filmed outside that country. The series was made by the same team behind the successful *Hill Street Blues* and *Lou Grant*. It starred Beau Bridges and Ian Ogilvy and centred on the exploits of a trio of spies working from a high-class restaurant in the South of France. An entire French street was built in the studio for the proposed thirteen part series. The first episode was to serve as a 'prototype' which would be used to test how a full series would fare in the States. Unfortunately the results were not encouraging and plans to make the series were shelved.

Despite a $320,000,000 takeover of MTM Enterprises by the British Television South Company, Ardmore was constantly in demand. It became the base for *The Real Charlotte,* a four part mini-series based on the novel by Sommerville and Ross. The series, with a three months shooting schedule, was produced by Gandon Productions with Tony Barry as director and Niall McCarthy as producer. Heading the strong Irish cast were Jeananne Crowley, Patrick Bergin, Sorcha Cusack and Aiden Grennell. *Like The Irish R.M.*, the setting was the Irish countryside at the end of the nineteenth century. The studio was also used by Ronan O'Leary to shoot a television version of the successful stage play *Fragments of Isabella* with Gabrielle Reidy.

Film and television production is labour intensive and employs a high proportion of technicians, actors and extras. MTM Studio also benefited with interiors for many of these productions utilising their stages and facilities. This additional business, together with the RTE produced *Glenroe*, pop videos and commercials proved to the sceptics that the re-opening of the studio was a sound commercial decision.

A form of film-making new to Ireland was animation and the American company Sullivan-Bluth was to introduce this industry to Dublin. In 1986 feeling dissatisfied with Hollywood animation producer, Don Bluth., who had served his apprenticeship with Walt Disney, joined with financier Morris F. Sullivan and explored various options before settling in Dublin with IDA backing. They brought 90 Canadian and American actors and recruited 260 Irish, mostly graduates from the arts colleges, and ultimately hoped to increase this figure to 600. Steven Spielberg contacted Bluth to discuss working together on an animated feature film. With Spielberg's support the company made *An American Tail* which was completed in the Dublin studio. The $9,300,000 film which told of a mouse who emigrated to America, became a smash hit at the American box-office where it grossed over fifty million dollars.

Their second feature was the fourteen million dollar *The Land Before Time Began*, a Spielberg / Lucas presentation of a Don Bluth film produced entirely at the Dublin studio. The film secured a complete American distribution and made the number one spot in the US box office. The story, in marked contrast to the action packed *An American Tail* set at turn of the century, is set in prehistoric times and recounts the adventures of five young dinosaurs who embark on the adventure of a lifetime to find a hidden valley.

Sullivan Bluth Ireland had tripled in size to become the largest animation studio in Europe. In 1988 the company secured a joint financing agreement of forty million dollars for three animated films with Goldcrest Films and Television. The studio completed their third feature *All Dogs Go To Heaven* featuring the voices of Burt Reynolds, Dom DeLuise, Loni Anderson and singing to the music of Charles Strouse.

Work then got underway at MTM Studio on *Rock A Doodle* which combined live action and animation and was released in November 1990. Voices included Glen Campbell, Phil Harris and Sandy Duncan. The constantly expanding company also planned to establish an entirely new division for television and commercial animation. The studio's principal aim - to make Ireland world centre of classical animation seems well on target. Due to a combination of factors Sullivan Bluth was forced to close.

Chapter 23

Academy Awards for Ireland

From the beginning of 1989 a number of major films with top-line stars and impressive budgets were announced to go into production in Ireland, but for a variety of reasons, chiefly financial, none came to fruition. Despite this disappointment a number of productions, mainly indigenous, did go before the cameras.

Director Pat O'Connor returned from success abroad with *A Month in the Country* and *January Man* to direct the film version of William Trevor's novel *Fools of Fortune*. Academy Award winning actress, Julie Christie, took the leading role with Mary Elizabeth Mastrantonio, Ian Glen, John Kavanagh and Rosaleen Linehan in support. Filming for the £2,500,000 production was completed in the Dublin, Mullingar, Aran Islands and Robertstown areas with interiors on sets at MTM, Ardmore Studios. This co-production between the international Polygram company and the successful London-based, Working Title opened in the Black and Tan era of the 1920s and told how the Troubles affected the Quinton family. Their tranquil life style is shattered with an outbreak of violence, the burning of their big house and cold blooded killing of some of the family.

Ronan O'Leary used MTM Studio for the entire six days shooting schedule of *Fragments of Isabelle* which he completed on a budget of £150,000. Gabrielle Reidy recreated her stage role of Isabelle Leitner, a survivor of Auschwitz. The one woman monologue, based on the best selling Pulitzer nominated book was interspersed with documentary clips from the harrowing days of the Holocaust in Germany and Hungary. The story which told of Isabelle and her family's arrest and imprisonment in Auschwitz was well received by both critics and the public. Within six months of its release the film was already in profit.

The Derry Film and Video Workshop was initially set up to counteract how life in the city was being portrayed in the media. They produced an impressive feature film entitled, *Hush-A-Bye Baby* directed by Margo Harkin. In the film, a young Derry girl (played by Emer McCourt) discovers she is pregnant and the dilemma she faces. Her boyfriend is arrested and her letter to him is censored because it is in Irish. The singer, Sinead O'Connor, appeared in a cameo role.

Thaddeus O'Sullivan, the well-known lighting cameraman, made his début as a feature

Producer Noel Pearson

film were Strangford Lough and Dublin with interiors again being filmed in MTM Ardmore Studios. The cast was headed by Donal McCann and Ciaran Hinds as Presbyterian farmer brothers who both fall in love with Saskia Reeves, who portrays a servant girl whom they employ. When she has a baby she refuses to disclose to the local rector which of the two is the father.

Within a week of collecting yet another award for *My Left Foot* producer Noel Pearson and director Jim Sheridan went into production on their second film, a screen adaptation of John B. Keane's successful stage play, *The Field*. Ray McAnally was cast in the central role of Bull McCabe but sadly died only months before filming commenced. He was replaced by Richard Harris, making a welcome return to the screen, who went very much into character by growing a bushy white beard and having his teeth blackened. Other roles were played by international stars, John Hurt as The Bird, Tom Berenger as the American and Sean Bean as the Bull's son. They were supported by a

film director with *December Bride*, from a screenplay by David Rudkin, based on the novel by Sam Hanna Bell, set in County Down at the turn of the century. Principal locations for the

John Hurt, Richard Harris and Sean Bean in a scene from *The Field*

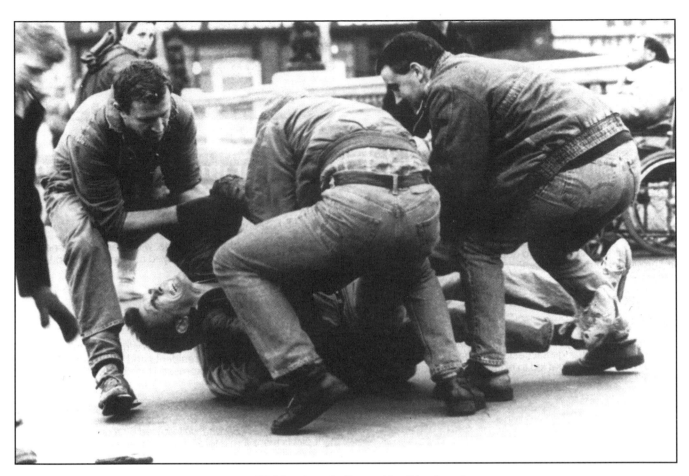

Hidden Agenda directed by Ken Loach

strong team of Irish players headed by Frances Tomelty, Brenda Fricker, John Cowley and Eamon Keane. The central theme in the film was the confrontation between the Bull and the American for possession of a field. Sheridan's screenplay greatly opened out the original plot, adding new characters and taking advantage of the misty beauty of Leenane in County Galway which was chosen for the bulk of the winter shoot.

In the latter part of 1989 Ken Loach filmed *Hidden Agenda*, a political thriller set in Northern Ireland, under a cloak of secrecy in Dublin, Belfast and London. The film, based on a screenplay by Jim Allen, deals with the murder of an American civil rights investigator and the subsequent investigation which uncovers a web of conspiracy. The leading roles were played by Brad Dourif as the American, Frances McDormand as his colleague and Brian Cox as a detective.

Early in 1990 there was more good news for the *My Left Foot* team when the ultimate

accolades in the film industry, the Academy Awards were announced. Not alone was Daniel Day-Lewis to receive a nomination for Best Actor for his portrayal of the handicapped writer, Christy Brown, but the film received a total of five nominations. They were Day-Lewis as Best Actor, Brenda Fricker for Best-Supporting Actress, Jim Sheridan for Best Director, Jim Sheridan and Shane Connaughton for best adapted screenplay and, most significantly, it secured a place on the important short-list of five for Best Picture of the year. At the British Academy Film and Television Awards (BAFTA), a week before the Oscar ceremony Daniel Day-Lewis received the Best Actor Award and Ray McAnally won a posthumous award as Best Supporting Actor for his portrayal of Christy's father.

On 26th March at the 62nd Academy Awards in the Dorothy Chandler Pavilion, Los Angeles, Kevin Kline announced the nominees for Best Supporting Actress:- Angelica Huston, Lena Olin, Julia Roberts, Dianne Wiest and Brenda

Fricker. He opened the envelope to announce . . Brenda Fricker. There was even better news for *My Left Foot* when Daniel Day-Lewis beat such formidable competition as Tom Cruise, Morgan Freeman, Robin Williams and Kenneth Brannagh to win the Best Actor Award. In his acceptance speech he thanked Hugh O'Connor who played young Christy and to Christy Brown himself. This was a remarkable achievement for the £1,700,000 budget film which was to receive an enormous box-office boost with world-wide receipts estimated at £20,000,000. The two Oscar recipients were to receive a civic reception on their return to Dublin. Following the amazing success of their first film, the producer, Noel Pearson and director, Jim Sheridan were approached by all the major Hollywood studios to sign attractive deals. They finally agreed a major contract with Universal under which they would produce a minimum of two films over the next three years for the studio, with an option to make five films in that period. Part of the agreement would be a fund to develop 'Irish craft industry to train directors, writers and cinematographers in a series of seminars'.

Due to the success of *My Left Foot*, post-production on *The Field* was delayed and the World Prémiere in Dublin was moved back to September. The film opened to rave reviews from the Irish critics and broke box-office records at Irish

Lorraine Pilkington in *The Miracle*

cinemas. Richard Harris received an Oscar nomination for his performance as the Bull McCabe. Pearson and Sheridan were onto another winner.

After directing *We're No Angels* with Robert de Niro and Sean Penn in Canada, Neil Jordan returned to his hometown of Bray to prepare for his sixth film, the first to be shot totally in Ireland since *Angel*. The film *The Miracle*, with a £2,500,000 budget was based on his own screenplay starred Beverly D'Angelo and Donal McCann and introduced two newcomers, Niall Byrne and Lorraine Pilkington. The drama set in summertime Bray told the story of two teenagers, Jimmy and Rose. Jimmy becomes obsessed with Renée, a blonde American, who is appearing in a musical. It later transpires that she is his mother whom he thought was dead. The film-makers transformed Bray's seafront with pink railings along the prom, fairy lights and new facades for cafes, hotels and amusement arcades. The tourist season commenced early with a protracted stay by Fossetts Circus and a carnival. Sightseers were treated to the sight of a lion in the sea and elephants on the prom. Hundreds of locals were hired as 'extras' and children were paid for attending the circus. Director of photography, Philippe Rousselot, captured the flavour and landscapes of the seaside town.

While the final 'cut' was being called on *The Miracle* another major film was going before the cameras in Dublin. British director Alan Parker whose hit films included *Fame, Midnight Express, Bugsy Malone* and *Mississippi Burning* was chosen to direct *The Commitments* based on Roddy Doyle's novel, set in the fictional north Dublin suburb of Barrytown. The film chronicled the effects of a group of young working-class Dubliners to form a soul band. Parker conducted an 'open audition' in the Mansion House and invited young Dubliners between 18 to 25 who could sing and play instruments to attend. Over 3,000 people were auditioned in exhaustive sessions before Parker finally chose his mainly unknown cast. They were Andrew Strong, Johnny Murphy, Michael Aherne, Dave Finnegan, Dick Massey, Felim Gormley, Robert Atkins, Bronagh Gallagher, Ken

McCluskey, Maria Doyle, Angeline Ball and Glen Hansard. The book was adapted for the screen by Dick Clement and Ian La Frenais and was shot in a variety of locations throughout the city. *The Commitments* won four BAFTA Awards, including Best Film, Best Director and Best Adapted Screenplay. The film was widely acclaimed and broke records at the Irish box-office.

By year's end technical crew were stretched to the limit with three other feature films going into production in Dublin. *Hear My Song*, directed by Peter Chelsom, based on the life of Joseph Locke was a Limelight/Windmill Lane Production with a £2 million budget. American character actor, Ned Beatty, played the elder Locke with Terry Mulligan as the young man. Others in the cast included David McCallum and Shirley Anne Field.

Fatal Inheritance, told the story of an American 'heir-hunter' who arrives in Ireland to trace the sole heir to a three million dollar fortune of a deceased relative in America. The suspense love story, set in Northern Ireland, was actually shot around Skerries, Rush and Laytown, starring Kevin Davies, who also wrote the script, Emma Samms, David McCallum and Irish actors Darragh Kelly, Anna Manahan and Jim Bartley.

In 1991 another entire village was constructed above Dunquin in County Kerry, by film-makers for the $40 million production *Far and Away*, starring Tom Cruise and Nicole Kidman and directed by Ron Howard. Many Irish actors including Colm Meaney, Cyril Cusack and Niall Tóibín had leading roles in the film. Local men grew beards and long hair for parts as villagers. The other main locations were Killruddery House in Bray, County Wicklow and the Temple Bar area of Dublin where a Boston street set was constructed. The American sequence of the film was shot in Montana. Cruise played Joseph Donnell, a young Connemara man who sets out in 1893 to avenge the death of his father, a tenant farmer, who had fallen victim to a landlord, and is forced to emigrate to America.

Rehills, County Cavan was the location for *The Playboys*, an entertaining drama set in a 1950s rural Ireland, about the impact of the arrival of a

Ruaidhrí Conroy and Ciaran Fitzgerald
Into the West

travelling theatre group on a small community. The middle-aged local sergeant is overcome with frustration when a strolling player falls in love with an unmarried mother. The film, from a screenplay by Shane Connaughton, was directed by Gillies MacKinnon. Albert Finney played the sergeant, Aidan Quinn the young actor, Robin Wright the unmarried mother and Milo O'Shea the owner of the travelling theatre.

Following mediocre reviews for *High Spirits*, *We're No Angels* and *The Miracle*, Neil Jordan returned to a low budget film based on his original screenplay. In Ireland Jordan found great difficulty in raising the budget for the film *The Crying Game*, originally titled *The Soldier's Wife*. Despite a short stint of location work in Ireland, with a carnival sequence in Bettystown, County Meath, the bulk of the production was shot in England. Jordan again teamed up with Stephen Rea. Rea played Fergus, an IRA man involved in kidnapping Jody, a British soldier and holding him as hostage. An understanding develops between the two men and when Jody is killed Fergus goes to London to console his wife, Dil. Fergus falls in love with her only to discover that Dil is a man. The surprise shock revelation was one of the drawing factors of the film in America where it grossed over $60,000,000 at the box-office. The film was nominated for six Academy Awards and Neil Jordan won an Oscar for best screenplay. Adrian Dunbar, Miranda Richardson and Jaye Davidson co-starred.

Donald Sutherland and Julie Christie were reunited for starring roles in *The Railway Station Man*, based on the novel by Jennifer Johnston. The quirky love story, filmed in Donegal, also starred John Lynch and was directed by Michael Whyte.

The years 1991 and 1992 were a lean period for Irish film production. There was only one investment of £2 million by Irish individuals and companies in films in 1992.

The Snapper was the second of Roddy Doyle's books based on the life of the Rabbitte family in the fictitious Barrytown, to be brought to the screen. In contrast to *The Commitments* which had a high budget and high profile, *The Snapper* was filmed for Channel 4's series of new films for a television screening. Due to the amazing critical reception the film received it was given a cinema release and won many plaudits for Colm Meaney as the father and Tina Kelleher as his pregnant daughter. Interior scenes for the production were filmed on stages at Ardmore Studios, with location work in Darndale and Kilbarrack. Colm Meaney was very much in form again as the father whose daughter Sharon announces she is pregnant but will not reveal the identity of the father. Ruth McCabe and Patrick Laffin played other leading roles with a group of young unknowns playing the younger members of the Rabbitte family.

Into the West, from a screenplay by Jim Sheridan, told the tale of two boys Ossie and Tito, who steal a white horse Tír na nÓg, after it has been acquired by a rich, unscrupulous horse stud owner. With his traveller friends, Kathleen and Barreller, the children's father, Papa Riley, sets off after the boys as they head *Into The West*. The film, directed by Mike Newell, on a £5 million budget, starred Gabriel Byrne as Papa Riley and Ellen Barkin as Kathleen. Following a nationwide search, two young boys were cast in the main roles. Ossie was played by six year old Ciarán Fitzgerald and Tito by eleven year Ruaidhrí Conroy. The film was shot on location over a ten week period in Wicklow, Dublin, Portarlington and Dog's Bay, near Roundstone in County Galway. Some tricks of the trade were employed during filming, with six identical white horses, three Irish and three French, being used as Tír na nÓg. For the riding sequences the boys were frequently replaced by a jockey with a beanbag strapped to his back. The film was an instant success in Ireland where it took over £1,000,000 at the box-office.

High Boot Benny saw a return of writer/director Joe Comerford with his first production since *Reefer and the Model*. The cast was headed by Mark O'Shea, Frances Tomelty and Alan Devlin. The film centred on Benny, a seventeen year old delinquent (O'Shea), who has found refuge in a radical school run by an ex-priest and matron on the southern side of the Irish border. When the body of a murdered police informer is discovered a political and psychological drama erupts. Frances Tomelty played the school's Protestant matron and Alan Devlin the ex-priest.

Bob Quinn, the veteran film director, based in Connemara, shot *The Bishop's Story* on location on Clare Island, County Mayo. For this production, filmed in black and white, Quinn was again united with actor Donal McCann, with whom he had worked on *Poitín* and *Budawanny*. In *The Bishop's Story*, McCann starred as an elderly bishop, in a retreat house, recalling the affair he had as a young curate on a western island. Margaret Fegan was cast as the young woman.

Richard Harris as Bull McCabe in a dramatic scene from *The Field*

Jim Sheridan as Jonathan Swift in *Words Upon the Window Pane*

Chapter 24

Film-making Boom

There was a marked improvement in 1993 with ten feature films going into production in Ireland. Several factors contributed to this upsurge in the industry.

Neil Jordan winning an Oscar for the best screenplay for *The Crying Game*, again focused attention on Ireland's small but talented band of film-makers. An equally significant factor was the appointment of the Labour Minister, Michael D. Higgins, as the first Minister for Arts, Culture and the Gaeltacht. The Minister immediately realised that given the correct infrastructure there was potential for growth in this sector. He re-established the Irish Film Board with headquarters in Galway. Lelia Doolan was appointed chairman and Rod Stoneman its chief executive. The Board had a budget of £10,000,000 for development and production over a five year period. The Department had a two-pronged strategy of building the skills and resources of the industry through attracting large budget foreign films, while encouraging the indigenous industry through development grants from the Film Board. The Film Board did not itself produce films, but provided loans and equity investments to independent Irish film-makers to assist them in the development and production of between six and eight Irish films a year. It could also co-operate with other agencies to improve the marketing, sales and distribution of Irish films, and to promote training and development in all areas of film-making. Another function of the Board was to raise public awareness of the cultural, social and economic benefits of a vibrant film-making industry in Ireland, making full use of Irish talents, creative and technical.

With the high profile and good financial return from film production, Section 25 of the Finance Act introduced in 1983 became an attractive proposition for investors. A private investor could invest up to £25,000 annually in an approved film project with tax relief available at the top rate of the investment. In order to qualify as a suitable investment, a substantial part of the work involved in the making of the production must be undertaken in Ireland. The Minister must also certify the film company as qualifying for the purposes of tax relief. The investment must be for a minimum of three years, except in the case of low budget productions or large corporate investors. Investors in productions with a budget of less than £1,000,000 could withdraw after a year without any claw back of tax relief, as can corporate investors who have invested more than £1,000,000 into a qualifying film.

Director Jim Sheridan

The first film to go into production in 1993 was *In the Name of the Father*, directed by Jim Sheridan, based on Gerry Conlon's book *Proved Innocent*. The film was based on the experience of Gerry Conlon, a young Belfast man, who along with friends and family members, was wrongly convicted by British Courts in 1975 for the terrorist bombing of two pubs in Guilford, a small town outside London. The film centred on a relationship between Gerry and Guiseppe Conlon, played by Daniel Day-Lewis and Pete Postlethwaite respectively. Emma Thompson co-starred as lawyer Gareth Peirce and singer Don Baker made his screen début as an IRA man. The bulk of the filming took place in Kilmainham Jail with Ringsend and Sherriff Street in Dublin doubling as working-class Belfast. Jim Sheridan co-wrote the screenplay with New York-based writer Terry George. Daniel Day-Lewis approached the role of Conlon with an intense level of preparation, including spending two days and nights in a cell, submitting himself to twelve hours of interrogation by a team of real detectives, to help perfect his Belfast accent. On its release *In the Name of the Father* became embroiled in a controversy over questions of accuracy. The film was a massive box-office success in Ireland, taking over £2,500,000. An even greater achievement was receiving seven Oscar nominations for best picture, director, actor, supporting actress, adapted screenplay and editing, but the film lost out to *Schlindler's List* which swept the boards.

On a more modest budget writer/director Barry Devlin filmed *All Things Bright and Beautiful* in the small village of Donoughmore, County Laois. The charming tale set in Ireland of the 1950s, told of nine year old Barry O'Neill, an altar boy and innocent, who has a vision of the Blessed Virgin Mary - or believes he does - and the ensuing snowball of religious euphoria that threatens to turn him into a saint. Young Ciarán Fitzgerald played the boy and was supported by Gabriel Byrne and Tom Wilkinson.

Another indigenous film was *Broken Harvest*, the first venture of director, writer and executive producer Maurice O'Callaghan. It took him ten years to raise the £1,250,000 budget to bring his bitter-sweet story about the effects of the War of Independence, the Civil War, emigration and politics on a small Cork community to the screen. The film shown in flashbacks recorded the memories of Jimmy O'Leary's 1950s rural childhood, darkened by the discovery that his father, a hero of the War of Independence, is locked into a thirty year feud with another man dating back to the Civil War. The screenplay was written by solicitor and part-time actor, Maurice O'Callaghan and his sister Kate and was produced by their brother Gerry. Filming began in West Cork in August 1993 and lasted six weeks. The leading roles were played by Marian Quinn as Catherine, Colin Lane and Niall O'Brien. The film was completely financed by Irish money. O'Callaghan sank a good deal of his own capital into the production and raised finance under Section 35. It had its first screening during the 1994 Dublin Film Festival and received generally encouraging reviews.

Shooting simultaneously in West Cork was *War of the Buttons*. The film, adapted by Colin Welland from a Louis Pergaud novel filmed by Yves

Robert in 1962 in a French setting was transferred to a rural Irish location. Producer David Puttnam, who has a home in West Cork, chose locations within a short radius of his base including Skibbereen, Union Hall and Castletownsend. Casting directors Ros and John Hubbard conducted a nation wide search for child actors before recruiting their troop of unknown youngsters led by Gregg Fitzgerald and John Coffey, with Eveanna Ryan as the tomboy caught in the middle. The adult stars were Colm Meaney as Geronimo's father, Johnny Murphy, the local postman and Liam Cunningham as the teacher. *War of the Buttons* was an engaging yarn directed by John Roberts, who won an Oscar in 1992 for his student film, *This Boy's Story*. The plot of *War of the Buttons*, told of children from two small towns located on either side of an inlet in West Cork who form small armies and battle against each other for supremacy. Their token of victory became the removal of an opponent's buttons and shoe laces: hence the title. The showdown with the children marching into battle in cardboard armour with dust-bin lids, was set in a Gothic ruin overlooking Rosscarbery Bay. Release of the film was delayed following a court injunction by parents of one of the children extras, who objected to him appearing briefly with his bottom bare in one of the skirmishs between the groups. The film took £0.5 million at the Irish box-office.

Also in production that summer was *Widow's Peak*, directed by John Irvin. Originally Hugh Leonard had written the screenplay of the film as a vehicle for actress Maureen O'Sullivan and her daughter Mia Farrow, but it took a decade to get the project into production with Joan Plowright playing the part intended for Maureen O'Sullivan. This comedy whodunnit was set in rural Ireland of the 1920s known as *Widow's' Peak* because it was ruled by women, almost all of them widows. Mia Farrow played Miss O'Hare, a spinster, who feels her position within the community is threatened with the arrival of Edwina, a beautiful rich American. Soon the ladies of *Widow's Peak* have murder on their mind. Adrian Dunbar and James Broadbent take the main male roles. The £14.5 million budget film was mainly shot around

Julia Brendler and Ruaidhrí Conroy in *Moondance*

the Blessington Lakes in County Wicklow and picturesque Inistióge, County Kilkenny. Locals in both venues were employed as extras.

Realising the potential of film, Wicklow Film Commission was established to promote the county as a film base and to find suitable locations, arrange street closures and generally to facilitate the requirements of film makers. The county was chosen as one of the locations for *Moondance*, a drama based on *The White Hare* by Francis Stuart. The film, directed by Dagmar Hirtz for Little Bird Production under co-producers James Mitchell and Jonathan Cavendish was also shot in West Cork and Dublin. The plot related how two brothers, 21-year old Patrick and 14-year old Dominic lived an idyllic lifestyle in a dilapidated country house in West Cork. They spent their time fishing and catching rabbits. Their only regular visitor was their Aunt Dorothy who brought Anya, a pretty German girl. Anya begins to play havoc with the boys' lives as both of them are attracted to her. Ian Shaw and Ruaidhrí Conroy played the brothers, with Julia

Brendler as the girl. Other leading roles were taken by Marianne Faithfull as the mother and comedian Brendan Grace as the publican. Van Morrison provided the music.

Controversial American director John Sayles adapted *The Secret of Roan Inish*, a favourite Celtic children's story for the screen. He filmed, with Academy Award-winning cameraman Haskell Wexler, entirely on location in Donegal over the summer months, building a cottage beside the beach. The film told how Fiona Connelly comes to live with her grandparents in a small fishing town in Donegal. There she meets her cousin Eamon and through the window she sees the distant island of Roan Inish, home of the Selkies . . . and so the magic begins. Mick Lally and Eileen Colgan played the grandparents and Jeni Courtney, the young girl. Mick Lally summed up his experience of worklng on the film. 'It was a children's film made by adults.' He felt it a most enjoyable experience, as Sayle was a pleasant character and his temperament perpetrated down through everyone working on the crew. The production came in under budget and the surplus was divided between cast and crew.

In November that year Bray born director, Paddy Breathnach, who served his apprenticeship

Director Paddy Breathnach

with the award winning short *A Stone of the Heart*, went into production with *Ailsa*, his first feature film. The film, adapted by Joseph O'Connor, from his own short story, was produced by Ed Guiney, on a budget of £200,000. Newcomer Brendan Coyle played the main role of Myles, a Dublin man, who becomes obsessed with a beautiful American woman who moves into the flat beneath his. The photography of Cian de Buitlear captured the starkness of the decaying Georgian house. Other roles were played by Andrea Irvine, O.Z. Whitehead and Juliette Gruber. The film was critically acclaimed and won the prestigious first prize of £250,000, towards their next project, at the San Sebastian Film Festival.

The incentives of filming in Ireland were to attract *An Awfully Big Adventure*, to be shot entirely in Dublin, although the story-line was set in the Liverpool of the 1950s. The principal locations were the Olympia Theatre, Henrietta Street, the docks and Bray. The film was based on the Beryl Bainbridge novel which was nominated for the Booker Prize in 1990. Despite its £3 million budget the production was able to gather a formidable cast headed by Alan Rickman, Hugh Grant, Peter Firth and Prunella Scales. Grant and

Brendan Coyle as Miles in *Ailsa*

director Mike Newell, who had previously directed *Into the West* in Ireland, were at the time enjoying a major box-office success in America with the comedy *Four Weddings and a Funeral*. The central character in *An Awfully Big Adventure* was Stella, a rebellious 17-year old who gets a job as an assistant stage manager on Peter Pan at a Liverpool repertory theatre, where she becomes infatuated with the gay actor-manager and falls in love with the actor playing Captain Hook. Georgina Coates made her film début as Stella.

Following a meeting with Minister Michael D. Higgins, actor Mel Gibson announced that production on his $53 million film *Braveheart* scheduled to be filmed entirely on location in Scotland would be, for the most part, made in Ireland instead. One of the attractions for Gibson was that 1,500 members of the defence forces were made available for the battle scenes. There was outrage in Scotland, particularly as the subject matter of the film, William Wallace, was a thirteen century Scottish rebel played by Gibson. The Minister also secured specific staffing requirements including the creation of twelve trainee-ships to work on different aspects of the production. £10,000,000 was raised from Irish investors under Section 35 of the Finance Act towards the budget. Mel Gibson, who had the dual role of director and

Alan Pentony and Gabriel Byrne in *Frankie Starlight*

starred as Wallace, transformed castles and landscapes into Scottish locations. Trim Castle became Stirling and the bloody battles were re-enacted at the Curragh and Ballymore Eustace. Leading critics regarded the battle scenes as some of the best ever filmed. The production team worked from July to October and along with the soldiers hundreds of extras were employed. Other leading roles were played by Patrick McGoohan as King Edward and Sophie Marceau as a French princess. A strong force of Irish actors had leading roles including Brendan Gleeson, Sean McGinley, John Kavanagh, Gerald McSorley and Niall O'Brien. *Braveheart* was nominated for ten Academy Awards and ended up winning five including Best Film and Best Director.

Frankie Starlight was producer Noel Pearson's first production since *The Field*. The £4 million film was based on Chet Raymo's novel *The Dork from Cork* with a screenplay written by Raymo, Ronan O'Leary and Michael Lindsay-Hogg. Director Lindsay-Hogg filmed the drama in Dublin, Cork, Kildare and Kingsville Texas. Henrietta Street in Dublin again featured as one of the main locations. The story, stretching from the end of World War Two to the mid-1980s was told by Frankie, a dwarf who recounts his mother's flight from France during the War and her love affair with two men. Ann Parillaud played the young woman, with Matt Dillon and Gabriel Byrne as her lovers. Dublin artist Corbin Walker made his début as Frankie and Alan Pentony as the boy.

Words Upon the Window Pane was an ambitious undertaking for first-time director Mary McGuckian. She had written the screenplay but it was at Pat O'Connor's suggestion that she became director. It took her three years to get the film into production and raise the $3 million budget. Funding came from a number of sources in Europe which meant the production had to utilise facilities in numerous countries. A complicated shooting schedule was arranged with exteriors filmed in Dublin at some popular venues including Trinity College, Dublin Castle and Henrietta Street and interiors in a studio in Luxembourg. Post-production was completed in Germany and

John Lynch and Geraldine Chaplin in *Words Upon the Window Pane*

Albert Finney in a scene from
A Man of No Importance

England. The Film was an adaptation of W. B. Yeats short play of the same name. It recounted the passionate lives of Jonathan Swift and his two lovers Stella and Vanessa which evolves at a seance in a drawing room in Dublin in which Swift's secret wife Stella lived and died 200 years previously. Mary McGuckian gathered an impressive cast of international stars including Geraldine Chaplin, Geraldine James, Ian Richardson, John Lynch, Donal Donnelly and Jim Sheridan as Swift. Niall Byrne's music provided the appropriate dramatic balance.

A Man of No Importance was an enjoyable film set in the Dublin of the early 1960s and was directed by Suri Krishnama. Albert Finney played Alfie Byrne, a Dublin bus conductor, an amateur theatre producer and a raconteur of the works of Oscar Wilde. Barry Devlin's witty script quoted liberally from Wilde. Finney was supported by a strong cast headed by Brenda Fricker, Michael Gambon, Tara Fitzgerald and Rufus Sewell. The

Victoria Smurfit and Matt Keeslar in
The Run of the Country

film was shot over a five week period on a £2 million budget by Little Bird Films.

Within months, Albert Finney was back filming in Ireland in *The Run of the Country*. On this occasion it was back to County Cavan for his second role as a sergeant in a rural drama by Shane Connaughton based on his novel *A Border Station*. Victoria Smurfit made her screen début as Annagh, a Protestant girl and Matt Keeslar was cast as the young man. The story centred on Danny, an 18-year old whose mother has recently died. Danny rebels against his father, the local sergeant, but falls in love with a Protestant girl. The film touched on many 'issues' from politics and religion to drink and emigration. In conjunction with the film Connaughton kept a diary on the progress of the film which was published in book form as *A Border Diary*.

Circle of Friends by best-selling writer Maeve Binchy was adapted for the screen by Andrew Davies and directed by Pat O'Connor. This was O'Connor's first film in Ireland since directing

William Trevor's *Fools of Fortune*. The Binchy novel was set in Ireland in 1957 and followed the romantic entanglements of three girls removed from the confines of village life when they go to college in Dublin. They were played by a trio of newcomers Minnie Driver, Saffron Burrows and Geraldine O'Rawe. The romantic interest was provided by Hollywood heart-throb, Chris O'Donnell. Many prominent Irish actors including Mick Lally, John Kavanagh and Tom Hickey played character roles. The film was shot in Kilkenny with the attractive village of Inistioge undergoing a transformation and Kilkenny city doubled as Dublin. The $9,000,000 budget film did exceptionally well at the American box-office and remained for many weeks in the top ten charts.

Another indigenous feature film to go before the cameras in 1994 was *Korea*. This film saw the return of Cathal Black to feature films following an absence of ten years, following his highly acclaimed *Pigs* and *Our Boys*. The film, based on a John McGahern story was filmed in Leitrim and Dublin, on a low budget, raised from a range of sources in Europe. The main roles were played by Donal Donnelly, Vass Anderson and two newcomers Andrew Scott and Fiona Molony. The story, set in rural Ireland of 1952, told of Eamon Doyle spending his last summer with his father, John, fishing in the lake. Eamon's exams will decide his future. Luke Moran, son of Ben, is killed in Korea, and his body is returned to the village for burial in a lake-side cemetery. When Eamon falls in love with Una Moran, his father feels betrayed, as he has been an arch-enemy of Ben Moran since the Civil War. The film won many awards including Special Jury Prize for Best Film at the Amiens Film Festival in France.

Undercurrent, shot on a shoe-string budget, over a two year period, was the first feature film for Brian O'Flaherty. The film, a thriller set in contemporary Dublin, featured a diverse group of characters. When the daughter of a prominent politician disappeared two cynical detectives are assigned to the case. The cast included Owen Roe, Stanley Townsend, Tina Kelleher, Orla Charlton, Ali White and Liam Cunningham.

Michael Gambon, Ian Hart & Gary Lydon in *Nothing Personal*

Luke Griffin and Jonathan Rhys-Myers in a scene from *The Disappearance of Finbar*

Chapter 25

Stembridge to Jordan

The first production to be filmed in 1995 was *Nothing Personal* originally titled *All Our Fault.* The film for Little Bird Productions in association with Film Four and British Screen was scripted by Daniel Mornin from his novel *All Our Fault* and directed by Thaddeus O'Sullivan. The leading roles were taken by Ian Hart, John Lynch, Michael Gambon, Maria Doyle Kennedy and James Frain. The film makers returned to Ringsend to once more transform its red-bricked terraced streets into the Belfast of 1972 during a ceasefire as Loyalist and IRA gangs attempted to provoke each other into breaking the truce. The film followed a squad of Loyalist paramilitaries led by war-weary Kenny and his psychopathic accomplice, Ginger. Tommy, a young teenager, impressed by the power and violence is invited by Kenny to go on patrol. This becomes a baptism of fire as the gang torture an innocent Catholic, who Kenny discovers was a childhood friend. Locals in Ringsend watched as slogans were sprayed on gable-ends and buses and cars were burnt out during rioting.

The film makers constructed a wooden fly-over in the suburb of Fettercairn in Tallaght,

County Dublin for *The Disappearance of Finbar.* On completion of the Irish segment the cast and crew moved to Swedish Lapland and Stockholm for further location work. The film, a co-

Kevin Moriarty, Chief Executive, Ardmore Studios

production between First City Features, Samson Films and Victoria Film was adapted by Dermot Bolger and Sue Clayton from the novel by Carl Lombard, originally titled *The Disappearance of Rory Brophy.* The film told of 18-year old Finbar who jumps off a flyover bridge in Dublin and disappears. No body is found and his best friend, Danny, reluctantly embarks on a journey to try to discover the truth behind Finbar's disappearance that brings him across Europe to Scandinavia. Jonathan Rhys-Myers, Luke Griffin, Fanny Risberg and Sean McGinley starred in the film, which was directed by Sue Clayton.

For *Driftwood*, his fifth film, director Ronan O'Leary assembled his cast of James Spader, Anne Brochet and Barry McGovern, for a week's rehearsal before shooting commenced. O'Leary co-wrote the screenplay with Richard Wearing and described the film as 'an unnerving love story, of obsessive and possessive love, and a Polanski-esque adaptation of the female psyche.' The psychological thriller with a $5,000,000 budget, was shot on the Aran Islands in March with interiors at Ardmore Studios. Rob Lowe was originally mentioned as the male lead, then William Defoe, but finally James Spader was cast as a mysterious stranger who arrives on an island and encounters a lonely French woman.

Writer-director Gerry Stembridge made his feature film début with *Guiltrip*, shot on location in Maynooth, County Kildare. Stembridge and his producer Ed Guiney, made the film on a modest budget of £850,000 which they had difficulty in raising because of its subject matter. The Irish-French-Italian co-production told of 'a fatal day in the life of a young Irish couple, with an army corporal applying army life discipline to his quiet wife.' Along with Stembridge, lighting cameraman Eugene O'Conn and film editor Mary Finlay, also made their feature film débuts on *Guiltrip*. In the gritty topical drama Stembridge drew brilliant performances from Andrew Connolly as the corporal and Jasmine Russell as his long suffering wife. They were superbly supported by Michelle Houlden and Peter Hanly. The film won awards at two international film festivals at Amiens in France, for best film, best

actor (Connolly) and best actress (Russell) and at Thessalonika in Greece for best screenplay (Stembridge). The film won widespread critical acclaim and acknowledged Stembridge as a major force in Irish film.

The population of Ballycotton, County Cork, was overjoyed with the news that *Divine Rapture*, a big budget film, starring Marlon Brando, Johnny Depp and Debra Winger was to be shot in their area over the summer months. Before filming commenced the production was involved in controversy when the Bishop of Cloyne, Dr. John Magee, refused permission for any scenes to be shot in the local Catholic church. Undeterred, the film crew, under director Thom Eberhardt, moved into Ballycotton and filming began. When financial backing from America was not forthcoming the producers were forced to halt filming. Following a period of confusion the production was finally wound up.

Another beneficiary of the enormous increase in film-making was Ardmore Studios in Bray. Chief executive, Kevin Moriarty was particularly pleased with the development. Many

Andrew Connolly and Jasmine Russell in *Guiltrip*

Garrett Flynn in *The Old Curiosity Shop*

major television series were based at the studio including *The Family, The Old Curiosity Shop, Scarlett, Kidnapped* and *Jake's Progress*, with elaborate interior and exterior sets being constructed to accommodate them. An adaptation of Daniel Defoe's romantic novel *Moll Flanders*, was based at Ardmore, with location shooting at Dublin Castle, Foster Place, Old Conna,

Some extras in costume for *Scarlett*

Powerscourt and Bantry, County Cork. A brothel sequence was filmed in Iveagh House in Dublin. The $14,500,000 production, written and directed by Pen Denshan, starred Robin Wright, Morgan Freeman, Stockard Channing, Geraldine James, John Lynch, Brenda Fricker and Jim Sheridan. Robin Wright played the title role of Moll Flanders, a woman born into hardship and heartbreak who gets an opportunity to re-invent herself.

Shooting simultaneously in Dublin on a modest budget was *Snakes and Ladders*, written and directed by Trish McAdam. The comedy centred around two street entertainers which starred Pom Boyd, Gina Moxley, Sean Hughes, Rosaleen Linehan and Paudge Behan and the unit also spent a week in Berlin.

Brenda Fricker in a scene from *Moll Flanders*

Joe My Friend, based on a screenplay by David Howard and Declan Hughes was also shot on location in south Dublin. The family film directed by Chris Bould, told of two children each of whom dream of belonging to the other's world. Chris is bored with his family and dreams of the adventure of a travelling circus. In contrast the mysterious Joe wants to be part of a normal family. The story depicted the cruel reality of the adult world in which Joe lives and the pleasant life style of Chris. The film ends with an exciting chase sequence. The film starred John Cleere, Joel Grey, Schuyler Fox and Stanley Townsend. In February 1996, *Joe My Friend* won the Crystal Bear Award for Best Children's Film at the Berlin Film Festival.

The most eagerly awaited film of the year

Liam Neeson in *Michael Collins* filming at The Four Courts, Dublin (Photo A. Flynn)

was Neil Jordan's *Michael Collins*. This was the cumulation of a twelve year quest for writer/director Jordan to bring the life of the Irish statesman to the screen, despite attempts by, amongst others, Michael Cimino and Kevin Costner to film the Collins story. Following the success of *Interview With the Vampire*, Warner Brothers were in a position to support the Collins project. Jordan assembled an impressive cast headed by Liam Neeson as Collins, Julia Roberts as Kitty Kiernan, Alan Rickman as Eamon de Valera, Aidan Quinn as Harry Boland and Stephen Rea as Broy. The film was shot over a fourteen weeks schedule in eighty locations throughout Dublin and County Wicklow as the film makers transformed City Hall, Dublin Castle, Henrietta Street and Gardner Row into the 1916-22 period. At Grangegorman a replica of the GPO and O'Connell Street were constructed in what was the largest set ever built in Ireland. To recruit extras for the large crowd scenes the film makers made an appeal for people who would receive no payment. Thousands turned up for the Collins address in Rathdrum, County Wicklow, the Dev speech in Grangegorman and for the dramatic Bloody Sunday re-enactment in the Carlisle Grounds in Bray. Along with a high calibre cast, Jordan surrounded himself with an award winning team headed by double Oscar-winning lighting cameraman, Chris Menges and Oscar-winning set designer, Josie McAvin.

Shooting on a £2.25 million budget and much lower profile around the north Dublin fishing village of Howth was *Last of the High Kings*. The film based on the novel of the same name by Ferdia McAnna, was directed by David Keating, making his directorial début and co-writing the screenplay with actor Gabriel Byrne. The latter headed the cast with Colm Meaney, Stephen Rea and Catherine O'Hara and the younger team was headed by Jared Leto and Christine Ricci. The film told of an amusing coming-of-age in the summer of 1971, when some young people experienced changing relationships with parents and friends. Frankie who believes he will fail his exams is obsessed by two girls, but his mother is the most powerful person in his life.

Director *Mary McGuckian*

Another indigenous film in production at the same time was *This is the Sea*, taking its title from the Waterboy's song. This was the second feature for director Mary McGuckian, who signed up Gabriel Byrne, Richard Harris and John Lynch for leading roles. Although filmed in Counties Dublin and Wicklow, the story was set in contemporary Northern Ireland. Hazel is a twenty year old, from a Protestant Plymouth Brethren background. Her best friend is Old Man Jacobs. He encourages her parents to allow her out and at the Balmoral Show she meets Malachy, a Catholic. His brother is in the IRA. Her mother's attempts at ending the relationship ends in tragedy.

Also on a five week summer shoot in Dublin was *The Boy from Mercury*, making the feature film writing and directorial début of film editor Martin Duffy. The production, the first Irish made science fiction feature film told of eight year old Harry Cronin, growing up in a Dublin working class suburb in 1960. Harry's father is dead, his mother is worn out and his brothers and sisters have little time for him. He lives in a world of fantasy and believes that he comes from the planet Mercury. He is really only happy when he can escape into the world of Flash Gordon at the local cinema or can signal the flashing lights of the Mercurian spaceship in the sky. When his friend is bullied, Harry seeks the help of the Mercurians. The film

produced by Marina Hughes for Mercurian Productions, featured in the title role nine year old unknown James Hickey from Saggart in West Dublin, and a predominantly Irish crew. Hugh O'Connor played his older brother, veteran British actress Rita Tushingham was cast as his mother and Tom Courtenay also starred.

James Hickey in a scene from *The Boy from Mercury*

British director Stephen Frears returned to north Dublin to direct *The Van*, based on the third book by Roddy Doyle, set in the fictitious Barrystown. In 1991 the book was short listed for the prestigious Booker Prize. The story centred around Bimbo who is made redundant. He goes into partnership with his pal Larry and buys a chipper van, hoping to make a killing during the World Cup. Colm Meaney returned to the familiar role of a Dublin character in his third Doyle film. Comedian Brendan O'Carroll, Ger Ryan and Donal O'Kelly co-starred. House interiors were shot in Ardmore Studios, with location work in Kilbarrack and Dollymount, County Dublin.

By contrast *Space Truckers*, with a budget of $23 million, moved onto extensive sets at Ardmore Studios. The only location scenes were shot on Dollymount Strand in Dublin, doubling for the Mojave Desert, and the civic offices at Wood Quay. Dennis Hopper played John Canyon, an interplanetary long distance haulier who agrees to take a black-market shipment of mysterious sealed containers to Earth. Stephen Dorff, Debi Mazar and Charles Dance played other leading roles. The production was directed by Stuart Gordon, whose previous credits included *Honey, I Shrunk the Kids*. The special effects team, headed by Brian Johnston, who won Oscars for *The Empire Strikes Back* and *Alien*, built a special effects warehouse where they assembled miniature sets for the space flight sequences. When the main shooting was completed the effects team continued for another five months.

In the second half of the year there was an even greater increase in the volume of films in production in Dublin. Terry George, who had received an Oscar nomination for co-writing the screenplay of *In the Name of the Father* with Jim Sheridan, made his directorial début with *Some Mother's Son*. The film was produced by Hell's Kitchen, the production company founded by Jim Sheridan. The story-line dealt with two women with sons on hunger strike in the H Block in 1981. Kathleen Quigley's only son, Gerard, a member of the IRA, is shot and captured by the British Army and charged with the murder of a British soldier. When Gerald goes on hunger strike, Kathleen is forced to find her own way amid

Helen Mirren in a scene from *Some Mother's Son*

complexed powerful political forces. Her well-ordered life turns into a brutal nightmare for her son's life, a life he is willing to sacrifice. The film starred Helen Mirren, David O'Hara and John Lynch. The producers were pleased by the response to their appeal for 'free extras,' for the funeral scene of a hunger striker filmed in Ballybough in Dublin. Other scenes were shot in North Dublin and in a warehouse on the quays. *Sons and Warriors* was the working title of the film during production.

The north Dublin seaside resort of Donabate was the setting for *The Sun, the Moon and the Stars*. This film was another first for an Irish writer-director, with Geraldine Creed at the helm. It starred Angie Dickinson, Jason Donovan, Elaine Cassidy, Gina Moxley and Aisling Corcoran and was produced by Brendan McCarthy for Blue Light Productions. The central character, twelve year old Sheiley, distressed by the break-up of her parents marriage, decides to dabble in a little witchcraft during a summer holiday by the sea. She declares war on the adult world and when a mysterious American woman arrives on the scene and befriends her mother, Sheiley is convinced she is a sea-witch and sets out to destroy her.

Another film with an Irish setting was *Spaghetti Slow*, an Irish-Italian co-production. Simone, a young Italian student comes to Dublin to learn English, his parents hoping the trip will knock some sense into him. He stays with the Fergus family in south Dublin and falls in love with their daughter. The couple set off on a bizarre journey across Ireland, pursued by their fathers. The young couple were played by Niamh O'Byrne and Guilio Di Marco, with Brendan Gleeson co-starring. Director Valerio Jalango co-wrote the screenplay with Barry Devlin and Lucinda Coxon and filmed for six weeks in Ireland and for one in Italy.

In mid-October director Gillies MacKinnon shot the first scenes for *Trojan Eddie* in Pearse Square in Dublin. The film based on a screenplay by Billy Roche, the award winning Wexford writer, had a strong cast headed by Stephen Rea, Richard Harris, Brendan Gleeson, Sean McGinley, Angeline Ball and Gladys Sheehan. Newcomer

Aislin McGuckin played a young traveller. The production had a six weeks schedule in Dublin and Wicklow. Rea played Trojan Eddie, a traveller and small town hustler, who becomes entangled in a web of deceit and betrayal when he crosses into a sub-culture of settled travellers and bare-knuckled fighters. When Eddie's boss (Harris), falls in love with Kathleen, a young and beautiful traveller, there are tragic consequences.

Within days of completing work on *Trojan Eddie*, Stephen Rea was heading the cast in a thriller, *A Further Gesture*, on location in Mountjoy Jail in Dublin. The film, also starring, Maria Doyle Kennedy and Brendan Gleeson, was directed by Robert Dornhelm on a £4,000,000 budget, based on a screenplay by Ronan Bennett. Samson Films co-produced with CSL Films (UK), Road Movies (Germany), Channel Four Films and NDF. Rea played an IRA man who escapes from the Maze Prison and finds a new life in America but becomes involved in an attempted assassination of a colonel responsible for murder and torture in Guatamala. Following three weeks work in Dublin the unit moved to New York for a further five weeks.

The Irish film sector welcomed the news that veteran Hollywood producer/director Roger Corman was to set up a permanent film studio in Connemara. Corman, anxious to establish a European base and to avail of Section 35 tax concessions, chose Tully in County Galway as the venue for his studio to be named Concorde Anois.

Richard Harris in *This is the Sea*

Corman who had made his reputation producing a series of horror films including *The Pit and the Pendulum* and *The Raven*, planned to produce at least six films a year in Ireland. Even before the studio was constructed, two films went into production in quick succession - *Bloodfist VIII: Trained for Action* and *Spectre*. The former was the eighth in the martial arts Bloodfist films starring American kick-boxing champion Don Wilson.

John Clarke and Schuyler Fox in *Joe My Friend*

Stephen Rea in a scene from *A Further Gesture*

A scene from *This is the Sea* directed by Mary McGuckian

Robin Wright in the title role of *Moll Flanders*

Albert Finney and Matt Keeslar in a scene from *The Run of the Country*

Filmography

Film **The Lad from Old Ireland** (1910)
Director Sidney Olcott
Cast Gene Gauntier, Robert Vignola

Film **Rory O'Moore** (1911)
Director Sidney Olcott
Cast Gene Gauntier, Jack P. McGowan

Film **The Colleen Bawn** (1912)
Director Sidney Olcott
Cast Brian MacGowan, Sidney Olcott

Film **Arragh-na-Pogue** (1912)
Director Sidney Olcott
Cast Jack P. McGowan, Robert Vignola

Film **The O'Neill** (1912)
Director Sidney Olcott
Cast Pat O'Malley, Gene Gauntier

Film **The Shaughran** (1912)
Director Sidney Olcott
Cast Gene Gauntier, Jack Clarke

Film **You'll Remember Ellen** (1912)
Director Sidney Olcott
Cast Gene Gauntier, Jack Clarke

Film **Shane The Post** (1913)
Director Sidney Olcott
Cast Jack Clarke, Pat O'Malley

Film **The Kerry Gow** (1913)
Director Sidney Olcott
Cast Gene Gauntier, Jack P. McGowan

Film **Ireland The Oppressed** (1913)
Director Sidney Olcott
Cast Robert Vignola, Jack Clarke

Film **The Kerry Dancer** (1913)
Director Sidney Olcott
Cast Gene Gauntier, Jack Clarke

Film **A Girl of Glenbeigh** (1914)
Director Sidney Olcott
Cast Gene Gauntier, Jack Clarke

Film **The Fishermaid of Ballydavid** (1914)
Director Sidney Olcott
Cast Gene Gauntier, Robert Vignola

Film **The Gypsies of Old Ireland** (1914)
Director Sidney Olcott
Cast Annie O'Sullivan, Valentine Grant

Film **Ireland A Nation** (1914)
Director Walter MacNamara
Cast Barry O'Brien

Film **Robert Emmet** (1914)
Director Sidney Olcott
Cast Jack Melville, Pat O'Malley

Film	**Bunny Blarneyed** (1914)		Film	**The Irish Girl** (1917)
Director	Larry Trimble		Director	J.M. Kerrigan
Cast	Johnny Bunny		Cast	Kathleen Murphy

Film **Bunny Blarneyed** (1914)
Director Larry Trimble
Cast Johnny Bunny

Film **Fun at Finglas Fair** (1915)
Director F.J. McCormick
Cast F.J. McCormick

Film **Puck Fair Romance** (1916)
Director J.M. Kerrigan
Cast J.M. Kerrigan, Kathleen Murphy

Film **Molly Bawn** (1916)
Director Cecil M. Hepworth
Cast Alma Taylor, Stewart Rome

Film **O'Neill of the Glen** (1916)
Director J.M. Kerrigan
Cast J.M. Kerrigan, Nora Clancy, Fred O'Donovan

Film **The Miser's Gift** (1916)
Director J.M. Kerrigan
Cast J.M. Kerrigan, Kathleen Murphy, Fred O'Donovan

Film **An Unfair Love Affair** (1916)
Director J.M. Kerrigan
Cast Nora Clancy, Fred O'Donovan

Film **Widow Malone** (1916)
Director J.M. Kerrigan
Cast J.M. Kerrigan

Film **Food of Love** (1916)
Director J.M. Kerrigan
Cast Kathleen Murphy, Fred O'Donovan

Film **Woman's Wit** (1916)
Director J.M. Kerrigan
Cast Kathleen Murphy, Fred O'Donovan

Film **The Eleventh Hour** (1917)
Director Fred O'Donovan
Cast Brian MacGowan, Kathleen Murphy

Film **The Upstart** (1917)
Director J.M. Kerrigan
Cast Kathleen Murphy, Fred O'Donovan

Film **Blarney** (1917)
Director J.M. Kerrigan
Cast Kathleen Murphy, J.M. Kerrigan

Film **The Byeways of Fate** (1917)
Director J.M. Kerrigan
Cast Nora Clancy

Film **The Irish Girl** (1917)
Director J.M. Kerrigan
Cast Kathleen Murphy

Film **In the Days of Saint Patrick** (1917)
Director Norman Whitton
Cast Ira Allen, Alice Cardinall, George Griffin

Film **Knocknagow** (1916)
Director John McDonagh
Cast Brian McGowan, J. McCarra, Alice Keating

Film **Rafferty's Rise** (1918)
Director J.M. Kerrigan
Cast Fred O'Donovan, Kathleen Murphy, Arthur Shields

Film **When Love Came to Gavin Burke** (1918)
Director Fred O'Donovan
Cast Brian Moore, Kathleen Murphy

Film **Willie Scouts While Jessie Pouts** (1918)
Director William Power
Cast William Power

Film **Rosaleen Dhu** (1919)
Director William Power
Cast William Power, Kitty Hart

Film **An Irish Vendetta** (1920)
Director William Power
Cast William Power, Kitty Hart

Film **Willie Reilly and the Colleen Bawn** (1919)
Director John McDonagh
Cast Brian McGowan, Kathleen Alexander

Film **The Life of Michael Dwyer** (1919)
Director John McDonagh
Cast F.J. McCormick

Film **The O'Casey Millions** (1922)
Director John McDonagh
Cast Jimmy O'Dea, Nan Fitzgerald, Fred Jeffs

Film **Wicklow Gold** (1922)
Director John McDonagh
Cast Jimmy O'Dea

Film **Paying the Rent** (1922)
Director John McDonagh
Cast Jimmy O'Dea

Film **Land of her Fathers** (1924)
Director John Hurley
Cast Mícheál MacLiammóir, Phyllis Wakeley

Film	**Cruiskeen Lawn** (1924)		Film	**Wings of The Morning** (1936)
Director	John McDonagh		Director	Harold Schuster
Cast	Tom Moran, Jimmy O'Dea, Fay Sargent		Cast	Annnbella, Henry Fonda, John McCormack

Film — **Cruiskeen Lawn** (1924)
Director — John McDonagh
Cast — Tom Moran, Jimmy O'Dea, Fay Sargent

Film — **Irish Destiny** (1925)
Director — I.J. Eppel
Cast — Dennis O'Dea, Una Shields, Daisy Campbell

Film — **Ireland's Rough-Hewn Destiny** (1929)
Director — Victor Haddick
Cast — Gearóid O'Lochlinn

Film — **Song of my Heart** (1930)
Director — Frank Borzage
Cast — John McCormack, Maureen O'Sullivan

Film — **Some May Change** (1933)
Director — Michael Farrell
Cast — Sheila Fay

Film — **Sweet Inniscarra** (1934)
Director — Emmet Moore
Cast — Sean Rogers, Mae Ryan

Film — **Guests of the Nation** (1934)
Director — Denis Johnson
Cast — Barry Fitzgerald, Shelagh Richards, Hilton Edwards

Film — **General John Regan** (1934)
Director — Henry Edwards
Cast — Henry Edwards, Chrissie White, W.G. Fay

Film — **Jimmy Boy** (1934)
Director — John Baxter
Cast — Jimmy O'Dea, Guy Middleton, Vera Sherburne

Film — **Irish Hearts** (1934)
Director — Brian Desmond Hurst
Cast — Lester Matthews, Nancy Burne, Sara Allgood

Film — **Riders to the Sea** (1935)
Director — Brian Desmond Hurst
Cast — Sara Allgood, Kevin Gutherie, Ria Mooney

Film — **The Luck of the Irish** (1935)
Director — Donovan Pedelty
Cast — Richard Hayward, Kay Walsh, Niall McGinnis

Film — **Irish for Luck** (1936)
Director — Arthur Woods
Cast — Athene Seyler, Margaret Lockwood

Film — **The Voice of Ireland** (1936)
Director — Victor Haddick
Cast — Richard Hayward, Victor Haddick, Barney O'Hara

Film — **Wings of The Morning** (1936)
Director — Harold Schuster
Cast — Annnbella, Henry Fonda, John McCormack

Film — **Irish and Proud of it** (1936)
Director — Donovan Pedelty
Cast — Richard Hayward, Dinah Sheridan, Liam Gaffney

Film — **The Early Bird** (1936)
Director — Donovan Pedelty
Cast — Richard Hayward, Jimmy McGeean

Film — **Man of Aran** (1936)
Director — Robert Flaherty
Cast — Tiger King, Maggie Dirrane, Aran Islanders

Film — **The Dawn** (1937)
Director — Tom Cooper
Cast — Tom Cooper, Eileen Davis, Brian O'Sullivan

Film — **Uncle Nick** (1938)
Director — Tom Cooper
Cast — Val Vousden

Film — **Blarney** (1938)
Director — Harry O'Donovan
Cast — Jimmy O'Dea, Myrette Morven

Film — **West of Kerry** (1938)
Director — Dick Bird
Cast — Eileen Curran, Cecil Ford

Film — **The Islandman** (1938)
Director — Patrick Heale
Cast — Gabriel Fallon, Brian O'Sullivan

Film — **Devil's Rock** (1938)
Director — Germaine Burger
Cast — Richard Hayward, Geraldine Mitchell

Film — **Henry V** (1943)
Director — Laurence Olivier
Cast — Laurence Olivier, Robert Newton, Leslie Banks

Film — **Hungry Hill** (1946)
Director — Brian Desmond Hurst
Cast — Margaret Lockwood, Dennis Price, F.J. McCormick

Film — **Captain Boycott** (1946)
Director — Frank Launder
Cast — Stewart Granger, Cecil Parker, Kathleen Ryan

Film — **Crime on the Irish Border** (1946)
Director — Maurice J. Wilson
Cast — Kieron Moore, Barbara White

Film	**Odd Man Out** (1946)		Film	**The Quiet Man** (1952)
Director	Carol Reed		Director	John Ford
Cast	James Mason, Kathleen Ryan, Robert Newton		Cast	John Wayne, Maureen O'Hara, Barry Fitzgerald

Film | **Odd Man Out** (1946)
Director | Carol Reed
Cast | James Mason, Kathleen Ryan, Robert Newton

Film | **The Courtneys of Curzon Street** (1947)
Director | Herbert Wilcock
Cast | Anna Neagle, Michael Wilding

Film | **Black Narcissus** (1946)
Director | Michael Powell, Emeric Pressburger
Cast | Deborah Kerr, Sabu, David Farrar

Film | **I See a Dark Stranger** (1946)
Director | Frank Launder
Cast | Deborah Kerr, Trevor Howard

Film | **Another Shore** (1948)
Director | Charles Crichton
Cast | Robert Beatty, Moira Lister, Stanley Holloway

Film | **My Hands are Clay** (1948)
Director | Patrick McCrossan
Cast | Shelagh Richards, Bernadette Leahy, Cecil Brook

Film | **The Greedy Boy** (1948)
Director | Richard Massingham
Cast | Joyce Sullivan, Jim Phelan

Film | **Transatlantic Flight** (1948)
Director | Joseph Ryle
Cast | Gene Kelly, Betsy Blair

Film | **At A Dublin Inn** (1949)
Director | Desmond Leslie
Cast | Valentine Dyall, Joseph O'Connor

Film | **No Resting Place** (1950)
Director | Paul Rotha
Cast | Michael Gough, Eithne Dunne, Noel Purcell

Film | **The Strangers Came** (1950)
Director | Alfred Travers
Cast | Seamus MacLocha, Gabriel Fallon

Film | **Jack of All Maids** (1951)
Director | Tomas MacAnna
Cast | Jack McGowran

Film | **The Promise of Barty O'Brien** (1951)
Director | George Freedland
Cast | Eric Doyle, Eileen Crowe, Harry Brogan

Film | **The Gentle Gunman** (1952)
Director | Basil Dearden
Cast | John Mills, Dirk Bogarde, Gilbert Harding

Film | **The Quiet Man** (1952)
Director | John Ford
Cast | John Wayne, Maureen O'Hara, Barry Fitzgerald

Film | **Knights of the Round Table** (1953)
Director | Richard Thorpe
Cast | Robert Taylor, Ava Gardner, Mel Ferrer

Film | **Captain Lightfoot** (1954)
Director | Douglas Sirk
Cast | Rock Hudson, Barbara Rush, Jeff Morrow

Film | **Jacqueline** (1955)
Director | Roy Baker
Cast | John Gregson, Kathleen Ryan, Jacqueline Ryan

Film | **Moby Dick** (1955)
Director | John Huston
Cast | Gregory Peck, Orson Welles, Richard Basehart

Film | **The March Hare** (1956)
Director | George More O'Farrell
Cast | Terence Morgan, Peggy Cummins, Cyril Cusack

Film | **Rising of the Moon** (1956)
Director | John Ford
Cast | Jimmy O'Dea, Noel Purcell, Cyril Cusack

Film | **Boyd's Shop** (1957)
Director | Henry Cass
Cast | Geoffrey Golden, Eileen Crowe

Film | **Professor Tim** (1957)
Director | Henry Cass
Cast | Ray McAnally, Márie O'Donnell

Film | **Rooney** (1957)
Director | George Pollock
Cast | John Gregson, Murial Pavlow, Barry Fitzgerald

Film | **Dublin Nightmare** (1958)
Director | John Pomeroy
Cast | William Sylvester, Marie Landi, Richard Leech

Film | **Home is the Hero** (1958)
Director | Fielder Cooke
Cast | Arthur Kennedy, Máire O'Donnell, Walter Macken

Film | **Sally's Irish Rogue** (1958)
Director | George Pollock
Cast | Julie Harris, Tim Sheely, Harry Brogan

Film | **The Big Birthday** (1958)
Director | George Pollock
Cast | Barry Fitzgerald, Tony Wright, June Thorburn

Film **Shake Hands with the Devil** (1958)
Director Michael Anderson
Cast James Cagney, Don Murray, Dana Wynter

Film **This Other Eden** (1959)
Director Murial Box
Cast Leslie Phillips, Audrey Dalton, Norman Roadway

Film **A Terrible Beauty** (1960)
Director Tay Garnett
Cast Robert Mitchum, Anne Heywood,
Dan O'Herlihy

Film **Gorgo** (1960)
Director Eugene Lourie
Cast Bill Travers, William Sylvester, Barry Keegan

Film **Fr. Brown** (1960)
Director Helmut Ashley
Cast Heinz Ruhmann

Film **The Siege of Sidney Street** (1960)
Director Roy Baker, Monty Berman
Cast Donald Sinden, Nicole Berger, Kieron Moore

Film **Ambush in Leopard Street** (1960)
Director J.H. Piperno
Cast James Kenny, Michael Brennan, Bruce Seton

Film **Johnny Nobody** (1960)
Director Nigel Patrick
Cast Nigel Patrick, William Bendix, Aldo Ray

Film **The Big Gamble** (1960)
Director Richard Fleischer
Cast Stephen Boyd, Juliette Greco, David Wayne

Film **Sword of Sherwood Forest** (1960)
Director Terence Fisher
Cast Richard Greene, Peter Cushing, Nigel Greene

Film **Middle of Nowhere** (1960)
Director Don Chaffy
Cast John Cassavetes, Elizabeth Sellars, David Farrar

Film **Lies My Father Told Me** (1960)
Director Don Chaffy
Cast Betsy Blair, Harry Brogan

Film **The Mark** (1961)
Director Guy Greene
Cast Stuart Whitman, Rod Steiger, Maria Schell

Film **Murder in Eden** (1961)
Director Max Varnell
Cast Ray McAnally, Norman Rodway

Film **A Question of Suspence** (1961)
Director Max Varnell
Cast Peter Reynolds

Film **Enter Inspector Duval** (1961)
Director Max Varnell
Cast Anton Diffring

Film **Freedom to Die** (1961)
Director Frances Searle
Cast James Maxwell, T.P. McKenna

Film **Stork Talk** (1961)
Director Michael Furlong
Cast Tony Britton, Anne Heywood

Film **Term of Trial** (1961)
Director Peter Grenville
Cast Laurence Olivier, Simone Signoret, Sarah Miles

Film **The List of Adrian Messenger** (1962)
Director John Huston
Cast George C. Scott, Dana Wynter, Kirk Douglas

Film **The Quare Fellow** (1962)
Director Arthur Dreyfuss
Cast Patrick McGoohan, Walter Macken, Sylvia Syms

Film **The Very Edge** (1962)
Director Cyril Frankel
Cast Richard Todd, Anne Heywood, Jack Hedley

Film **The Running Man** (1962)
Director Carol Reed
Cast Laurence Harvey, Lee Remick, Alan Bates

Film **Dead Man's Evidence** (1962)
Director Frances Searle
Cast Conrad Phillips, Jane Griffith

Film **A Guy Called Caesar** (1962)
Director Frank Marshall
Cast Conrad Phillips, George Moon

Film **The Playboy of the Western World** (1962)
Director Brian Desmond Hurst
Cast Siobhan McKenna, Gary Raymond,
Liam Redmond

Film **The Devil's Agent** (1963)
Director John Paddy Carstairs
Cast McDonald Carey, Peter Van Eyck,
Christopher Lee

Film **Dementia 13** (1963)
Director Francis Ford Coppola
Cast Patrick Magee, Eithne Dunne, William Campbell

Film **Of Human Bondage** (1963)
Director Ken Hughes, Henry Hathaway
Cast Laurence Harvey, Kim Novak, Robert Morley

Film **I Thank A Fool** (1963)
Director Robert Stevens
Cast Peter Finch, Susan Hayward, Diane Cilento

Film **Never Put It in Writing** (1963)
Director Andrew Stone
Cast Pat Boone, Milo O'Shea, Fidelma Murphy

Film **Girl With Green Eyes** (1963)
Director Desmond Davis
Cast Peter Finch, Rita Tushingham, Lynn Redgrave

Film **Ballad in Blue** (1964)
Director Paul Henreid
Cast Ray Charles, Mary Peach, Tom Bell

Film **The Spy Who Came in from the Cold** (1964)
Director Martin Ritt
Cast Richard Burton, Claire Bloom, Oscar Werner

Film **Finnegan's Wake** (1964)
Director Mary Ellen Bute
Cast Martin J. Kelly, Jane Reilly

Film **Face of Fu Manchu** (1965)
Director Don Sharp
Cast Christopher Lee, Tsai Chin, Nigel Green

Film **Sherlock Holmes and the Deadly Necklace** (1964)
Director Terence Fisher
Cast Christopher Lee, Senta Berger, Thorley Walters

Film **Ten Little Indians** (1964)
Director George Pollock
Cast Hugh O'Brian, Shirley Eaton, Stanley Holloway

Film **Young Cassidy** (1965)
Director Jack Cardiff
Cast Rod Taylor, Julie Christie, Maggie Smith

Film **The Blue Max** (1965)
Director John Guillermin
Cast George Peppard, James Mason, Ursula Andrews

Film **I Was Happy Here** (1965)
Director Desmond Davis
Cast Sarah Miles, Cyril Cusack, Julian Glover

Film **Rocket to the Moon** (1966)
Director Don Sharp
Cast Burl Ives, Troy Donoghue, Gert Frobe

Film **Robbery** (1966)
Director Peter Yates
Cast Stanley Baker, Joanne Pettet, James Booth

Film **The Viking Queen** (1966)
Director Don Chaffy
Cast Don Murray, Carita, Andrew Keir

Film **Casino Royale** (1966)
Director John Huston, Val Guest, Ken Hughes, Joseph McGrath
Cast David Nevin, Deborah Kerr, Peter Sellers

Film **Ulysses** (1966)
Director Joseph Strick
Cast Milo O'Shea, Barbara Jefford, T.P. McKenna

Film **Sinful Davey** (1967)
Director John Huston
Cast John Hurt, Pamela Franklin, Nigel Davenport

Film **30 is a Dangerous Age, Cynthia** (1967)
Director Joseph McGrath
Cast Dudley Moore, Suzy Kendall, Patricia Routledge

Film **The Lion in Winter** (1968)
Director Anthony Harvey
Cast Peter O'Toole, Katherine Hepburn, Jane Merrow

Film **Lock Up Your Daughters** (1968)
Director Peter Coe
Cast Christopher Plummer, Susannah York, Glynis Johns

Film **Guns in the Heather** (1968)
Director Robert Butler
Cast Glenn Corbett, Kurt Russell, Alfred Burke

Film **Darling Lili** (1968)
Director Blake Edwards
Cast Julie Andrews, Rock Hudson, Jeremy Kemp

Film **The Prince and the Pauper** (1968)
Director Elliott Geisinger
Cast Cast of unknown

Film **Where's Jack?** (1968)
Director Jack Clavell
Cast Stanley Baker, Tommy Steele, Fiona Lewis

Film **The Italian Job** (1968)
Director Peter Collinson
Cast Michael Caine, Noel Coward

Film **Alfred the Great** (1968)
Director Clive Donner
Cast David Hemmings, Michael York, Prunella Ransome

Film	**The Violent Enemy** (1968)		Film	**Zeppelin** (1970)
Director	Don Sharp		Director	Etienne Perier
Cast	Tom Bell, Susan Hampshire, Ed Begley		Cast	Michael York, Elke Sommer, Anton Diffring

Film **The Violent Enemy** (1968)
Director Don Sharp
Cast Tom Bell, Susan Hampshire, Ed Begley

Film **Wedding Night** (1969)
Director Piers Haggard
Cast Dennis Waterman, Tessa Wyatt, Eddie Byrne

Film **The Girl with the Paleface** (1969)
Director Paul Gallico Jr.
Cast Fidelma Murphy, Donal McCann, Lee Dunne

Film **McKenzie Break** (1969)
Director Lamont Johnson
Cast Brian Keith, Ian Hendry, Helmut Griem

Film **Underground** (1969)
Director Arthur Nadel
Cast Robert Goulet, Daniele Gaubert

Film **Paddy** (1969)
Director Daniel Haller
Cast Des Cave, Derbhla Molloy, Milo O'Shea

Film **Country Dance** (1969)
Director J. Lee Thompson
Cast Peter O'Toole, Susannah York, Michael Craig

Film **Ryan's Daughter** (1969)
Director David Lean
Cast Robert Mitchum, Sarah Miles, Trevor Howard

Film **Quackser Fortune has a Cousin in the Bronx** (1969)
Director Warris Hussein
Cast Gene Wilder, Margot Kidder, Seamus Forde

Film **Ace Eli and Rodgers of the Skies** (1969)
Director Cliff Robertson
Cast Cliff Robertson, Jack Watson

Film **Philadelphia Here I Come** (1970)
Director John Quested
Cast Donal McCann, Des Cave, Siobhan McKenna

Film **Flight of the Doves** (1970)
Director Ralph Nelson
Cast Ron Moody, Jack Wild, William Ruston

Film **Black Beauty** (1970)
Director James Hill
Cast Mark Lester, Walter Stezack, Patrick Mower

Film **The Red Baron** (1970)
Director Roger Corman
Cast John Phillip Law, Don Stroud, Tom Adams

Film **Zeppelin** (1970)
Director Etienne Perier
Cast Michael York, Elke Sommer, Anton Diffring

Film **Act Without Words** (1971) (Unfinished)
Director Tom Blevins
Cast Rod Steiger

Film **Sitting Target** (1971)
Director Douglas Hickox
Cast Oliver Reed, Ian McShane, Jill St. John

Film **Images** (1971)
Director Robert Altman
Cast Susannah York, Rene Auberjonois, Hugh Millais

Film **A Fistful of Dynamite** (1971)
Director Sergio Leone
Cast Rod Steiger, James Coburn

Film **The Hebrew Lesson** (1972)
Director Wolf Mankowitz
Cast Milo O'Shea, Patrick Dawson, Alun Owen

Film **And No One Could Save Her** (1972)
Director Kevin Billington
Cast Lee Remick, Milo O'Shea, Frank Grimes

Film **A War of Children** (1972)
Director George Schaffer
Cast Jenny Aguter, Vivien Merchant, Aideen O'Kelly

Film **Catholics** (1973)
Director Jack Gold
Cast Trevor Howard, Cyril Cusack

Film **The Mackintosh Man** (1973)
Director John Huston
Cast Paul Newman, James Mason, Dominque Sanda

Film **Zardoz** (1973)
Director John Boorman
Cast Sean Connery, Charlotte Rampling,
        John Alderton

Film **A Quiet Day in Belfast** (1973)
Director Milad Basada
Cast Barry Foster, Margot Kidder

Film **Horowitz of Dublin Castle** (1974)
Director William Kronick
Cast Harvey Lembeck, Cyril Cusack, Sinead Cusack

Film **Barry Lyndon** (1974)
Director Stanley Kubrick
Cast Ryan O'Neal, Marisa Berenson

Film	**The Next Man** (1975)		Film	**North Sea Hijack** (1979)
Director	Richard Sarafin		Director	Andrew V. McLaglen
Cast	Sean Connery, Cornelia Sharpe		Cast	Roger Moore, James Mason, Anthony Perkins

Film **The Next Man** (1975)
Director Richard Sarafin
Cast Sean Connery, Cornelia Sharpe

Film **Victor Frankenstein** (1975)
Director Calvin Floyd
Cast Per Oscarsson, Leon Vitali, Stacy Dorning

Film **Portrait of the Artist as a Young Man** (1975)
Director Joseph Strick
Cast Bosco Hogan, T.P. McKenna, John Gielgud

Film **The Last Remake of Beau Geste** (1976)
Director Marty Feldman
Cast Marty Feldman, Ann Margaret, Michael York

Film **The Purple Taxi** (1976)
Director Yves Boisset
Cast Peter Ustinov, Fred Astaire, Charlotte Rampling

Film **The Inn of the Flying Dragon** (1977)
Director Calvin Floyd
Cast Curt Jurgens, Niall Tóibín

Film **Down the Corner** (1977)
Director Joe Comerford
Cast Joe Keenan, Declan Cronin, Kevin Doyle

Film **The First Great Train Robbery** (1978)
Director Michael Crichton
Cast Sean Connery, Lesley Anne Down,
Donald Sutherland

Film **The Outside** (1978)
Director Tony Luraschi
Cast Craig Wasson, Patricia Quinn, Sterling Hayden

Film **Cry of the Innocent** (1978)
Director Michael O'Herlihy
Cast Rod Taylor, Cyril Cusack

Film **Exposure** (1978)
Director Kieran Hickey
Cast Catherine Schell, T.P. McKenna, Bosco Hogan

Film **The Big Red One** (1978)
Director Samuel Fuller
Cast Lee Marvin, Mark Hamill

Film **Poitín** (1978)
Director Bob Quinn
Cast Cyril Cusack. Niall Tóibín, Donal McCann

Film **McVicar** (1978)
Director Tom Clegg
Cast Roger Daltry, Adam Faith

Film **North Sea Hijack** (1979)
Director Andrew V. McLaglen
Cast Roger Moore, James Mason, Anthony Perkins

Film **The Flame is Love** (1979)
Director Michael O'Herlihy
Cast Linda Purl, Timothy Dalton

Film **Tristan and Isolt** (1979)
Director Tom Donovan
Cast Richard Burton, Kate Mulgrew, Nicholas Clay

Film **The Hard Way** (1979)
Director Michael Dryhurst
Cast Patrick McGoohan, Lee Van Cleef, Edna O'Brien

Film **Excalibur** (1980)
Director John Boorman
Cast Nicol Williamson, Nigel Terry, Helen Mirren

Film **Inchon** (1980)
Director Terence Young
Cast Laurence Olivier, Jacqueline Bisset

Film **It's Handy When People Don't Die** (1980)
Director Tom McArdle
Cast Garret Keogh, Bob Carisle, Brendan Cauldwell

Film **Light Years Away** (1980)
Director Alain Tanner
Cast Trevor Howard, Mick Ford

Film **Wagner** (1981)
Director Tony Palmer
Cast Richard Burton, Vanessa Redgrave,
Gemma Craven

Film **Fire and Sword** (1981)
Director Keith Von Fuerstenberg
Cast Peter Firth, Leigh Lawson

Film **Angel** (1981)
Director Neil Jordan
Cast Stephen Rea, Honor Heffernan, Ray McAnally

Film **Educating Rita** (1982)
Director Lewis Gilbert
Cast Michael Caine, Julie Walters

Film **The Outcasts** (1982)
Director Robert Wynn Simmons
Cast Cyril Cusack, Mary Ryan, Mick Lally

Film **Attracta** (1982)
Director Kieran Hickey
Cast Wendy Hiller, Kate Thompson

Film **State of Wonder** (1983)
Director Martin Donovan
Cast Anne Chaplin, Martin Donovan

Film **Pigs** (1983)
Director Cathal Black
Cast James Brennan, George Shane,
Maurice O'Donoghue

Film **Anne Devlin** (1983)
Director Pat Murphy
Cast Brid Brennan, Bosco Hogan

Film **The Country Girls** (1983)
Director Desmond Davis
Cast Sam Neill, Maeve Germaine, Niall Tóibín

Film **Cal** (1983)
Director Pat O'Connor
Cast Helen Mirren, John Lynch, Ray McAnally

Film **Eat the Peach** (1985)
Director Peter Ormrod
Cast Stephen Brennan, Eamonn Morrissey,
Catherine Byrne

Film **The Fantasist** (1985)
Director Robin Hardy
Cast Timothy Bottoms, Moira Harris, John Kavanagh

Film **Rawhead X** (1986)
Director George Pavlov
Cast David Dukes, Kelly Piper, Niall Tóibín

Film **Budawanny** (1986)
Director Bob Quinn
Cast Donal McCann, Margaret Fegan

Film **The Dead** (1987)
Director John Huston
Cast Anjelica Huston, Donal McCann,
Dan O'Herlihy

Film **The Courier** (1987)
Director Joe Lee, Frank Deasy
Cast Gabriel Byrne, Padraig O'Loingsigh,
Cait O'Riordain

Film **Reefer and the Model** (1987)
Director Joe Comerford
Cast Ian McElhinney, Carole Scanlan, Ray McBride

Film **The Lonely Passion of Judith Hearne** (1987)
Director Jack Clayton
Cast Bob Hoskins, Maggie Smith, Marie Kean

Film **Taffin** (1987)
Director Francis Megahy
Cast Pierce Brosnan, Alison Doody, Ray McAnally

Film **Da** (1987)
Director Matt Clark
Cast Martin Sheen, Barnard Hughes,
Doreen Hepburn

Film **The Dawning** (1987)
Director Robert Knights
Cast Anthony Hopkins, Jean Simmons,
Trevor Howard

Film **Now I Know** (1987)
Director Robert Pappas
Cast Matthew Modine, Maeve Germaine

Film **High Spirits** (1987)
Director Neil Jordan
Cast Peter O'Toole, Daryl Hannah, Steve Guttenberg

Film **Joyriders** (1988)
Director Aisling Walsh
Cast Andrew Connolly, Patricia Kerrigan,
Billie Whitelaw

Film **My Left Foot** (1988)
Director Jim Sheridan
Cast Daniel Day-Lewis, Brenda Fricker, Ray McAnally

Film **Fragments of Isabella** (1989)
Director Ronan O'Leary
Cast Gabrielle Reidy

Film **Hidden Agenda** (1989)
Director Ken Loach
Cast Brad Dourif, Brian Cox, Frances McDormand

Film **Fools of Fortune** (1989)
Director Pat O'Connor
Cast Julie Christie, Mary Elizabeth Mastrantonio,
Ian Glen

Film **Hush-A-Bye-Baby** (1989)
Director Margo Harkin
Cast Emer McCourt, Sinead O'Connor

Film **December Bride** (1989)
Director Thaddeus O'Sullivan
Cast Donal McCann, Saskia Reeves, Ciaran Hinds

Film **The Field** (1989)
Director Jim Sheridan
Cast Richard Harris, John Hurt, Tom Berenger

Film   **The Miracle** (1990)
Director   Neil Jordan
Cast   Beverly D'Angelo, Donal McCann, Niall Byrne

Film   **The Committments** (1990)
Director   Alan Parker
Cast   Andrew Strong, Angeline Ball, Johnny Murphy

Film   **Hear My Song** (1990)
Director   Peter Chelsom
Cast   Ned Beatty, Shirley Ann Field, Adrian Duncan

Film   **The Railway Station Man** (1991)
Director   Michael Whyte
Cast   Donald Sutherland, Julie Christie, John Lynch

Film   **Far and Away** (1991)
Director   Ron Howard
Cast   Tom Cruise, Nicole Kidman, Colm Meaney

Film   **Into the West** (1991)
Director   Mike Newell
Cast   Gabriel Byrne, Ellen Barkin, Ciarán Fitzgerald

Film   **The Playboys** (1991)
Director   Gillies MacKinnon
Cast   Albert Finney, Aidan Quinn, Robin Wright

Film   **The Crying Game** (1992)
Director   Neil Jordan
Cast   Stephen Rea, Adrian Dunbar, Jaye Davidson

Film   **High Boot Benny** (1992)
Director   Joe Comerford
Cast   Mark O'Shea, Frances Tomelty, Alan Devlin

Film   **The Bishop's Story** (1992)
Director   Bob Quinn
Cast   Donal McCann, Margaret Fegan

Film   **The Snapper** (1992)
Director   Stephen Frears
Cast   Colm Meaney, Tina Kelleher, Ruth McCabe

Film   **In the Name of the Father** (1993)
Director   Jim Sheridan
Cast   Daniel Day-Lewis, Emma Thompson,
              Pete Postlethwaite

Film   **Broken Harvest** (1993)
Director   Maurice O'Callaghan
Cast   Colin Lane, Niall O'Brien, Marion Quinn

Film   **Widow's Peak** (1993)
Director   John Irvine
Cast   Mia Farrow, John Plowright,
              Natasha Richardson

Film   **All Things Bright and Beautiful** (1993)
Director   Barry Devlin
Cast   Gabriel Byrne, Tom Wilkinson, Ciarán Fitzgerald

Film   **War of the Buttons** (1993)
Director   John Roberts
Cast   Colm Meaney, Johnny Murphy, John Coffey

Film   **Moondance** (1993)
Director   Dagmar Hirtz
Cast   Ruaidhrí Conroy, Julia Brendler, Ian Shaw

Film   **The Secret of Roan Inish** (1993)
Director   John Sayle
Cast   Mick Lally, Eileen Colgan, Jeni Courtney

Film   **Aisla** (1993)
Director   Paddy Breathnach
Cast   Brendan Coyle, Andrea Irvine, Juliette Gruber

Film   **An Awfully Big Adventure** (1994)
Director   Mike Newell
Cast   Alan Rickman, Hugh Grant, Peter Firth

Film   **Braveheart** (1994)
Director   Mel Gibson
Cast   Mel Gibson, Sophie Marceau,
              Patrick McGoohan

Film   **Words Upon the Window Pane** (1994)
Director   Mary McGuckian
Cast   Geraldine Chaplin, Geraldine James,
              Donal Donnelly

Film   **Frankie Starlight** (1994)
Director   Michael Lindsay-Hogg
Cast   Ann Parillaud, Matt Dillon, Gabriel Byrne

Film   **A Man of No Importance** (1994)
Director   Suri Krishnama
Cast   Albert Finney, Brenda Fricker, Tara Fitzgerald

Film   **The Run of the Country** (1994)
Director   Peter Yates
Cast   Albert Finney, Matt Keeslar, Victoria Smurfit

Film   **Circle of Friends** (1994)
Director   Pat O'Connor
Cast   Chris O'Donnell, Minnie Driver,
              Gerladine O'Rawe

Film   **Korea** (1994)
Director   Cathal Black
Cast   Donal Donnelly, Andrew Scott, Fiona Molony

Film   **Undercurrent** (1994)
Director   Brian O'Flaherty
Cast   Owen Roe, Stanley Townsend, Tina Kelleher

Film	**Nothing Personal** (1995)	
Director	Thaddeus O'Sullivan	
Cast	Ian Hart, John Lynch, Michael Gambon	

Film	**The Disappearance of Finbar** (1995)
Director	Sue Clayton
Cast	Jonathan Rhys-Myers, Luke Griffin, Fanny Risberg

Film	**Driftwood** (1995)
Director	Ronan O'Leary
Cast	James Spader, Anne Brochet, Barry McGovern

Film	**Guiltrip** (1995)
Director	Gerry Stembridge
Cast	Andrew Connolly, Jasmine Russell, Michelle Houlden

Film	**Moll Flanders** (1995)
Director	Pen Densham
Cast	Robin Wright, Morgan Freeman, Stockard Channing

Film	**Michael Collins** (1995)
Director	Neil Jordan
Cast	Liam Neeson, Julia Roberts, Alan Rickman

Film	**The Last of the High Kings** (1995)
Director	David Keating
Cast	Gabriel Byrne, Colm Meaney, Christine Ricci

Film	**This is the Sea** (1995)
Director	Mary McGuckian
Cast	Gabriel Byrne, Richard Harris, John Lynch

Film	**Joe My Friend** (1995)
Director	Chris Bould
Cast	John Cleere, Joel Grey, Schuyler Fox

Film	**The Boy from Mercury** (1995)
Director	Martin Duffy
Cast	Tom Courtenay, Rita Tushingham, James Hickey

Film	**The Van** (1995)
Director	Stephen Frears
Cast	Colm Meaney, Donal O'Kelly, Brendan O'Carroll

Film	**Space Truckers** (1995)
Director	Stuart Gordon
Cast	Dennis Hopper, Stephen Dorff, Debi Mazar

Film	**Some Mother's Son** (1995)
Director	Terry George
Cast	Helen Mirren, John Lynch, Fionnula Flanagan

Film	**The Sun, The Moon and The Stars** (1995)
Director	Geraldine Creed
Cast	Angie Dickinson, Jason Donovan, Elaine Cassidy

Film	**Spaghetti Slow** (1995)
Director	Valerie Jalango
Cast	Niamh O'Byrne, Guilio Di Marco, Brendan Gleeson

Film	**Trojan Eddie** (1995)
Director	Gillies MacKinnon
Cast	Stephen Rea, Richard Harris, Angeline Ball

Film	**A Further Gesture** (1995)
Director	Robert Dornhelm
Cast	Stephen Rea, Maria Doyle Kennedy, Brendan Gleeson

Film	**Bloodfist VIII - Trained for Action** (1995)
Director	Rick Jacobson
Cast	Don Wilson, J.P. White

Scene from *Man of Aran*

Roibeard Ó Flatharta in *Man of Aran*

James Joyce, pictured in 1902

Scene from *Riders to the Sea*

Index